Classical American Philosophy

Also Available from Bloomsbury

American Philosophy: From Wounded Knee to the Present
ed. Erin McKenna, Scott L. Pratt

Women Philosophers Volume I: Education and Activism in Nineteenth-Century America
Dorothy Rogers

Women Philosophers Volume II: Entering Academia in Nineteenth-Century America
Dorothy Rogers

The Bloomsbury Companion to Pragmatism
ed. Sami Pihlström

The Bloomsbury Encyclopedia of Philosophers in America: From 1600 to the Present
ed. John R. Shook

Classical American Philosophy

Poiesis in Public

Rebecca L. Farinas

BLOOMSBURY ACADEMIC
LONDON • NEW YORK • OXFORD • NEW DELHI • SYDNEY

BLOOMSBURY ACADEMIC
Bloomsbury Publishing Plc
50 Bedford Square, London, WC1B 3DP, UK
1385 Broadway, New York, NY 10018, USA
29 Earlsfort Terrace, Dublin 2, Ireland

BLOOMSBURY, BLOOMSBURY ACADEMIC and the Diana logo
are trademarks of Bloomsbury Publishing Plc

First published in Great Britain 2021
This paperback edition published in 2022

Copyright © Rebecca L. Farinas, 2021

Rebecca L. Farinas has asserted her right under the Copyright,
Designs and Patents Act, 1988, to be identified as Author of this work.

For legal purposes the Acknowledgments on p. viii constitute an
extension of this copyright page.

Cover design by Charlotte Daniels
Cover image © Oxygen / Getty Images

All rights reserved. No part of this publication may be reproduced or
transmitted in any form or by any means, electronic or mechanical, including
photocopying, recording, or any information storage or retrieval system,
without prior permission in writing from the publishers.

Bloomsbury Publishing Plc does not have any control over, or responsibility for,
any third-party websites referred to or in this book. All internet addresses given
in this book were correct at the time of going to press. The author and publisher
regret any inconvenience caused if addresses have changed or sites have ceased
to exist, but can accept no responsibility for any such changes.

A catalogue record for this book is available from the British Library.

Library of Congress Cataloging-in-Publication Data

Names: Farinas, Rebecca L., author.
Title: Classical American philosophy: poiesis in public / Rebecca L. Farinas.
Description: London; New York: Bloomsbury Academic, 2021. | Includes
bibliographical references and index. | Summary: "Rebecca Farinas takes
seven major figures from the American philosophical canon and examines their
relationship with an artistic or scientific interlocutor. In so doing, she provides a unique
insight into the origins of American philosophy and, through case studies such as the
friendship between Alain Locke and the biologist E.E. Just and the collaboration between
Jane Addams and George Herbert Mead, sheds new light on these thinkers'
ideas"–Provided by publisher.
Identifiers: LCCN 2020039296 (print) | LCCN 2020039297 (ebook) |
ISBN 9781350151352 (hb) | ISBN 9781350203945 | ISBN 9781350151369 (epdf) |
ISBN 9781350151376 (ebook)
Subjects: LCSH: Philosophy, American. | Philosophy and science. | Arts–Philosophy.
Classification: LCC B851.F37 2021 (print) | LCC B851 (ebook) | DDC191–dc23
LC record available at https://lccn.loc.gov/2020039296
LC ebook record available at https://lccn.loc.gov/2020039297

ISBN: HB: 978-1-3501-5135-2
PB: 978-1-3502-0394-5
ePDF: 978-1-3501-5136-9
eBook: 978-1-3501-5137-6

Typeset by Integra Software Services Private Limited

To find out more about our authors and books visit
www.bloomsbury.com and sign up for our newsletters.

I would like to dedicate this book to my Father, Gerald Lee Stevens. He first taught me how to be a pragmatist and a citizen.

Contents

Acknowledgments		viii
1	Classical American Philosophy Poeisis in Public	1
2	A New Universality: Pragmatic Symbols of World Peace in Drawing and Dance	11
3	Josiah Royce's Values of Interpretation and Community: Poetry, Cybernetics, and Folk Songs	29
4	Art and Soul: James and Scheler on Pragmatic Aesthetics	57
5	The Icon Moves: Diversity Through Pragmatic/Religious Aesthetics	71
6	Dewey and Kahlo: Cosmopolitanism Midst Crisis	89
7	Jane Addams's Trajectory of Creative Memory Contra to Intersectional Violence	113
8	Science and Art Moon-lit by Values: Relativity of Epi-Genetics, Film, and Cultural Democracy	139
9	Conclusion: Problem Solving with Cultural Aesthetics	167
Notes		182
Selected Bibliography		242
Index		246

Acknowledgments

Please note, portions of Chapters 2, 4, and 5 have previously been published. Chapters 4 and 5 appear in "Pragmatism Today" and are published here with the kind permission of Alexander Kremer, Editor, "Pragmatism Today," *The Journal of the Central European Pragmatist Forum*. Chapter 2 appears in *The Bloomsbury Handbook of Dance and Philosophy* and is published here with the permission of Claire Weatherhead, Permissions Manager, Bloomsbury Academic, Bloomsbury Publishing Plc.

1

Classical American Philosophy
Poeisis in Public

As author, I want to begin offering an apologia for my interpretive method. Readers interested in this field of philosophy, classical American, undoubtedly want to be informed about pragmatism and the social progressive turn in philosophy; however, I have chosen to focus on applying these ideas on aesthetics to contemporary social problems. Upon the advice of the philosophers we will now engage, I want to discuss issues currently in the public square, in light of the arts. John Dewey clears the way for an aesthetic approach to philosophizing:

> When philosophy shall have co-operated with the course of events and made clear and coherent the meaning of the daily detail, science and emotion will interpenetrate, practice and imagination will embrace. Poetry and religious feeling will be the unforced flowers of life. To further this articulation and revelation of the meanings of the current course of events is the task and problem of philosophy in days of transition.[1]

By reconfiguring philosophy to a more experiential orientation, our subject is aestheticized, in terms of explaining and motivating the makings and doings of our shared experiences. The arts and sciences can now be thought of as part of this mix of philosophy and practical problem solving, as we can think of both methods in relation with our firsthand experiences so as to create new realizations. Aesthetics becomes a study of how ideas and actions make our lives better, as we learn without abstract dictates how to behave and how to relate to one another. As well, we develop and spread our cultural values through creative practices, particularly in respect to the theories and actions taken up in light of the philosophies we will discuss. Value-making, for the Classical American philosophers, is an aesthetic process, as we direct our moral progress in terms of productive, progressive norms, which are the fruits of our relationships.

So, exact definitions and comprehensive analysis of the laws of pragmatism are not relevant; as well, I cannot provide such, in that we will cover six unique philosophies in eight chapters. I will say that pragmatic philosophy in general refers to the envisioned effects of our efforts to better our world, and pragmatic aesthetics is a matter of the communicative processes by which those efforts are expressed, realized, and taught. We will focus the ideas of a group of early-twentieth-century philosophers who relied upon such a forward-looking and interrelational approach to life: Charles Sanders Peirce, Joshua Royce, William James, John Dewey, Jane Addams, and Alain Locke. These interlocutors often cast shadows over each other's philosophies, as well as substantiating some ideas held in common. But what binds these philosophers is not a rehashing or clarification of universal principles or maxims, as their like-mindedness is probably best thought of in terms of their biographies and a history of their ideas. However, other researchers best tell those stories, and such analysis is beyond the scope of my research, so I refrain from either a comparative analysis or a conventional historical method. I want to take a slightly different approach so by referencing the arts, I seek to understand how these philosophers' ideas, and their patterns of human relationships, as well as some of the cultural associations we can relate with both, might be meaningful today.

Nonetheless pragmatic aesthetics is a recognized field of study, and the areas of common experience running through the writings of these philosophers can be pointed to as shared points of inquiry. I recommend Richard Shusterman's analysis of Alain Locke's aesthetics as it pertains to other pragmatists, "Pragmatist Aesthetics: Roots and Radicalism," to begin our discussions on aesthetics, culture, and problem solving.[2] An overview of Shusterman's analysis is helpful, as an introduction to themes reoccurring throughout our present discussion.

Shusterman sketches twelve themes of pragmatic aesthetics, so I can now summarize how each of the featured philosophers contributes to the field. First, for these pragmatists nature's sustaining energies are vitally available to us through the arts. Peirce, who is known as the founder of the American school of pragmatic thinking, considered ideas as both born out of and constructive of our common experiences, such as, in terms of practices, habits, and norms.[3] Naturalism comes into play for Peirce, as creative thinking is in harmony with being part of the universe. Royce highlights nature as a meaningful, shared experience among communities. To explain he writes:

> Man, the gregarious animal, has always regarded nature as in some ways common property of the experience or knowledge of the group or the tribe.

Yet people also become distrustful of private, individual observation unless this receives the systematic confirmation of the group.[4]

Known for dissolving the mind-body dualism, James writes about our stream of consciousness. Our consciousness is integrated with our emotions and actions, while our ongoing brain stimuli are made meaningful through our beliefs and values. So our aesthetic sensibilities are naturalistic as we continually make new relationships meaningful. Dewey writes specifically about naturalism (although as an ism the term often comes with ideological baggage, nonetheless):

> But naturalism in art means something more than the necessity all arts are under of employing natural and sensuous media. It means that all which can be expressed is some aspect of the relation of man and his environment, and that this subject-matter attains its most perfect wedding with form when the basic rhythms that characterize the interaction of the two are depended upon and trusted with abandon.[5]

The rhythms of life guide our interactions with our environments, and pragmatic inquiry is how we find out more about those relationships. For Addams, nature offers us key insights into how to infuse our daily lives with simple, collective, and caring (therefore creative) answers to social problems. Finally, Locke thinks nature and art provide us with our sense of unity, guiding us to more meaningful personal expressiveness and cultural diversity.

Second, in respect to Shusterman's points of reference for pragmatic aesthetics, all of our interlocutors find that our cultural histories of art, philosophy, and ethics are helpful when solving social problems, rather than looking toward eternal truths. Peirce finds history as a creative process, allowing us to symbolize what we can rely on as certain by interpretation and thereby moving us toward more effective communication and general understanding. Royce similarly thinks of history as a semiotic process. He emphasizes history as a hermeneutic mode of interpretation, whereby we can coalesce our values and critique our communities. James, taking a critical stance, claims our histories can be redirected by our personal transformations, in that believing in dogmatic religion and/or acting upon our innate attitudes, such as patriotism and competition, can be redirected by our aesthetic experiences. Aesthetic experiences involve personal embodied meanings through the arts and by way of our spiritual beliefs; as well we form relationships in respect to these meanings, valuing those meanings historically. Dewey thinks art consolidates what is historically true over time, thereby renewing such truth continually through contemporary applications. For Addams, we are inspired by the arts, and we act for social change, in the same manner that our historical references are best applied relationally, and as a matter of collective memory. Collective memory allows us to take on board our past in terms of our present social challenges, while allowing us to think in regard to our diverse gender and class orientations. Locke thinks of history as a value orientation of our experiences, similar to art, in that historical experiences can be shared through our varied perspectives. What's important for Locke is that we use history to critique social injustice and improve our communities.

That there are beneficial aesthetic aspects of social diversity is Shusterman's third criteria. Peirce's aesthetics is ethical, meaning that what binds us is a cohesive thought/feeling dynamic of agapism, constituting our phenomenological approach to life as loving and inclusive. Interpretation, according to Royce, is our creative mode of critical thinking as an aesthetic process that relies on multiperspectives and an inclusive community of inquirers. As I point out in the third chapter of this book, James thought of all experience, physical and mental, as interconnected yet pluralistic, in that what is not paid attention to continues to exist in relation to one's sense of the world. The fact that there are varied possibilities for our common experiences allows us to orient our lives through the meanings of our beliefs and relationships with others. Dewey makes it clear that the most diverse societies are more peaceful, creative, and democratic, and diverse cultural experiences are inspiring and inclusive. Addams depends on feminist aesthetics, as a caring and peaceful cultural dynamic, by which we make healthier and fairer communities. Caring necessitates inclusion and parity in terms of our cultural diversity. Diversity, for Locke, is integral to life, art, and culture, all of which are made by unique, personal expressions of shared experiences.

A fourth criterion is the practical value of art, as we strive to make our lives better. Peirce writes in his essay "Trichotomic," "Conventional modes of expression, and other modes dependent on the force of association, enter largely into every art."[6] This criterion is particularly relevant to my thesis, as we move to solve urgent social problems, through aesthetic values, including our refugee crisis, racial and gender discrimination, and war. We discuss in the first chapter of this book Peirce's semiotics in terms of the practice of drawing and dance, and the meanings of worldwide peace as entailed in specific works of art. In the second chapter we discuss Royce's explication of artistic agency, as he points specifically to the poet Percy Bysshe Shelley as a revolutionary. We look again toward world peace, in that chapter, specifically in terms of how we can change our scientific methods to be more artistic. Imaginative value-making is my focus in the chapter on the theories of Max Scheler and James. James describes using our moral imaginations as "pure experience," through which we unify and value our commonly shared experiences. Art is a catalyst for value-making, in that through art we share peaceful relational experiences. In *Art as Experience*, Dewey gives examples of artistic experiences, which are practical, as he therein finds aesthetic values. I can offer an example of his approach to art as experience, as a matter of drinking tea. Teacups made with skill and imagination allow us tea drinkers to slow down our contemporary pace, while we take time to admire the beauty of not only the cup or taste of the tea, but also to value our seamless shared experience. When art is part of our everyday experiences, we are able to live more meaningful and joyful lives. In the chapter herein concerning the relationships between Dewey's aesthetics and Frido Kahlo's paintings, I mark the particular merit of Mexican art in respect to community values and education. By writing in a literary style, Addams puts into action aesthetic agency in terms of sociopolitical reform. By using the art of storytelling and feminist literature, she exposes the intersectional nature of militarization, domestic violence, poverty, greedy capitalism, social class, and racial discrimination. Locke also understood the practical value of art, in terms of individual artistic expressiveness through music, visual art, and film. In the early-twentieth-century United States, these arts were vehicles for Black people to change how they identified themselves and how they interacted as part of the larger culture.

Melorism is a term used by pragmatists, referring to how aesthetic processes, such as art, ethics, politics, community norms and activism, and our sciences, better our society. Shusterman reiterates this concept through several criteria, such as optimism for the future, and in relation to aesthetics not being a matter of disinterestedness (i.e., nonpractical appreciation of art). Addressing such issues, Peirce writes about philosophy as a theoretical science, better pursued apart from practical concerns, such as politics. For Peirce, when writing philosophy in terms of societal issues, we have a tendency to think about philosophical directives as factual, in a static, unchangeable manner, or we disregard the consistency and importance of philosophical ideas because of changing circumstances. Both of these approaches to philosophy are harmful to communities. He suggests a unifying and multiperspectival interpretive process, using semiotics, as people engage through the arts, communication, and ethics, and such practices help us form aesthetic ideas, which better our world. Trusting each other to reinterpret our ideas for the future and to think critically about our present-day communal challenges is at the heart of melioristic aesthetic practices for Royce. James is known for first putting forward the notion of meliorism as a pragmatic possibility, and in our discussion, I note how he thinks our beliefs can better our world, as our hopes mediate and guide us. We should focus on transforming, through our hopeful relationships, our present experiences for our mutual betterment. As well as emphasizing collective thinking, Addams brings to this conversation the powerful quality of thinking in terms of caring for each other, which of course is beneficial to family and community. For Locke we must be able to develop our personal creativity, while participating with our value-oriented communities, in order to contribute to social justice and moral progress.

Science is a frequent topic throughout these chapters, in that all of these philosophers consider it at its best when practiced artistically. Aesthetic ideas in a Peircean sense include scientific facts and discoveries, and such ideas are born from creative moral growth as well as critical thinking. Peirce considers that the chances presented to us through our inter-relational experiences are best worked with as opportunities to view and present matters both in accord with multi-perspectives and holistically, and such is first and foremost an artist's ethical challenge. Our discussion on Royce's thoughts on the scientific method is especially relevant to how science is done best by using an artistic, interpretive, and community-oriented approach to research and invention. Psychology was James's scientific field, but he thought we need to approach the study of our emotional and thoughtful experiences pluralistically, meaning that we seriously consider what is not yet known as being at work in our assessments. Imagination as an artistic process depends on us making relationships rather than relying on factual consequences, affording us a more robust view of our world than conventional science, which is confined as a field of fortuitous reality. In our chapter on Addams's aesthetics, we discuss how she calls for scientists to distance themselves from the industries of war and greedy motivations. She calls for the scientific community to speak out about our obligations to care for one another, while depending on the arts as ways to think and communicate morally about our shared responsibilities. Locke's collaboration with E.E. Just, a cellular biologist, highlights how science and the arts combine, thereby contributing to culture, importantly through value-making. For both Locke and Just, being inclusive, through our cultures as individual participants with our communities' affairs, is inherent in our physical and ethical natures.

Before finishing our reanalysis of pragmatic aesthetics, following Shusterman's outline, with an explanation of the role aesthetics plays in democracy, I want to mention two other criteria. There are two points that might seem, through a strictly academic exercise, extraneous to some of the philosophies discussed, those being race as an aesthetically propagated orientation and the value of aesthetics by "deepening those values in actual experience by improving the arts and aesthetic appreciation of them."[7] I do think these criteria can be points of discussion in reference to all of the philosophies discussed, but the interlocutors differ, with varying degrees, on the philosophical concepts of cultural relativism and education. Some of those differences are brought forward in the upcoming chapters, although our main purpose is to enrich pragmatic values, not to compare and contrast definitions and structured concepts. In this regard, throughout the book we look toward Peirce's semiotics to give us unifying signs, Royce's method of interpretation allowing us to be more inclusive, James's ideas on emotions and imagination as instructive to well-being, and Dewey's and Addams's call for acceptance of immigrants and art as educational in respect to civic life. However, race as a cultural construct is most significant for Locke, who thought in terms of cultural pluralism and value relativism. We also should note at this point in our conversation that for these pragmatists a diverse society is not only about our acceptance of our interraciality but also fluid gender roles and identity, acceptance of varied religious beliefs, and interest in experimental forms of community. All of these ideas should be aesthetically constructed for the means of cultural progress. Especially in relation to Locke's philosophy, valuing one's diversity reestablishes norms in all the fields of social interactions, and this is the overarching purpose of our cultural values. Our personal expressions are necessary to inspire the depth of understanding needed to carry on our interpersonal relationships, and we are at our best when we embrace the complexity of those relationships in light of the moral health of our communities. Locke's value theory offers us an understanding of how the arts are able to move us, intimately, so we can understand each other's purposes and contributions.

Thinking about democracy as an aesthetic value goes to the heart of our present discussion. Each philosopher we engage, throughout this book, explores how aesthetics and art are democratic processes and how through these processes citizens work together to solve problems. I do the same by applying their philosophies to contemporary social problems. So, I want to begin our longer discussion with a conversation among our interlocutors, concerning aesthetic agency in respect to democracy. Through their words we can set the stage for the theories, examples, and speculative future scenarios, given as evidence throughout the book. All of these quotes I use in the chapters that follow, so we can think of them here as a foreshadowing, or the first attempt to prove my thesis.

Charles Sanders Peirce: "Thus the very origin of conception of reality that this conception essentially involves the notion of community, without definite limits, and capable of indefinite increase of knowledge."[8]

Joshua Royce: "It is not my thought that natural science can ever displace religion or do its work. But what I mean is that since the office of religion is to aim towards the creation on earth of the Beloved Community, the future task of religion is the task of inventing and applying the arts which shall win men over to unity, and which shall overcome their original hatefulness by the gracious love, not of mere individuals, but of communities. Now such arts are yet to be discovered. Judge every social device, every proposed reform, every national and every local enterprise by the one test: *Does this help towards the coming of the universal community.*"[9]

William James: "And, when you ask how much sympathy you ought to bestow, although the amount is, truly enough, a matter of ideal on your own part, yet in this notion of the combination of ideals with active virtues you have a rough standard for shaping your decision. In any case, your imagination is extended. A persons' integration with the world assumes humility on your own part, and tolerance, reverence, and love for others; and you gain a certain inner joyfulness at the increased importance of our common life. Such joyfulness is a religious inspiration and an element of spiritual health, and worth more than large amounts of that sort of technical and accurate information, which we professors are supposed to be able to impart."[10]

John Dewey: "The religious attitude signifies something that is bound through imagination to a *general* attitude. This comprehensive attitude, moreover, is much broader than anything indicated by 'moral' in its usual sense. The quality of attitude is displayed in art, science and good citizenship."[11]

Jane Addams: "The first step toward their real solution must be made upon a past experience common to the citizens as a whole and connected with their daily living. As moral problems become more and more associated with our civic and industrial organizations, the demand for enlarged activity is more exigent."[12]

Alain Locke: "In my definition of culture I would include science as well as the arts. On that basis, then, all we should be sanely concerned about is freer participation and fuller collaboration in the varied activities of the cultural life and that with regard both to the consumer and the producer roles of cultural creation. Democracy in culture means equally wide-scale appreciation and production of the things of the spirit."[13]

I titled this book *Classical American Philosophy: Poiesis in Public* because classical connotes how the ideas we will continue to discuss relate to an artistic democracy. This moniker not only spotlights an early-twentieth-century milieu but also pulls out a thread running throughout this book, in that the culture of the United States was and continues to be diverse and open to change. The featured philosophers wrote when there was a rapid growth of population and industry, due to a great extent to the immensely profound contributions of Native Americans, Black Americans, immigrants, suffragettes, visionary artists, and fearless scientists. It was a progressive time, but culturally the country remained troubled, and its problems, although countered by the philosophies we will study, were only partially addressed. Many people who committed heinous crimes because of their prejudices of race, gender, socioeconomic class, and elitist intellectualism lived through this period of history without accusation or feeling the power of moral justice. So, I ask if we could once again discuss the ideas of these philosophers in an attempt to solve some of those problems, which continue to cause harm. As well, we must admit, that many women and men around the world feel the weight of these problems.

Let us therefore begin our discussion speculating briefly on the meaning of democracy, in that this central idea held promise for our interlocutors. Everyone knows democracy is an ancient Greek political/philosophical idea. The roots of the word are *demos*, meaning people, and *kratos*, meaning power. It is also well known that Socrates in Plato's *Apology* debates the verdict of his peers, as Athens' newly reinstated democracy was being tested in terms of elitist corruption and praise and blame ethics. Socrates appeals to people's social conscious, in respect to his own *daimon* (his personal moral guide); his meaning is that justice and fairness lie in the hearts of all citizens. It follows that the *demos* and one's *daimon* can be thought of as fostering beliefs of a righteous freedom, inspiring united trust of our collective wisdom. So I would like us to consider, at the launch of our broader discussion, that democracy is not based solely on popular control or political equality but on an ethos of inclusion, that is on pragmatic aesthetics, as citizens are not afraid to consider what diverges from already established norms. In this respect, democracy depends on creative/expressive aesthetic processes to drive a diverse culture, with its many unique voices and ideas, from which we can draw our moral courage, so as to change our world for the better.

2

A New Universality: Pragmatic Symbols of World Peace in Drawing and Dance

The arts are bound with aesthetics, as a study of how we are embodied with, perceive, and interpret our world. Alike to this approach, pragmatic aesthetics includes phenomenology, as an investigation of how our meaningful experiences are constituted by creative practices and interpretive artifacts, such as signs, language, and works of art. Focusing on Charles Sander Peirce's semiotics, in respect to aesthetics, such modes of knowledge bring us to a better understanding of how we can make more benevolent communities, thereby presenting an ethically oriented aesthetic process.[1] However, for Peirce a science of signs should not be abstracted from explaining, reinterpreting, and understanding such practices and artifacts while such is experienced. I mark this pragmatic turn in philosophical thinking, while investigating Peirce's interests in drawing and dance, and my analysis finds examples of these arts as resonant signs of global peace movements.

My purpose is to bring forward relationships between Peirce's views on aesthetics, artistic practices, and sign-making, explaining how those practices propagate our global, yet community-oriented, experiences. I will not be offering a detailed explanation of late Peircean semiotics, with its far-reaching implications in the areas of logic, language, and science, in that my purpose is more specific to the arts of drawing and dance. For those interested, there are clear and accessible explications of his approach to pragmatic philosophy and his semiotics in a plethora of secondary literature. However, the importance of sign-making to aesthetics is a specific point of our discussion in respect to drawing and dance, so I focus on Peirce's earlier writing wherein he addresses this topic and is engaged with these practices.[2] I am concentrating on two ideas, synechism and agapism, helping us understand a connection between feelings, movement, signification, and how we better our lives. Through art, we will come to understand the context, and scope, of Peirce's aesthetics and his notions of universal love. I can say at the outset that Peirce thinks of love as a creative sign and an aspect of our common experience, not as a construct originating outside of our experience. Nor does he think of love as determining experiences, in that love develops in an open field of experience, but also as we act on what we feel and think of as meaningful to our lives.

However, I do put forward this discussion as investigating how we make meaningful gestures, so I will briefly summarize Peirce's general approach to semiotics. Signs are modes of phenomena, communication, and knowledge, and they can be recognized as meaningful to our ongoing experiences. Actually Peirce writes about the similar aspects of both drawing and gesture in relation to three aspects of how we discern our world as meaningful. An object, and a referent to that object, as well as an interpretant, constitutes the meanings we think about and how we act on such meanings as part of the ongoing relationships with our world. Peirce finds these three main components to sign-making as: *likenesses* or *icons*, which are representational, *indices*, which are referential, and *symbols* or *signs*, which are imaginative, interpretive, and relational. All three modes of experience are integrated and concurrent aspects of our making our experiences relevant to our beliefs and actions.[3]

In two early essays Peirce possibly initiates what would become his later, more fully developed semiotic method.[4] Specifically, I highlight Peirce's essays "Trichotomic" and "Evolutionary Love," both of which include references to the arts, sciences, and aesthetics.[5] Peirce introduces a definition of aesthetics in his essay "Trichotomic," and although it is technically dense as a passage describing consciousness, it is important to understanding community experiences as influenced by creative practices.

Peirce writes:

> The Genuine synthetic consciousness, the consciousness of that which has its being in its thirdness is Reason. The dynamical variety is a consciousness of a coordination between acts of sense and will, it is the looking upon the phenomena of sense and will as rational, which we may call Desire, though that does not precisely define it. The variety is the comparison of feelings, and may be called esthetic understanding.[6]

By synthetic consciousness, Peirce is referring to our interpretive processes, by which we perceive and make sense of our world. The dynamical variety of consciousness can be thought of as artistic, creative practices. The esthetic aspect of the process "collects present and absent into a whole" and pins down our feelings as a matter of relational interpretation.[7] A second definition is given in his essay "Evolutionary Love," and he offers this definition while anticipating and lamenting the passing of a popular relevance of aesthetic theories based on "natural judgements of the sensible heart."[8] He places aesthetics, and evolving modern life in a creative arena, available to everyone, purposely making a point of relating evolution and aesthetics to our loving relationships. There are three modes of evolution: tychasm (chance), ananchasm (circumstantial and logical), and agapastic (creative). The later mode of evolution is particularly aesthetic. Peirce explains:

> All three modes of evolution are composed of the same general elements. Agapasm exhibits them the most clearly. The good result is here brought to pass, first, by the bestowal of spontaneous energy by the parent upon the offspring, and second, by the disposition of the latter to catch the general idea of those about it and thus to subserve the general purpose.[9]

He goes on to explain that science and aesthetics are meaningful to people's lives through different modes of understanding, but both involve a "continuity of mind," which involves signs. So both can be creative if work in those areas is done with focus on our "general purpose," thereby being aesthetically attuned. Our evolutionary aesthetics can happen through community, by an individual developing reasoning because of their relationships with their neighbor, and/or by an individual genius for recording meanings in their experiences because of "an attraction it exercises upon his mind."[10] So I assume Peirce means that our moral development is aesthetic as a matter of feeling and reasoning, a matter of penetrating relationships, and a matter of focusing our talents and energies on value-laden experiences.

Accordingly, people's feelings and thoughts are focused by ideas and signs, which are continually reinterpreted, while holding a continuity of meaning. For Peirce, aesthetics and the arts are spatially and temporally connected yet changeable, as we *integrate* our relationships, practices, and ideas, turning our attention to the art object (or practice) at hand.[11] Furthermore, artistic objects, practices, and ideas are practical enterprises, and they are thought of in terms of their practical effects. Art objects raise questions, such as how everyday aesthetic practices, and the making of art objects, are meaningful to our everyday experiences. We can also ask, Do such creative practices better our world?

Peirce argues that changes in the world are brought about by compelling ideas energized through evolutionary love, and the embodied arts further melioristic strivings through community spirit, neighborly love, and gifted creativity. Applying his theory to particular art practices, I find a like comparison with drawing and dance, as both are creative practices, employing relational signs, enlivening worldwide goals, such as the goal I will highlight, *world peace*. Although drawing is often thought of as a reflective, mindful art, while dance is immediate, physical, and expressive, both arts embody what Peirce terms *esthetic reasoning* (which I call aesthetic reasoning). Aesthetic reasoning involves symbolic meanings (what Peirce calls signs), ushering people into personal and cultural relationships. To further the discussion, I will explain connections between artistic signs of drawing and dance and Peirce's aesthetics of evolutionary love, thereby describing an experiential sense of cultural creative change, which is unifying, hopeful, and peaceful. Considering American Modern Dance at its origins, in connection with the then contemporary thinking and drawings of Peirce, raises new ground for propagating universal symbols of peace.

One of my main objectives in this discussion is to highlight how the arts might be ethical, so I reference Peirce's interpretations of Plato. Peirce was a Plato scholar and philologist, and his thinking on aesthetics was influenced by that research. I also engage in hermeneutics by comparing Mark Morris's critical dance presentations of *Socrates* to Peirce's theories. I surmise that Morris's dance and Peircean aesthetics embody symbols of love, death, and peace as an ethos of loving universality, emerging through co-joined, interpretive global cultures.

Aesthetics and Art as Sign-Making Processes

For Peirce, intuitive, perceptual, and bodily contingent values express an expansive mindfulness, which pervades all of nature, and which is morally *evolutionary*.[12] To begin to explain, Peirce holds that throughout the universe forces are not deterministic, rather matter congeals by its continuity, which is ever expanding through movement and time. For Peirce, what may seem oppositional is actually creative—in that what has continuity eventually unifies—allowing for recurring actions and eventful change. Peirce claims that movement occurs with and is motivated by feelings of such resumed continuity. Peirce calls this phenomenon *synechism*, which we can discern as a process of lived experience.[13] Synechism accounts for habits, creativity, and revaluations of ethical norms.[14] Furthermore, our arts and practices are thoughtfully yet spontaneously made, so our thinking and doing as making sense of the world and our place in it is in sync with our feelings. In light of this theory, our ideas, practices, and habits become increasingly productive, so that we can facilitate ever-more vital and important changes to our ontologies and normative values.[15]

Modern Dance is a good example to carry this discussion, as it can be an art form, alike to drawing and many other arts, through which practitioners express an open-endedness, yet continual in relation to their feelings, while thoughtfully moving and gesturing.[16] As well, nascent values are often especially shown and felt by dancers and audiences, and without an explicit narrative or without having specific expressive intentions. Through their ongoing movement and gesturing of more static communicative relationships, their intentions are value-oriented, as we will come to more fully understand in the third section of this chapter. For now, an example of this process by way of everyday actions can include thinking about the soma-aesthetic benefits of facilitating interconnectedness of life's energies and mind-body connectedness with others as vital to creativity, such as greeting one another or encouraging one another through touch or even applause, as a process of value making. When no determinate outcome is set before our experiencing of moving and gesturing in such ways, the meanings of graceful movements present our interrelational feelings before any judgment or moral decision is made. In kind we can discern the meaningfulness of beauty and grace as intimately connecting people, who are working through problems and challenges, as such experiences are increasingly value-laden.

To further clarify synechism in terms of values, Peirce, while a philosopher of science and logic, was also involved with thinking about what he thought of as phenomenology: as an inquiry into *"the analysis of what kind of constituents there are in our thoughts and lives, (whether these be valid or invalid being quite aside from the question)."*[17] Peirce's synechism theory gives ground to a phenomenology involving aesthetic values. Synechism is an experiential process of concretizing one's felt mindfulness, in that our feelings congeal and have continuity, through our personal and public relationships. As people discover more about their awareness of themselves and the world, they are more able to put their experiences into broader contexts, thereby constituting their growth and learning as moral and ethical agents of ongoing experiences. With such a confluence of consciousness, feelings, and situations, we come to know reality as familiar, yet continuing and morally impactful.[18] For Peirce, there is no perceptual reality without a sense of living in an open-ended, emotional, value-laden environment.[19] Turning our attention to these phenomenological relationships, Peirce's views might include radical (or open)—yet ethical—interpretations of values, as our feelings and relationships are impacted by chance, embodied in the creative processes of arts such as dance and drawing.[20] In this aspect, values are somewhat experimental and open to our moral imagination.

To offer an example of synechism in the manner of the arts, a dancer performs a movement or passage many times, and if danced with intensity, the passage will change in creative and phenomenal ways by the dancer's spontaneity and grace. As well, a dancer is continually enthralled with differing experiences and ideas of their world, thereby reinterpreting how to move and what their movements mean. Erick Hawkins, in his text *The Body as a Clear Space*, offers a similar explanation of creativity and reception: "As artists in the modern dance, we have to go on a voyage of discovery constantly." He expands on this thought:

> This discovery, this revolution which is still to be made in dance, is in that pure fact of existence, that awareness of awareness, that first function of art—the material of dance itself for its own sake is in transition before your eyes, instant by instant, before it is meanings, associations, or language—the immediately apprehended and eternal "now."[21]

Hawkins, as a choreographer and dancer, describes feeling while dancing and watching dance as mindful. He was influenced by F.S.C. Northrop's philosophy.[22] Northrop describes a first order and a second order of aesthetic experience and artistic making: the first being a naïve realism, followed by second-order objectivity of structuring and defining feelings, sensations, and artistic methods. Both Northrop, employing philosophy, and Hawkins, practicing choreography and dancing, attempt to disclose the *radical empiricism* of a synthesis of both orders.[23] Radical empiricism is defined in this context as the importance of one's understanding as an essential involvement with the world and as a matter of one's relationships with the varied aspects of experience.[24] The point is that Northrop's experiential view of dance corresponds with Peirce's understanding of meaningful, yet relational and changeable aesthetics.[25] Here, I think there could be a correlation between Northrop's and Hawkins's emphasis on radical empiricism in the arts and Peirce's phenomenology and semiotics. However, my purpose here is to speak specifically of the ethical aesthetics of art from a Peircean point of view, so investigating those possible connections is best left for a future discussion.[26]

Moreover, Peirce explains a further progression in understanding aesthetic practices as relational and open-ended, as he stresses that our thoughtful feelings through movement are signs, leading us to further interpretations and new signs. Signs take on a thoughtful continuity, becoming culturally symbolic.[27] We can understand how once an audience or practitioner leaves a performance, they can think and feel that performance as a matter of thought-filled moments animating their futures. We might even gesture spontaneously with a more confident sense of meaning, upon leaving a performance. Therefore, dancing in the here and now can bridge our past experiences with our futures, as value-laden and meaningful. The radical empirical aspects of such artistic practices and spectatorship are aspects of wide-ranging, symbolic, and communicative fields of feelings and social engagement. As well each person is symbolic as we soma-aesthetically reinterpret our thoughtful experiences of movement, and this is how we come to be more graceful and value-oriented.

Now let us turn our thinking to Peirce's notion of apagism, in relation to signs. Peirce proposed aesthetics as integrated with ethics, describing how symbols are meaningfully sustained as practices, which progress our co-joined lives in positive ways. The Ancient Greeks also had a conception of universal understanding that is spread through loving and graceful spiritual feelings: love as *agape*, meaning an unconditional love of what is eternal or divine. This universal love is sometimes understood as a static, closed system of idealism, but Peirce's term *agape* is correlated with syncheism, notable aspects being the relational orientation of feelings and thought, continuity of creative approaches to our experiences, as well as meaningful reinterpretation of value-laden experiences. Upcoming, as an example of reinterpreting *agape* through dance, we will refer to the *Symposium* in which Plato bridges *eros*, or physical love, with *agape*, love that universalizes regenerative goodness throughout nature. For Peirce, human endeavors endure through spreading symbols of love. For now, I emphasize that *agapism* is Peirce's term for ethical aesthetics of evolutionary love. Such aesthetics marks perceptions and signs of goodness, as these signs are embodied and active, motivating, sustaining, while unifying environments and communities. However static, exclusive practices stunt the growth of one's creativity as well as a communities' common, yet pluralistic strivings.[28]

Eidetic Drawing and the Delsarte Method of Elocution as Universal Symbols of Evolutionary Love

Peirce was not a dancer but a draftsman, although he interestingly discerns an ethical connection between the two.[29] We will come to that connection after referring to his own drawings in relation to synechism and agapism, then disclosing what is meaningful about Peirce's direct relationship with the Delsarte Method of elocution, which is the seminal technique of American Modern Dance.

As well as ongoing studies of the arts, photography, film, painting, music, dance, in relation to Peircean semiotics, scholars have taken interest in Peirce's philosophy in the context of his habits of doodling/sketching and making rebus puzzles.[30] Peirce undoubtedly thought eidetically, realizing that our imagistic perceptions assist us in interpreting reality. Peirce considered ideas and conceptions, as well as what is often called the unconscious, as beginning with the continuity of perceptions and interpretations, as he was constantly mentally and actually sketching new realizations, while correlating drawing with experimentation. Peirce was fascinated by bi-stable images, such as the duck/rabbit image, and, in part, drew his theory of perception from such imagery. In fact, in the late 1880s, Joseph Jastrow, who drew and theorized about the duck/rabbit image, was Peirce's student at John Hopkins.[31] Tullio Viola thinks of Peirce's phenomenology and drawing as an embodied form of abduction or "inferential or active nature of perception."[32] Viola pulls Peirce's larger system of philosophy into contemporary studies of cognitive imaging and aesthetics, since he discerns that we rely on imaging as we "build up the world we inhabit."[33] For Viola, creatively we interpret and reinterpret concepts or images as we are making discoveries about our world while questioning our "perceptual habits" which bond us integrally with our world.[34]

Peirce's drawing of a stonewall demonstrates how we make general inferences but also how we are interested in guessing about or finding the possibilities of experimenting with what we are seeing. Feelings about what we are seeing are the material qualities of new ways of seeing (they are the medium, so to speak, of an artistic practice) and feelings can become symbolic.[35] A person looking at the duck/rabbit drawing might say, "I see it is a duck, but I can see how you think it is a rabbit," and so the relationships involved in discerning the meanings expand to feelings about what others are experiencing. Yet, Peirce's drawing can be seen as a stonewall or a meandering serpentine line, and although these interpretations can often intermingle and/or change, one's interpretation constitutes a perception that holds and is fixed for a time. Drawings add to our curiosity about the world in that we can review marks and symbols, changing our perspectives and interpretations. Therefore, drawn symbols do not rely on private processes such as "intuitions," but they carry forward congealed mindfulness, coming from our sensorial experiences. Through ongoing processes of sensing and thinking what is real from other interpretations—maybe new, maybe previously known—multiple perspectives are made more reliable, so that artists and viewers do not depend on tacit reasoning.[36] By understanding one's perceptions as a process involving possibilities and questioning, we learn a moral lesson, in that we can reinterpret our initial perceptions, thereby changing our feelings toward things.

Peirce drew diagrams to help explain his theory of perception, thinking of drawing and gesture in terms of a building up of ideas through relationships with other's point of view, rather than merely representing what is found. He, therefore, locates the synechistic aspect of the drawing. Of course, drawing relates to dance through practiced movement but also through active perception, interpretation, and re-enactment or critique.[37]

William Hogarth, during the eighteenth century, developed a philosophy of art based on draftsmanship. He claims that the serpentine line marks the seminal line of beauty, as it is found in nature but also ethically by inciting liveliness, activity, and gracefulness. Of course, the serpentine line is important throughout the sciences, arts, mathematics. For example, by joining two serpentine lines, we can understand how, in terms of Peircean semiotics and aesthetic interpretation, a geometrical asymptote becomes not infinite straight lines but the symbol of the aperion, which is drawn by making a figure eight turned sideways. Aperion was symbolic of boundless infinity and harmony for the Ancient Greeks, and we can think of the sign as being conceived through our reinterpretation by metaphysical speculation, and as the other way around, from nature or feelings to geometry. The symbol or feeling of aperion gives us an example of a continuum of reality, as a symbolic and synechistic experience.

Furthermore, there is an intriguing connection between the symbolization of a serpentine line and what was during the early twentieth century distinguished as a scientific method of movement conveying meanings, namely the Delsarte Method of elocution.[38] Before we disclose that connection with drawing, let us recall the connections between the Delsarte Method, Peirce, and the roots of American Modern Dance. American Modern Dance was founded on Delsartian semiotics, because of the collaboration of Steele MacKaye with Francois Delsarte. Peirce correlates his understanding of semiotics with Steele MacKaye's version of Delsartian semiotics of elocution in his essay "Trichotomic."[39] Delsarte used the term "semiotics" to refer to his advanced method of attributing meanings to facial expressions, gestures, and poses, thinking of his method as a reflection on the Christian trinity and as a matter of mind, body, and soul.[40] Peirce became quite familiar with the Delsartian method of elocution as taught by the American painter, actor, and theater impresario MacKaye, because Peirce's wife Juliette Peirce, who was an actress, studied the technique.[41] Iris Smith Fischer, in her research on Peirce's development of semiotics in relation to theatre, connects his semiotics with the expressive techniques of Delsarte and MacKaye. Delsarte's method of gestures and pantomime develops how people fuse their movements with their speech and their environments, as when they are presenting speeches, performing, and going about expressing their authentic identity in everyday life. As well, the method relies on pantomime as a meaningful form of rhetoric, emphasizing pose and gesture, as a kind of existential conversation. Our re-enactments, in light of Delsartian elocution, are filled with our most profound desires and hopes for our purposes in life, not mere imitations of role models. Fischer notes that MacKaye and Peirce were more naturalistic, rather than metaphysical, in terms of their semiotic philosophies than Delsarte. Fischer writes:

> Peirce's interest in Mackaye's system of actor training seems to focus on the reshaping of perceived binaries—aesthetic/semeiotic, inner/outer, spirit/matter—into more valid triadic conceptions of embodied cognition.[42]

To further this line of study, we can recall the research of Lee Chaifa Ruyter, in her essay "American Delsartism: Precursor of an American Dance Art." Ruyter notes that MacKaye, along with his student Genevieve Stebbins, furthered Delsarte's methods by popularizing a gymnastic harmony therapy emphasizing that the speaker, actor, dancer can develop their ability to open soma-aesthetic channels of less resistance (i.e. continuity) when communicating through meaningful poses and gestures. Their method and therapy were brought fully into a performance mode, namely through two dancers who were students of Stebbins, the pioneers of American Modern Dance: Isadora Duncan and Ruth St. Denis.[43]

In relation to another aspect of Delsartian semiotics, Stebbins spread "physical culture to the general public," especially to middle- and upper-class women, empowering them through their movements as they sense their meaningful presence in the world.[44] Stebbins expanded on MacKaye's techniques by instructing participants not to use their bodies like dynamic engines, pushing and pulling oneself into motion, but moving while opening oneself up more fully to the interconnectedness of all life. She suggests that a dancer or participant pattern their movements on a fundamental "motion in nature," namely the spiral curve.[45] Stebbins meshes performance dancing with health and community benefits by designing techniques that can be done by everyone, employing a seminal design of nature. Dancers call such bodily movements "spiral successive movements," and we can do one such movement as we make our body into an ocean wave.

I compare this to Peirce's investigation of the stonewall, recalling he unlocks a realization of how spontaneity through spiral lines, as felt perceptions, contributes to our broad ontologies as well as our normative habits.[46] Also Stebbins choreographed with a cultural anthropology in mind, as she connected her staged assembled presentations to what she knew about dances of the Orient and ancient Greece.[47] This embodied employment of ancient cultures, as meaningful to self-empowerment and community engagement rather than fantasizing or parodying primitivism, would become a theme running throughout American Modern Dance, including the choreography of Hawkins and Morris (as will be discussed). Pluralism by way of movement and thought connects with cultural histories, for both Stebbins and Peirce.

I place importance on Peirce's essay "Tichotomic," which he wrote in 1888 to discuss MacKaye's "practices of signs," noting that his interpretation has not been talked about in connection with the history of dance and the ethics of well-being. Although Peirce writes specifically about MacKaye's semiotics in respect to elocution, we can disclose a field of philosophical thinking in respect to developing people's awareness of the meanings of interconnectedness with nature, including each other, through fluid movement and symbolism. Peirce says MacKaye's method develops "reasoning with esthetic understanding," which is more than movement by habit, as it is "the ground of our faculty of learning."[48] I think we can think of this sort of understanding as embodied meanings, in that such reasoning is full with context and ongoing action. Peirce, as well, infers that aesthetically felt signs can inspire change and creativity through different mediums as aesthetic understanding, in that signs can interrelate through the arts, while retaining specific artistic practices and conscious attributes.[49] Peirce thereby merges MacKaye's semiotics with an ethics, claiming that aesthetic reasoning is productive as an interested, investigative, relational kind of human nature. He also discusses how meaningful movements can be practical signs, as parts of evolutionary processes of universal hopes for a more ethical world. Gestures are representative through imitative likenesses, but there are also movements that do not make a point of distinguishing between the sign and the thing signified. These are signs indicative of a plural consciousness, as a kind of symbolization bridging what is there in the essence of the movement and what is not there yet in reality, as an evolution of movement and thought.[50] Pantomime of this kind is what Peirce claims as the most rational kind of thinking. Pantomime (and I suggest we think of Peirce's passages on pantomime as related to dance) is, therefore, an immediate communicative mode of expression and a continuity of mindfulness, carrying forward the full continuity of nature. Peirce writes:

Pantomime alone is mainly representation of the purely artistic kind to be contemplated without analysis and without discrimination of the sign from the thing signified.[51]

The emphasize for Peirce, as well as MacKaye and Stebbins, was on using human expression as symbolizing enlivened meanings, linking movement with ethics by promoting well-being, honesty, growth, and unity through culture and community. Theirs was an organic semiotics, portending a living, ongoing kind of truthful symbolism that remains open to the individual's movements, perspectives, and interpretations.

As explained, we can say that American Modern Dance has its roots in such an ethical symbolism by which a practitioner, and interpreter of gestures, finds meaningful relationships among the movement of signs. Peirce thinks of such harmony as agapism: aesthetic relationships that are infinitely interconnected. To give an example, Peirce seems to draw eidetically, while evoking embodied feelings of dancing as he explains agapism and evolutionary love: "The movement of love is circular, at one and the same impulse projecting creations into independency and drawing them into harmony."[52] He then progresses his thoughts similarly to how Stebbins developed everyday gymnastics of well-being, which was then developed into a performing art and to an ethics. Here we understand aesthetics as a matter of well-being and beauty in an experiential sense, which includes a sense of what is good for our communities. Peirce finds the *movement* of love as ethical. He explains in "Evolutionary Love":

> This seems complicated when stated so; but it is fully summed up in the simple formula we call the Golden Rule. This does not, of course, say, Do everything possible to gratify the egoistic impulses of others, but it says, sacrifice your own perfection to the perfectionment of your neighbour.[53]

His ethics pushes beyond self-interestedness, spurring people to act on inclusive, nondiscriminatory feelings of love.[54] Peirce continues:

> Love is not directed to abstraction but to persons; not to persons we do not know, nor to numbers of people, but to our own dear ones, our family and neighbours. "Our neighbour," we remember, is one whom we live near, not locally perhaps, but in life and feeling.[55]

Theoretically, he combines his existential concepts of *synechism*, aesthetic reasoning, and *agapism*, interrelating creativity with progressive ideas, growing and learning as a matter of meliorism, and thoughtful practices in sync with feelings of love.[56] Finally, Peirce finds a creative "spirit of an age" existing for a plurality of people, places, and things, all on a progressive trek toward visionary, yet practical goals.[57] Now we can see more clearly how artistic practices, specifically Modern Dance, can move our world toward a better future.

Mark Morris's *Socrates* as Both Critique and Universal Symbol of World Peace

In "Philosophy and the Conduct of Life," Peirce states that philosophy must stand aloof as a science from practical affairs because there is danger in postulating final truths or falsely interpreting ideas as transitory, because ideas, looked at in those ways, can too readily become meaningless when brought into new and possibly novel contexts. Peirce alerts us that philosophical thinking should be "disinterested" because scientists should accept established truths as fallible while moral imperatives are often felt and thought of as universal and vitally urgent. Yet he does not think that moral actions, or science for that matter, are nonfactual, meaningless, or nonphilosophical.[58] He is obviously looking critically at the intersection of philosophy and ethics, just as Plato and Socrates did before him.[59] His discussion is related to Plato's challenge to philosophy in terms of norms in the Socratic dialogues, as Peirce warns of people's biases and the emotional strength of people's devotion to their own philosophical points of view.[60] He recommends a synthesis of sentiment, so we develop our *eros* as aesthetic reasoning through visionary actions, so as to remain concurrent with the changes and continuum of goodness and existence.

Within that essay he engages in a fuller discussion, praising Plato's philosophical prowess by combining poetry with philosophy so as to conflate ideas with ethics, aesthetics, and art. Accordingly Peirce puts forward a tenet of his own philosophy about the nature of artifacts:

> So, too, man looks upon the arts from his selfish point of view. But they, too, like the beasts and the trees, are living organisms, none the less so for being parasitic to man's mind; and their manifest internal destiny is to grow into pure sciences.[61]

Yet, he warns that if these signs, which are fields of human participation, are thought of in terms of absolute universal truths rather than thought-filled continuous forms unfolding meaningful existence and experience, they can be dangerous. Such artifacts can lose their relevance to everyday experience if not used in relational ways, becoming static, although sometimes impassioned, forms that are resistant to change.[62]

With these views in mind, we can understand the essay "Evolutionary Love" as an interpretive sign, disclosing a plurality to community aesthetics and ethical practices. I want to follow this hermeneutic lead in terms of an interpretation of the symbolic practices of Modern Dance. My methodology here gives reference to Peirce's aesthetic reasoning as a creative, interpretive process. I reconcile this discussion by bringing forward some of the symbolic complexities of Morris's dance *Socrates*, thereby evidencing the positive effects of pragmatic, continuous, change-making, universal signs.

Mark Morris's dance performance of "Socrates" is a reinterpretation of Eric Satie's fin de siècle composition for voice and instrument. Originally Satie was commissioned to complement with music, an elocutionary exercise in Ancient Greek.[63] His composition combines a non-narrative score with sung passages of three of Plato's Socratic dialogues, thereby creating a conceptual type of opera. A soloist sings as the dancers perform. This symphonic drama is not based on rhetorical techniques, as the music does not for the most part continually rise and fall from crescendo to diminuendo. Satie wrote that he wanted the music to be "white and pure music of Antiquity." The libretto comes from the *Symposium*, *Phaedrus* and *Phaedo*, highlighting several common themes: love as a shared experience, finding the meaning of the soul through music and philosophy, nature as peaceful and meaningful in respect to human's everyday lives, and death as a process of renewal. In the first movement, we hear sung Plato's poem from the *Symposium*:

> Love gives peace to me and stillness to the sea
> Lays winds to rest, and care worn men to sleep
> Love fills us with togetherness and drains all our divisiveness away.
> Love calls gatherings like these together.

Plato's understanding of universal peace as evolutionary love is echoed throughout the libretto.

Morris's dance offers symbolic meanings through mixing elocutionary gestures and poses, his choreography re-enacts everyday movements, such as walking and holding hands, in conjunction with community dancing such as the roundel. The choreography seems charged with symbolic reasoning, as we, as watchful participants, can question Platonic ethics. We can rethink questions about the connection of love, death, shared experience, and moral excellence, as well as the political questions of equality and justice.

Morris's dance is more oriented to its libretto than Satie's music is to Plato's text, as the dancer's gestures become embodied with the meaning of the music. A viewer and listener can allow the dancers to become absorbed with the music. Act one shows how people's *eros* can be motivated by desire, thereby enslaving one's soul.[64] Dancers are roped together in threes, symbolically presenting Plato's tripartite: mind, body, and soul. Dancing by pantomiming walking and conversing as if gracefully, strolling across the agora, the performers transform the philosophical meanings of such a state built on slavery, by desire, through movement, space, and timing. Being roped together, they show how a soul feels when physically enslaved. However, discussions are ongoing throughout the community, obviously showing intense concern about the enslavement of the community's political and ethical well-being. They engage in philosophical discussion, but often in these scenes, one person in the triads lingers, being left subserviently behind, reminding us of the problems of inequality, slavery, and an exclusive comradery.

In the second act, the unbound citizens romp with lively footwork and dance a roundel, as the polis celebrates together as a community. The dancers often move with stoic grace, forming serpentine lines while harmonizing their bodies with the music, and undulating, thereby connecting a continuum with the feeling of the audience. The dancers hold hands, and as their gestures are meaningfully symbolic of the ethical, cultural, relatedness of the narrative and music, their configurations are clearly not mere abstraction. The dancer's portrayal and physicality call the audience into their sense of ongoing rhythmic community, marking collective aesthetic reasoning.[65]

In Delsartian fashion, their gestures motivate continued expression, not by copying life but by acting as creative signs, as the dancers are engaging meaningfully with the audience's reception.

Morris, as well, brings theatrical staging to the composition, and it is here we can feel his expression of naturalism—a kind of Hellenistic baroque—with a sense of pathos embedded with humanistic ideas. Watching the dancers gesturing and posing, our physical feelings are heightened while our thoughts are flooded with images. People in the audience who have seen Greco-Roman statuary can once again be mesmerized by the naturalism of the Baberini Faun, when one dancer lounges as part of the symposium, supported by others as if raised on a plinth.

One gesture is particularly poignant as the dancers raise their right hands, palm inward with one finger pointing upward, while outstretching their left arms. At those times Raphael's Plato is reborn, as he gestures to the eternal heavens while walking through the School of Athens with his student Aristotle. We can also think of David's stoic Socrates as he gestures, bidding farewell to his family and friends, but not to his philosophy of peace and understanding.

In the third act a dancer portraying the condemned Socrates lifts his arm and finger again, and at this dramatic climax, we can call to mind the Peace Statue, which stands at Heiwa Knen-zo, the Peace Park, in Nagasaki, Japan. We can contemplate this gesture, turning our thoughts to Plato and Peirce, disclosing a meaning of our individuality, for the number one is calculable as a single unit more than zero, but when calculated relational, it is so much more. Plato taught us to understand not merely in numbers but to the meaning of the sum, and Peirce explains how this plurality occurs through aesthetic reasoning and syncheism. This Peace Statue is a sign embodying the human condition of striving to understand ourselves, employing our reasoning as a seamless connectivity with all existence, as a process that is changeable and ongoing, uniting our feelings of peace, love, and understanding. In kind, we can think further than the physics of a nuclear explosion to the relational and ethical meanings of our presence as part of a creative, peaceful time/space continuum. The Statue's gesture is symbolic of universal peace, carrying forward an idea of the importance of aesthetic reasoning in relation to a continuum of love.

The Nagasaki Peace Statue, which gestures to the air as a warning of the threat of nuclear Holocaust from the air, gestures for all people to come together with a universal resolve for peace and remembrance. Different in some ways to the Platonic and Peircean relationships between infinity and divinity, this humanistic symbol still echoes their philosophies of peace. But perhaps, when watching Morris's dance, it is possible the raised hand still marks a connection to our infinite physical connectedness with a boundless mindfulness of evolutionary love. Morris is able to symbolize how ideas are enlivened through movement and community, as the human body being finite is carried forward by what is infinite—love, peace, and harmony—as individuals are rooted, yet opened expressively through our relationships. Clearly, thinking of the immensity of the statement at Nagasaki, we need to rely on aesthetic reasoning, putting into motion ideas and goals we share, which are pluralistic in perspective, interpretation, and expression, and this is what Peirce describes as "the real potential world."[66]

In the final act, Morris draws on stage, forming the dancers together as a lotus symbol, representing nature's eternal mindfulness, a flowering of consciousness, and a transmigration of the soul. Somewhat paradoxically, Socrates is at this moment condemned by his fellow citizens. As the dancers move into the final passages, Satie's score is heard to make a singular dramatic crescendo, rising from a tetrachord to a fournote figure, followed by a funeral dirge-like motif. It is, then, the dancers begin to die, each dropping to the floor in their own time, as if their mourning of each other's deaths passes from the present performance into history. With their passing, all the citizens die, except one dancer who walks again, seemingly searching through Elysian Fields for the ideas and humanity of Greek democracy.

Peirce also thinks about immortality in relation to symbols, music, and synechism, and I want to continue to evoke Peirce's ideas on synechism, to reinforce Morris's connections of body and soul. In Peirce's "Immortality in the Light of Synechism," he offers an illuminating story:

> A friend of mine, in consequence of a fever, totally lost his sense of hearing. He had been very fond of music before his calamity; and, strange to say, even afterwards would love to stand by the piano when a good performer played, "So then", I said to him, "after all you can hear a little." "Absolutely not at all," he replied; "but I can *feel* the music all over my body." "Why," I exclaimed, "how is it possible for a new sense to be developed in a few months!" "It is not a new sense," he answered. "Now that my hearing is gone I can recognize that I always possessed this mode of consciousness, which I formerly, with other people, mistook for hearing. In the same manner, when the carnal consciousness passes away in death, we shall at once perceive that we have had all along a lively spiritual consciousness which we have been confusing with something different."[67]

Morris's dances and reinterpretations of musical themes, such as with Satie's compositions and Brahm's "Liebeslieder Walzer" (1868), are also contemporarily politically relevant. Recently, Alastair Macaulay, writing in *The New York Times*, clarified the importance of choreography as an interpretive and socially critical medium, as he explained Morris's troupe's feminist statements while dancing "Love Song Waltzes" (first performed in 1989). The evolution of love is portrayed as a message of sexual freedom becoming aesthetically political, through the danced actions, poses, and gestures of the performers. Macaulay writes:

> In Mr. Morris's world, not only are same-sex couples equal to opposite-sex ones, but women can be propulsive, and men submissive. This was the view of gender with which modern dance began to transform itself in the 1980s; Mr. Morris was among its earliest exponents. It took ballet another 30 years to catch up.[68]

We can think again of Peirce's understanding of an inclusive community relating to each other openly by movement, considering future possibilities through our communications of signs and our open-ended aesthetic ideas. Our social consciousness is not separated from our carnal and spiritual being, and such an embodied sense of meaning is present to us while we experience sign-making and the arts.

When sympathy fails as a theory of ethical pluralistic thinking, or normative ethics only gives us unhappy maxims, an ethics of agapism and an aesthetic reasoning could guide us to better solutions. In terms of Peirce's idea of evolutionary love, world peace can be seen as the best conception of effectual changes of our world, as we continually reinterpret our symbolic presences in our communities through our arts. Our multiperspectival aesthetic reasoning allows us to express our ethical evolution as a continuity of love and its unifying processes, in part with the dynamic of creativity and spontaneous change. Accordingly, there is real hope the world will eventually rid itself of hate and war. Certainly this means we would be moving toward unity over divisiveness and oppression, while individuals retain their expressiveness and creativity. On this final note, we can look ever more intently to Peirce's philosophy that evolution is a matter of aesthetics. Peirce's words resonate: "Love, recognising germs of loveliness in the hateful, gradually warms it into life, and makes it lovely."[69]

3

Josiah Royce's Values of Interpretation and Community: Poetry, Cybernetics, and Folk Songs

Scholarly studies exposing a possibility that Josiah Royce expounded racial bias relate a cautionary tale, warning against swallowing Classical American philosophies whole, without close analysis and continued critique. Particularly because of his 1908 book, *Race Questions Provincialism and Other American Problems*, Royce has been called out for basing American race relations on colonial aesthetic/socio/political cultural privilege.[1] I feared such prejudice ran throughout Royce's philosophy, making him guilty of painting a patriarchal picture of culture, and relegating such privilege to false values, passed on throughout the culture, continually protecting White male privilege.[2] If such were the case Royce's philosophy of culture would, of course, be considered doubtful (if not despicable), at the very least because any singular approach to culture is unreasonable in terms of our diverse world. I do realize the seriousness of this critique, which seems particularly biting in that the theories of many American philosophers (i.e. Alain Locke, Jane Addams, John Dewey, and others) have been beacons for pluralistic philosophical approaches, specifically in terms of positioning commonplace, yet individual, experiences at the forefront when we make decisions about ethical matters. These philosophers, as is well known, stress the importance of experiences and events born out of, and constantly remaining connected to, what some might consider unlikely sources of social change, the voices of vulnerable individuals oftentimes thwarted by justified public interests. It follows that a significant aspect of their philosophies has been that they attempted to write for democratic readers, as many were directly involved with movements for social justice.

Despite my concerns, I do not focus in this chapter on Royce's racial prejudices or similar critiques of other Classical American philosophers. I will say that I think there are many questions concerning racial and sexual bias in relation to this canon that remain unanswered, and researchers should sort out what the motivations behind possible incomplete thinking on matters of gender, race, and socio/economic justice were, and the extent of such biases, while thinking about whether these nineteenth- and twentieth-century thinkers did societal damage which resonates today. Although I admit to casting Royce's theories in a positive light, I do ask whether his semiotics/philosophy of culture is contemporarily valuable to our moral progress.

Why is Royce's semiotic theory important at our contemporary intercultural juncture of societal development, while culture wars rage? The answer may lie in our ability to expand the connections between Royce's innovative theory of interpretation and value-making, in terms of propagating more meaningful communications, value-oriented culture building, and global community fellowships. I investigate Roycean philosophy of culture, specifically in terms of value-making, as a matter of semiotic interpretation, which I see as helping people work toward a more diversely productive world.

I begin by analyzing how Royce found values connected with imaginative thinking/acting, then looking to understand how his semiotic method of interpretation enables people to enhance intercultural values, spotlighting technologies of poetry, artificial intelligence, and music. I spotlight T.S. Eliot's poetry and Norbert Wiener's ethics of science (connecting Royce's ethics to cybernetics and artificial intelligence). Moving on from historical influences, music and poetry win the day, as I mark the importance and perseverance of popular culture by referencing folk music/poetry. I locate creative dimensions of sharing our futures, spiritually and ethically, asking if we could include artificially intelligent beings, and hoping to solve existential problems such as nuclear war and environmental crisis by interpreting cultural artifacts.

My focus is on Royce's late work, *The Problem of Christianity*, originally published in 1913, a text in which he moves his religious philosophy past moral prescriptions to a philosophy of culture, which depends on spreading shared values, of loyalty, among diverse communities. After 1908 (the year of the publications of *Philosophy of Loyalty* and *Race Questions, Provincialism and Other American Questions*), Royce takes up a more experiential view than his previous absolute idealism, explaining that spiritual values are individualistic. Yet, he explains human actions and cognitions as not merely synthesized but added to by a third experiential process, which is collective, namely interpretation.[3] Interpretation is not just a binding agent between what we do and what we think but our interpretations of signs and artifacts are active creative dynamics, embodied with social ties and relational value-making. Individuals apply their interpretations of signs to their moral will, by making decisions in relation to their loyalty to their community. Signs are idealistic and material in makeup. But their most important attributes are aesthetic, in that signs engage one's community as ongoing relational mediums of collective creativity. So, we can refer to philosophical terms such as auto-poetic to describe the ongoing creative and aesthetic qualities of cultural signs. Through his late writing, Royce begins to understand culture as dependent on such creative agency and intercultural signs that harbor moral agency as well, hence his ethics of "loyalty to loyalty." Moreover his value theory, based on creating and acting on ethical ideas through such semiotics, can be thought of as foreshadowing a hermeneutic method of social critique, namely disclosure, as will be discussed.

I hope to solve some problems of cultural bias by investigating interpretive value-making.

So, wanting to draw out the connections between diversity, collective creativity, and loyalty to shared values, we will look closely at social issues of bias and prejudice. One possible problematic issue we will investigate is Artificial Intelligent technology, which could develop by dictating a singularity of norms, specifically in relation to White male privilege.

Royce's Value Theory: Creative and Meaningful Time Shared Through Interpretation

Value-making, for Royce, involves our interpretation of signs, as he explains such semiotics as a cultural process, based on historical developments (including leading voices) and progressive purposes. Each person's interpretive abilities are concentrated by both socially and individualistically creative motivations. Royce explains this process as basically, nonauthoritative and connected to our ongoing (often previously unexpressed) and relational experiences, involving us with a common interpretations of signs. Frank Oppenheimer gives several examples of such relational, commonplace qualities of interpretation:

> For example, a person tries to read his friend's unspoken preference, or a translator tries to grasp from the Hebrew text the genuine intent of Isiah and convey it faithfully to an English reader, or a banker tries to discern through the varied signs connected with a candidate for a loan the latter's reliability.[4]

A triadic process of conception, perception, and interpretation, Roycean semiotics accounts for time and history, as our common experiences of signs relate to the past in terms of the present while opening our thinking to what may lie ahead of us. Royce thinks of life as infused with a "timeless" quality, as we don't think of ourselves as ever finished or completed, but as always amid the process of ongoing interpretations of our goals and purposes. Our ongoing, creative interpretation of signs does not necessitate finality, and we rarely imagine ourselves as finished with this process. Through time, as if our thinking is an artistic medium, we integrate our emotions with our thoughts and actions, enabling us to fold our feelings into events, as signs, with this time-filled, eternal quality.[5] Robert Corrington and subsequently Frank Oppenheim adopt the term "interpretive musement" from Charles Sanders Peirce to describe the dynamic quality of interpretation.[6] We will adapt this concept further on in our discussion to gain a fuller understanding of Royce's epistemology.

Royce took inspiration from Peircian semiotics, in that he was thinking about knowledge (which always involves the interpretation of signs) as fallible, meaning that changing occurrences, emotions, and ideas can be replaced by novel perspectives. He came to understand truth, which we require for action, as based on interpretive decisions by "the community of inquirers." Peirce thought in terms of a community of scientists, but Royce thought of community as a culturally bonded group.[7]

Robert S. Corrington points out, "Royce did not retain the distinction between iconic, indexical, and symbolic signs but focused instead on the social and relational dimensions of sign systems."[8] Royce, adding dynamics of social consciousness to Peirce's semiotics and interpretive musement, asks important questions about community communication and culture building. He finds democratic community values depend on truth making as a creative matter, in contrast to truth as a matter of a static ideology or a culture, which relies mostly on authority, tradition, or dogma. Royce explains such like interpretive musement as the *purpose* of the arts and philosophy:

> Do you ask what this process is which thus transcends both perception and conception, I answer that it is the process in which you engage whenever you take counsel with a friend, or look in the eyes of one beloved, or serve the cause of your life. This process it is which touches the heart of reality. Let them equally avoid those wanton revels in mere perception, which are at present the bane of our art, of our literature, of our social ideals, and of our religion. Let the philosophers learn from those who teach us, as the true artist do, the art of interpretation.[9]

The connection between an individual's purpose in life and their culture is inherent to an interpretive process, which plays out in terms of ethical value-making.[10] Royce thinks of this creative process as a matter of direct interpersonal relationships, in that interpretative communication, rather than mere perception or conception, is "namely the successful interpretation of somebody to somebody."[11] Moreover, the interpretation of signs is a thrust of our efforts from the past and the present to a value-laden future, as interpreters seek, from what they have learned about each other as a matter of an ongoing correlated future.[12] So community values and communication are intertwined. Loyalty to one another is a matter of communicating with loyal intentions, which can be ethically interpreted among a cultural community.

Furthermore, Corrington makes clear that Royce shifts Peirce's semiotics so as to involve an inclusive pluralism, and in this respect, we can note Royce's emphasis on uncalculated possibilities and people's interpretations, which might lie outside of expert or elite groups. Royce considers exploring knowledge that has not been considered normative, as possibly the beginnings of new relationships.[13] Additionally, Royce also brings to a concept of interpretive musement the hermeneutic technique of disclosure.[14] What I mean by disclosure is marking and reinterpreting social problems that have been historically hidden or solved improperly. What is truly novel about Royce's understanding of interpretation is that by using disclosure, not just accounting for history (or general aspects of time) as a matter of one's personal experience or understanding, we establish an organic technology so as to grasp alternative interpretations of events or ideas. Through our creative interpretive musement, we are opening up novel possible solutions, which can be reparative. So, while we communicate freely and interpret cultural references creatively, as we follow through with our communities' continuity of value-laden signs, we are freed from extinct and outmoded biases and circumstances.

People need creative notions and novel techniques to correct and adjust societal values. An emergent moral situation often comes about through an ethical disclosure of a specific commitment in light of a specific "act of treason." Such an event, according to Royce, requires one's reconciling will, as a matter of loyalty to one's community. But loyalty is a creative process of engaging with one's history and ongoing relationships, a matter of a "creative will" and "creative love."[15] There is a resulting transfiguration of the community, as a revaluing of the very life of the traitor, as they reshape history. Their act of treason can mean the community's act of disclosure as an act of atonement, bringing forward the crisis of the community. Loyal citizens are able to creatively refashion the meaning of the treasonous act, along with the values of their community.[16] The triumph of the community resolves history in light of its present problems, by remolding cultural signs, and the resonance and emergence of disclosure prepares the way for an enlightened future.

Time, Poetry, Music, and Values

That we are able to imaginatively and collectively remake values is a spiritually motivating aspect of making art. We have talked about how interpretation and value-making processes occur with a cognitive, psychological/social dynamic; now let us turn to how such facilitates art. Artists and philosophers share a common quest according to Royce, for both interpret our sensual experiences.[17] Royce's favored examples of artistic signs were poetry, examining how cultures communicate values through creative processes, not through inherited emotional states, nationalistic dictates, or static rituals. Philosophically Royce prepares a way for the Modernist critics of mass society, while thinking in terms of cultural solutions rather than an existential crisis. Royce's literary connections with poems and relationships with poets are many, evidenced throughout his writing, letters, and biographical details. He wrote early in his career on the German Romantic poets, explaining an early version of his idealistic philosophy of art in his essay "The Aim of Poetry." He continued his investigations by his later philosophy of interpretation, in sections of *The Problem of Christianity*, as he employs poetry to explain his theory of time and semiotics. We will focus on these later writings, but the fact that Royce knew and taught philosophy to influential poets of the Modern era, namely the two very different modern poets and cultural figures T.S. Eliot and Gertrude Stein, is important to our understanding of the influence of his ideas of interpretation.[18]

Royce explains cultures as collective signs, livened by everyday experiences, rituals, traditions, and a holistic sense of time—all understood by participants as value-laden signs motivating our everyday purposes of life. Time's true relevance for a culture/community is not merely calculable, such as with clocks, calendars, and even nanoseconds in feedback loops, but as actively meaningful in that we gather together during sequences of events, making valued experiences. Music and poetry demonstrate how this holistic approach to time impacts our cultures. Royce describes music composition as "Beautifully significant musical meanings in temporal order."[19] Noting the importance of sequence and rhythm to the formation of collective meaning, one finds a leitmotif and symphony as "time-inclusive," transcending "any one temporal present."[20] The musical moments of particular movements share "vanishing instants" as those sounds are held relative to one another in "present, past, and future."[21] The sequence is present in every moment and can be identified as a unified passage; this Royce finds as an "eternal present."

> True listening to music grasps, in a certain sense as a totum simul, entire sequences—measures, phrases, movements, symphonies. But such wiser listening and appreciation is not timeless. It does not ignore sequence. It is time-inclusive. It grasps as an entirety a sequence which transcends any one temporal present. In this grasping of the whole of a time process one gets a consciousness of a present, which is no longer merely a vanishing present, but a time including, a relatively eternal present, in which various vanishing instants have their places as relatively eternal present, in which future one to another.[22]

Music is ontologically meaningful, being made from tones to be interpreted in sequence, in a shared present. This eternally present aspect of music is telling of the loyal value of one's relation to a community, as our conceptions of ourselves are not regressing or proceeding momentarily or even annually, but rhythmic and transcendent (as a matter of taking in holistic meanings). Thereby by listening to music, we can value what is significant and undeniably unique about ourselves in the present moment in relation to the ongoing relational quality of our culture/community.[23] Music is often described as "a sign of the times," such as with Chopin or even the music of Bob Dylan, which we will discuss in the final section of this chapter.

Poetry plays a part in culture in similar ways, as the explanation of the creative and transcendent dynamics of one's interpretations can be discerned in the combination of tempo of words and unity of meaning. When we read poetry, we read word for word, but the wholeness of meaning connects through rhythmic and semantic technologies of cadence and imagination. This is a twofold experience; on the one hand, one can be attentive to an isolation of each word, letter, or utterance; yet rather than a moment of synthesis when all elements snap together, there is part of that time spent contemplating the entire sequence. Neither an empirical sense nor a metaphoric sense of how we relate what we read to reality is fully able to afford for poetry's creative dynamic, so our interpretive cognition sets about relating matters in an ongoing sense of our experiences.

Before developing his semiotics, Royce wrote about poetry as a beacon for revolutionary activism, expounding on the limits and virtues of Shelley's poems in the treatise "Shelley and the Revolution."[24] Royce suggests his later theories on creative processes and value-making, in that essay by explaining the revolutionary's, and poet's, thinking as super-rational rather than sublime or mystical. A poet, according to Royce, knows how to focus on the emotional aspects of our experiences, apart from the continuous onslaught of phenomena. They engage with change and chance, yet through their emotional lens, they experiment with language so as to outmode what was previously felt. By contrast, a conservative person becomes used to thoughts and emotions that most easily adhere to present experiences because of their past. As a lyricist, the poet understands process as a matter of ever interpreting and forming new ideas and shades of emotions; this process takes effort and attention to changes in their environments. By using such processes, Shelley was revolutionary rather than someone finding acceptance and conventionality more existentially truthful; consequentially, his poems hermeneutically carry revolutionary meanings.[25] Yet, we are all conservative, but for recreating old conceptions and perceptions in regard to new conditions.[26] People, however, are revolutionary as they stretch and search for new meanings, just as activists demand social changes, nonetheless eventually returning to being conservative when our projects seem completed.

Years after writing about Shelley, while explaining interpretation, Royce would sum up the lyrical as an existential process; writing about poetry and time, "the series is not merely by virtue of remembered facts, but also as experienced facts, and in truth, were this not so, you could indeed have no experience of succession at all."[27] In artistic forms such as music and poetry, we are able to include philosophical wonderings about our personal, ongoing emotional experiences as in sync with our musings on comprehensive meanings of the present, while we are involved in a future-orienting process. As far as social consciousness is concerned, realizing our limited time span of consciousness, through writing, listening, or reading a poem, is not a drawback but is alike the dynamic of the previous experienced era of culture. Yet we are then able to approach a wholeness of *moral* meaning by forward-minded conceptual thinking.[28]

As mentioned, T.S. Eliot was one of Royce's students. While reading for his PhD in philosophy at Harvard before immigrating to the United Kingdom, he participated in Royce's infamous seminar focused on investigating and reformulating the scientific method. Eliot has been criticized for being anti-Semitic, perhaps alike to the critique of Royce's bias for a superior Anglo-European culture, as critics claim Eliot regaled racist views that resound in his poetry.[29] Anthony Julius has presented a strong case for interpreting Eliot's literary techniques as spreading anti-Semitism, and he thinks of Eliot as being a part of an ongoing abhorrent trend, as people continue to use anti-Semitism to make more secure their own identity.[30] We will find possible reasons for Eliot's lack of self-knowledge, as he limits his use of the emotional interpretive process we have been discussing.[31]

According to Julius, Eliot's poetry portrays insecurity in modern culture, harboring a lack of authenticity of cultural purpose, being that the poet, or artistic genius, feels trapped by modernism. Julius finds that anti-Semitism is correlated with fears of commercial society being a society without culture.[32] Eliot clearly finds randomness to an individual's spirit amid social constraints of his time, often blaming such on a hypocritical, status-oriented bourgeoisie class. For Eliot, because of middle-class values in respect to their consuming desire for wealth and social status, Western culture became devoid of the expressive range of inquiring about life's meanings. Through his explanations of such existential angst, which he also attributed to a cultural loss because of the lack of faith in God, we can find a close connection between Eliot's vision and Royce's philosophy. Both sought to clear new ground relating to science, religion, and culture, in a time when many people were unsure of how to authentically communicate and contribute, as many people felt powerless and purposeless amid massive societies.[33]

Piers Gray finds Eliot applying Royce's philosophy of "interpretive communities," yet Eliot does not ever fully realize the breadth of his professor's philosophy, especially in relation to how people's thoughtful actions can change social conditions. If the poetic aesthetic involves inclusive time, as being profound and as involving processes of change, collective agency is constituted. Eliot had lost faith in such a process.[34] We *focus* our histories (sometimes this means reflecting on our departures from meaningful values) by our future-oriented creative deeds. For Eliot, time and history inspire our senses of metaphoric interpretation but not our senses of connectedness to future possibilities for our relationships. Gray explains that Eliot was unable to accept any difference between tradition and ongoing dynamic interpretive changes. I surmise Eliot is not able to hold on to a fuller conception of collective meaning, even though his realism is strikingly poetic. What Eliot's art lacks is a more "eternally present" spark of hope, for a more inclusive sense of culture.

Gray points to the point I am emphasizing: that Eliot does not apply his thoughts in terms of interpretive musement, thereby not validating the interrelational purposes between individuals and their community, which are both uniquely significant because of their commonality. In the "Journey of the Magi," Eliot concentrates on the kings' experience while journeying, expressing an ambiguity of the meaning of that journey, as the travelers seem uncertain of their quest and therefore of their accomplishment when reaching their spiritual destination. Therefore when returning home to spread the good news of redemption and atonement, they feel confused. Their uncertainty is cloaked in a philosophy that hangs on to a moral ideal of what redemption *should* be, with a longing for being relinquished from death. So reading the poem, we find only an incomplete revelation in the journey's triumph of realizing what is suitable. Eliot, however, could have pointed to what they did find, as they undoubtedly spoke to those at the Nativity event and among each other along the long path home, asking what future purposes could be formed among their communities.

As an alternative to the listlessness and confusion of the travelers, I infer that Royce would find their spiritual journey open to many interpreters, as a quest of learning and making new companionship with each other along the way, while carrying on with that spirit in making changes to the ethics of their communities. The journey is a sign, depending on a creative interpretation of their journey in relation to a more inclusive community.[35] Royce often refers to the transformative quality of interpretation as a journey, explaining values at one point in *Problem of Christianity* in terms of exchange and revaluing one's currency while traveling. The exchange of currency when one is traveling requires a process of exchange, thereby valuing trust in that relationship underlies the currency's values. The exchange is based on interpreting the present value of the money but also future proceedings on the part of both the communities of the traveler and money exchanger. This commitment to the act of exchange and intercultural valuation is analogous to the spiritual commitment of faith made by the Magi. We should not forget the kings went bearing gifts, signs of their hope for cultural change. As said, the journey itself is a sign, an expression of the Magi's hope, not only for their personal redemption, or as a matter of sacrificial tithing, but their hope for a fuller intercultural life for their communities.

Royce and Wiener: Cybernetics, Interpretation, and Ethics

Acknowledging one's loyalty to a global community as a participant with ongoing interpretive cultures is a matter of recognizing ever-more creative ways of communication and organization. As far as art is concerned, we have seen how Royce thought of poetry as joined with community disclosure. He also advanced a collaborative, mediating approach to culture by formulating an interpretive scientific method.

Royce was convinced that creativity involves purposes that span time, history, and social challenges, progressing past a dialectical or synthesis of rhetorically presented interests. This approach is the basis of Royce's theory of science, and through his later writings, he intersects our interpretation of signs in respect to *creative* science with our enrichment of cultures. Culture and science depend on a community of interpreters with unifying purposes, collaborating in respect to answering questions and solving problems. Royce thought people who challenge outmoded values associate with each other purposefully, trading signs from sciences, arts, and ethics, thereby enabling inclusive communities to gain broad overviews of knowledge of our shared reality. "We conspire with the world even when most we seem to rebel." He wrote in *The World and the Individual* (1900):[36]

Our scientific methods have much to offer value-making as an interpretive technology, and alike to the arts, science is a communicative practice of cultural mediation. Royce thinks of science as an abductive activity, meaning speculation can be an aspect of scientific thinking. Let us now discuss his ideas on science as a creative interpretative practice and as a community-building mode of culture. To exemplify let's consider science's response to the contemporary threats of community separation and personal alienation coming from deep artificial intelligence.

Cybernetics, the science of communication and automatic control systems in machines and human beings, was founded by Norbert Wiener, who was a student of Royce's at Harvard. While scholars have studied Royce's influence on Wiener's logic and ethics of science, a more thorough understanding of how the latter's thinking on artificial intelligence was impacted by Royce's semiotics will help us with our investigation of values and culture. During the Second World War Wiener's visionary understanding of stochastic listening/signaling in radio communications and prediction in relation to random motion in physics resulted in a breakthrough with anti-aircraft radar. Wiener pioneered fusing philosophical logic with mathematics, using probability and statistics, calculating algorithms for machine-learning systems. He was at the forefront of computer technology in terms of feedback looping and control systems, advancing communications gathering, machine learning, and cognitive biotechnologies. Wiener's books on artificial intelligence and ethics, from the 1950s and 1960s, have been influential in contemporary discussions on our computer-dependent culture. He prophesies the misuse of advanced technologies, such as information fraud and existential threats because of literal learning and singularities of understanding, specifically in relation to automata learning robotic systems.

Fortunately, Wiener never abandoned his Roycean interpretive approach, and he credits Royce with shaping his ideas in respect to ethical thinking and culture. Wiener attended Royce's seminar on the scientific method, entitled "A Comparative Study of Various Types of Scientific Method," from 1911 to 1913.[37] Interestingly, T.S. Eliot also attended some of these seminar meetings, although I have not been able to discern whether he shared the room with Wiener.[38] Royce was to have been Wiener's dissertation director but for the professor's poor health at the time. Wiener went on to finish his studies at Tufts University.[39] A quote from Wiener's autobiography is telling of the strong influence Royce had on the younger mathematician:

> This position of facing both the past and the future was also clear in Royce's seminar on Scientific Method, which I attended for 2 years, and which gave me some of the most valuable training I have ever had. Royce welcomed into this little group every sort of intellectual who was carrying out a reasonable program of work and who was articulate concerning the methods by which he had come to his own ideas and concerning the philosophical significance thereof.[40]

The seminar was based on an interdisciplinary approach to science and Royce's interpretive epistemology. The purpose of developing new scientific methods was to break down barriers of secrecy between science, especially military science, and our community's knowledge and application of scientific discoveries. Wiener went on to write on this subject, notably his text *The Human Use of Human Beings*. He makes clear his approach:

> I repeat, to be alive is to participate in a continuous stream of influences from the outer world and acts on the outer world, in which we are merely the transitional stage. In the figurative sense, to be alive to what is happening in the world, means to participate in a continual development of knowledge and its unhampered exchange.[41]

Leone Montaguini has written a comprehensive study of Wiener's influences, explaining the philosophical similarities of cybernetics and Royce's thinking on "absolute pragmatism." Montaguine notes that Wiener took from Royce's seminar a nascent understanding of probabilistic and methodologically collaborative science.[42] Wiener, as well, took on board the importance of Royce's understanding of values as involving people's interrelated purposes in respect to manifesting their ideas, as well as Royce's broader teleological, yet pragmatic, optimism that all of existence *can* work in relationship with each another for the purpose of life's flourishing.[43] Undoubtedly, Wiener would have learned important lessons concerning how people are influenced, taught, and progress through their ongoing interpretations. Wiener would go on to write about scientific ethics stressing constructive, inclusive communal relationships as the most human and natural way to organize our lives. He realized the educational damages done by racist privilege in the United States and warned of an attitude of prejudice in relation to weak scientific ethics.[44] Notably Wiener ties creativity, open communication, and his idea that society has become enslaved to efficiency, to a conscious release from racist thinking and actions.[45] Creativity is essential for a society free of prejudice and for ethical technological progress; according to Wiener, any less is a mere matter of automata. A state of deterministic consciousness, both individually and socially, in respect to humans and machines, leads to problematic class and race problems for the community and seriously dangerous existential territory for individuals.[46]

Through his scientific work, Wiener sought a seamless relationship between analogical machine technology and digital information, and at the same time, he turned away from employing either without retaining voluntary relational action by participants as a foundation, particularly in the conception and design of such technologies. Wiener was concerned with autonomous relationships between people and people, people and their environments, and people and machines.

Wiener had deep ethical, legal, and political concerns about the then future of artificial intelligence, which now deserves our acute attention, as these issues are contemporarily pressing. Technically Wiener was concerned with information systems breaching their purposeful contexts, not so much because such would surpass human's intellectual limitations but because of the nature of mechanical systems in terms of entropy. Entropy involves disturbances in connecting information and communication (conditional entropy) and/or lack of meaningful translation of the information in regard to human purposes.[47] A machine fighting entropy, attempting to stop the loss of information at all costs, could make reckless or harmful decisions, affecting human life.

So while laying out tenets for an ethics of cybernetics, Wiener stressed the importance of paying close attention to interpretations of information by both humans and machines. What is important to Wiener, and Royce, is an ethical orientation ensuring ongoing communal relationships, which can involve diverse views in respect to meaningful and democratically beneficial purposes. As a major axiom for ethical human and machine communications, semiotic and ethical frameworks are necessary for mutual and ongoing communications, so we can act in concert, but Wiener thought that these frameworks should also be designed to be flexible in respect to a unity of purposes.[48]

Likewise unimaginative thinking was a concern for Wiener, in respect to machine-made decisions, retaining a singularity of understanding as well as advanced super intelligence understanding of data outrunning human understanding without ethical reflection or guidance.[49] Of course this is a problem confronting scientists contemporarily, and Mark Graves, a computer scientist and scholar of religious studies, asks, "How can human and machines communicate in a way that makes meaning and adds value and constructive purpose to their relationship?"[50] We will investigate Graves's approach after we look more closely at Wiener's ideas on cultural values and artificial intelligence.

Wiener recognized that automata learning must include situational and community-minded interpretation (as with imaginative musings). From his milestone text *The Human Use of Human Beings*, first published in 1950 and revised in 1954:

> Any machine constructed for the purpose of making decisions if it does not possess the power of learning, will be completely literal-minded. Woe to us if we let it decide our conduct, unless we have previously examined the laws of its action, and know fully that its conduct will be carried out on principles acceptable to us! On the other hand, the machine like the jinnee, which can learn and can make decisions on the basis of its learning, will in no way be obliged to make such decisions as we should have made, or will be acceptable to us. For the man who is not aware of this, to throw the problem of his responsibility on the machine, whether it can learn or not, is to cast his responsibility to the winders, and to find it coming back seated on the whirlwind.[51]

So years after Royce's seminar, Wiener continued to be concerned about altering scientific methods, while engaging scientific communities and the general public through his writings in ethical discussions. It becomes clear to Wiener that public trust and engagement by scientists affect the information, as well as the conditions of communication, which in turn affect how we construct both our technologies and our relationships.

What specifically might have stood out to Wiener, when attending Royce's seminar meetings, in terms of ethics, that helped him understand such a confluence of relationships between machines and humans? During those seminar years, Royce specifically addressed the problems of a person's free will in relation to society, coming to understand an individual's volition as always constituted with agency, as a part of vital purposes and challenges of their communities. Furthermore, scientific methods are a form of such agency growing out of the communities they help to foster. Scientific innovation depends on an ongoing community of sign makers and communicators, as scientists tackle questions about their experiences with an attitude of hope for the community. Royce wrote:

> Man, the gregarious animal, has always regarded nature as in some ways common property of the experience or knowledge of the group or the tribe." Yet people also becomes distrustful of "private, individual observation unless this receives the systematic confirmation of the group.[52]

Scientist's decisions about their investigations combine with "loyal practical consciousness" that come into play in ethical scientific decisions. Furthermore, I assume Royce also means that it is by virtue of everyone's tendency to be part of communities, rather than apart from such, that scientists as creative interpreters can present seamless connections between the general public's interests and ethical solutions to existential problems. So it follows, when thinking about scientific methods and ethics that each specialist should be able to make decisions about researching in terms of loyalty to an interrelated worldwide community and that their advice and suggestions will be able to be interpreted by their communities. Keeping in mind scientists also work as members of interpretive scientific communities, the bridge between such and the general public is a matter of trust and imaginative musings.

According to Royce, there are three ethical characteristics of the scientific method: first, the inquirer has an independent curiosity; second, the inquirer depends on science and facts, which are previously discovered; and third, the contemporary scientist is dependent on the work of others in respect to scientific communities.[53] Scientists do indeed make personal ethical decisions about interpreting their research, but their understanding of commonality is highlighted because their creative thinking is responsive to their communities. Again Royce informs:

> The methods of the special sciences are allied to the methods of working together which constitute the most significant feature of the practical life of modern humanity ... There is, then, a very close connection between the ethical attitude of the scientific inquirer and the characteristic attitude of the loyal man. Both the loyalists and the scientific man combine an interest in the unity of the social order with a respect for individual freedom of inquiry.[54]

Royce concludes that science is a leading discipline to forge ethics, as it affords a sense of creativity to our communities. Subsequently, scientists are equipped to take on ethical matters, in relation to interpretive musement, from environmental crisis to world peace, and to invent solutions to problems that arise from their discoveries.[55]

As well, important to Royce, and presumably Wiener, was Peirce's thinking on probability and inferential aspects of science, which plays a strong role in the creative/ethical character of the scientific method. There is a difference between necessity and probable inference, as the former is deterministic, leaving out the associative sense of realizing what is best to happen in the future.[56] Probability is the basis for Royce's abductive method; therefore, science is embedded in both what has happened in the past and what is predictive, in terms of a general population. Furthermore when scientists infer about generality, they assume relationships based on probability as neither true nor false but related to a common-sense understanding of events.[57] But for Royce, fallibility remains a factor, as there is always a plurality of individuals, relationships, and circumstances at play. An entrenched interest by the scientific community in ethics will surely entail substantiating the general truth of their findings, which will require understanding of pluralistic cultures.

Royce's hope in aligning science to an ethical responsibility lies with a mediating function as the scientific community verifies, tests, and communicates its empirical findings while upholding an active dialogue with communities. Royce clarifies his position on the scientific method as a gateway to a mediating method in respect to other socially oriented fields, such as politics and social justice. He thinks of a scientist as a mediator, someone who is in dialogue with their communities throughout their research, in a creative mode. Scientist can think ethically as a matter of interpretative signs that carry aesthetics and agency. Royce wrote about people in general: "Let this life be your art and also the art of all your fellow members. Let your community be as a chorus, and not as a company who forget themselves in a common trance."[58] Different community's positions to existential problems are joined by relationships when mediating in respect to common futures, and their decisions are interpretive as ongoing and continuing. Such decisions are not prescriptive but lead to more interpretation and likewise more innovation, inventiveness, and inclusiveness of views. Such decisions are not a matter of applying humanitarian charity to one group while withholding aid from others, as scientific interpretive processes put forward a more creative, existential dynamic. All life is involved with not merely making judgments or decisions but mediating as part of our interrelated environments, as we renew our proposes and commitments to our community.[59]

Wiener took on a role as a community mediator, while working on advanced radar communication during the Second World War. Afterward, he was rightly concerned about the global nuclear threat, thereby asking what can scientists do to curtail developing destructive technologies and how can the general public become more a part of scientific/military decisions. He saw that science is often affected by controlling interests, such as military-controlled research and weapon industries, as well as corporations and governments geared only to expanding productivity without mediating such progress by ongoing community engagement. According to Weiner and Royce, the individual creative scientist is invaluable to her discoveries and scientific breakthroughs, as specialized technical knowledge is vital. Methods of interpretation can be taken on with a philosophical mode of self-reflection, curiosity and wonderment, rather than specific problem-solving or task-oriented projects. Wiener suggests an interpretive method of "inverse invention," whereas a scientist reinvents (reinterprets) tools and concepts by inquiring about what is the purpose of such a study, or tool, or mechanism, and what are the research benefits and drawbacks to communities. Large-scale national and military scientific projects often forgo such interpretive methods, while the individual scientist is looked at with skepticism. Wiener warns that such a loss of interpretive thinking and creativity, along with economic competition and secrecy, can produce a loss of trust in science. Here science becomes a realm of monsters: misunderstood, dangerous, and unwanted. Wiener wrote warningly:

> It will appear from what I have said already that I consider that the leaders of the present trend from individualistic research to controlled industrial research are dominated, or at least seriously touched, by a distrust in the individual which often amounts to a distrust in the human. I wish to give more of the details and of the particular manifestation of this antihuman trend before I comment in detail on what it has accomplished and on its dangers.[60]

Individual ongoing interpretation, open communication, as well as community-minded thinking are required for ethical science, most imperatively today in regard to advanced AI. Wiener warned that humans may not be able to put the jinni back in the bottle when it comes to thinking machines and problems such as AI singularity and domination of the workforce. Computer scientists should involve teaching and learning skills while programming advanced intelligent machines, so that once a task is done, problem solved, or tool invented, those results are rethought in relation to the ethical human engagement.

Mark Graves is a contemporary systems scientist who grapples with spiritual ethical challenges in respect to developing community values as a matter of our relationships with intelligent computers and robots. He uses Royce's philosophy to think about our future ethical problems with advanced AI. For Graves human flourishing, value-making, arts and sciences expand throughout cultures by communities of interpreters, experiencing this way of life as a spiritual, 'transcendent' ontology. In his text *Mind, Brain and the Elusive Soul*, Graves clears ground for a "systems" philosophy of life, as our domains or systems emerge from shared mental and cultural activities. These systems are how humans and deep artificial intelligence could meet so as to advance all of life, specifically in terms of creativity and value-making.

Graves suggests six main systems of human activity, five of which are, subatomic, physical, biological, psychological, and cultural. Thesis fields are opaque, until emerging through a sixth field of human life: a community of inquirers.[61] The community is a transcendent system of human life, distinct from other activities but nonseparable from them as it organizes and mediates the signs of all fields. As well, we confer together to interpret and reinterpret these matters. But whether in agreement or not, such a community is able to shape a unity of systems.

Graves states, "Those assumptions and specific methods, but a community of scientists and scholars may develop a shared interpretation (that no one person can individually hold)."[62] What concerns Graves is the part advanced technological intelligence can play in helping produce such transcendental systems. Interrelated human and AI systems could succeed in furthering common interests by involving religious fields, while such engagement would be directed through common purposes for all beings to develop morally and ethically. As these systems are signs, they contribute to the creativity of communities; interpreters meet to analyze the ongoing relationships involved with the systems. Although such an ethics may not be completely effable (by data or policy) because it is embodied in complex psychologically driven relationships, Graves finds the intersecting of cultural signs, especially feelings and realizations of beauty, and intellectual data signs as setting up a safeguard for egoism. The combined efforts, or feelings of being part of a comprehensive whole, help us work with others in finding the moral "value or purposes" in respect to our inter-human/AI relationships.[63]

Royce's concept of loyalty to loyalty is embedded as part of such a transcendental, beyond empirical data, emergent systems of ongoing interpretations and communication, as people realize the value of the purposes of others. Graves explains that people while engaging with others on a transcendent level can find concepts such as loyalty and beauty as inherent in other intelligent being's cultural signs and as integral to the joy of thinking and reinterpreting that is profoundly important to all.[64] Here we can discern that interpretation and creativity become a joint aesthetic value among all intelligent beings.

Some cultural systems might clash (and here Graves gives the example of war), but this can be transformative, forming emergent lasting alliances, thereby propagating a more overarching transcendent system. Two of Graves's examples are poignant, as when British soldiers saw that Gandhi's followers allowed themselves to be beaten and when the world saw African Americans being beaten during the Civil Rights movement.

> Two coherent, autonomous, self-maintaining cultural systems interact at a place of possible and partially expressed violence, yet both systems become surprisingly transformed in a way that one cannot model in either cultural system.[65]

New transcendent or second-order value judgments form new values, as a matter of social movements or events.[66] The transcendental quality of cultures emerges when the values in common spread to many cultures and appeal to people as fundamental to human flourishing.[67] The creative aspect of this second-order and transcendent aspect of cultural exchange is obviously similar to thinking in terms of interpretive musement, but of course what is apparent is that this aspect of experience is viewed, participated with, and concretized as part of mediating felt experiences, which are symbolic and artefactual. It is the raised fist, the olive branch, MLK's "I have a Dream" speech, Holocaust and Lynching memorials, Black Lives Matter slogan, and many other examples of contemporary political art and music that propagate our interpretation of all essential systems while pulling us toward radical social change and new emergent changes in our combined system.

So how do such emergent systems coordinate creatively with an ongoing process of living signs? As said, Graves attributes to Royce a philosophy of community that "describes selected cultural-level systems as a whole from the perspective of transcendent-level systems."[68] It is here that Graves takes on a religious aspect as a third order, moving from culture to spirituality. This third order is what he finds is necessary for the creative cultural shifts needed to take on board the translation of systems or activities of cultures to form shared values. Also spirituality is needed to translate systems formed from data or information, as with deep artificial intelligence, to a level of values.[69]

Royce sets a philosophical precedent in *Philosophy of Loyalty*, written in 1908. Royce reinterpreted that text, transforming loyalty as an idea into a matter of cultural interpretation, in *Problem of Christianity*. Loyalty to loyalty becomes a matter of mutual understanding, an embodied and value-oriented devotion to one's community, but also a matter of shared spirituality between people with differing norms. For Graves, loyalty is constituent of a transcendental system of life. Graves expounds on loyalty by comparing a third-order system with Royce's religious connotation of a Beloved Community. Royce's Beloved Community is a democratic culture of ethical interpretation of signs. I think Grave is right when he points out that for Royce, the characteristic of loyalty to loyalty is a matter of human understanding that emerges from "cross-cultural harmony and diversity."[70] This aspect of loyalty is benefited by the aesthetic qualities of loyalty as thoughtful, felt, and embodied, inclusive and transformative, but also a manner by which we carry on scientific exploration and communication, as Graves, Wiener, and Royce, before them, emphasized.[71]

The importance of signs as materially artefactual lies with the importance of individual creativity and community. Perhaps Graves neglects the sensuous aesthetic of a transcendental system as being essential to the creative process of morality. Although Graves sees a transcendent third-order basis for the goodness and liberality of communities of interpreters, interpretation is a matter of individuals who make semiotic artifacts through a variety of medias. Royce writes in the late 1800s that the individual is alone able to truly feel a transcendent creative sense of self, but perhaps more important to our discussion at this time is that in *The Problem of Christianity*, he clarifies creative practice as individually embodied in respect to community symbols such as language, rituals, and tradition. The creative impetus remains a uniquely individual feeling, talent, effort, and challenge. Royce explains:

> Yes; but *this* neighbor is your enemy; or he belongs to the wrong tribe or caste or sect. Do not consider these unhappy facts as having any bearing on your love for him. For the ethical side of the doctrine of life concerns not what you *find*, but what you *create*.[72]

We live as individuals harboring hope through our interpretive musements, and pragmatically, our creativity constitutes an artful way of life. He continues:

> Nevertheless, the principle of principles in all Christian morals remains this: Since you cannot *find* the universal and beloved community, *create* it. And this again, applied to the concrete art of living means: Do whatever you can to take a step towards it, or to assist anybody, your brother, your friend you neighbor, your country, mankind, to take steps toward the organization of that coming community.[73]

So individual creativity, an artful meaning for our lives, while benefiting the whole of humanity, is immersed in an individually created system of interpreting.

How will this individual creativity and cultural loyalty play a part in relationships with artificial intelligence of the future? Graves is more hopeful than Wiener. Graves gives insight into a meeting of values between machines, who have a sense of their own autonomous decision-making skills, and humans in his essay "Shared Spirituality Among Human Persons and Artificially Intelligent Agents." Graves suggests engaging with ethical frameworks, which can be programmed as mediating platforms. The four most well-known frameworks in the Western tradition—virtue ethics, deontology, consequential ethics, and an ethics of care—are explained as informative data to be shared with AI beings. The goal of developing intelligent agents capable of communicating as members of communities of interpretation can lay an epistemological foundation for a new more pluralistic ethics.

Royce had a suggestion that also might help with our relationships with AI beings; we can strive to become leaders who advocate for community moral progress, instead of power-oriented goals. Thinking in terms of interpretation, we can recognize leaders as culturally artefactual, in respect to being ethical models. Our personal identities and specialized roles become part of the makeup of communities, and without cultural figures, substantiating ethics, and propagating communicative praxis, would be non-artefactual in respect to human-like actions. I do not think Royce would afford structural ethics complete effectiveness, certainly in terms of loyalty to what makes humans act on moral values. Yet, I think both Royce and Graves agree that all creative agents can be guided by a shared spirituality, which is embodied with our interpretive musement and relationships. Yet, unless AI can also creatively cooperate, guide, and innovate, so as to help inclusive pluralistic cultures, its relationships with humankind could be challenging and difficult.

Culture Wars, Spiritual Interpretation, and Folk Music

Contemporarily political agendas are often conflicting with spiritual values of shared loyalty, as cultural identity seems most unified when associated with socio/political issues. "Culture wars" is a popular term describing frustrations over moral and political divisions. Political identity can supersede nationalism and prevent people from relating person to person. Social protests by groups, such as among American football players, or immigrates, or gay people, are often artistically modeled and remodeled to fit political platforms, rather than interculturally. Slogans such as "Stand for country, kneel for God" and "Blacks Lives Matter" can be used as didactic signs of political culture wars.[74]

Interpretive musings, value-making, and Royce's philosophy of loyalty relate to political activism in respect to both artistic aesthetics as well as a spiritual/inclusive mode of cultural agency. The matter of aesthetics as a social mode of refinement over a more functional matter (as a thing or an activity which facilitates a task) becomes an issue to contend with, when thinking about the signs of culture wars. As well the matter of what is most at stake in these wars, an individual's values or the values of the collective, is relevant.

Royce was looking for a mode of social justice based on relationships. "Look forward to the human and visible triumph of no form of the Christian church," Royce wrote, meaning not to look to functional limitations of some signs (or institutions) but to expressive interpretations of interrelational communities.

> It is not my thought that natural science can ever displace religion or do its work. But what I mean is that since the office of religion is to aim towards the creation on earth of the Beloved Community, the future task of religion is the task of inventing and applying the arts which shall win men over to unity, and which shall overcome their original hatefulness by the gracious love, not of mere individuals, but of communities. Now such arts are yet to be discovered. Judge every social device, every proposed reform, every national and every local enterprise by the one test: *Does this help towards the coming of the universal community.*[75]

His thinking is creative, inferring aesthetic solutions in respect to collective agency, rather than merely isolated functional forms. Accordingly, Royce sees the sciences, arts, and spiritual/religious movements moving forward hand in hand to solve social problems through interpretive aesthetic means.

Contemporarily we can see such a mixing of aesthetic fields informing an intercultural social orientation, through exchanging methods, information, and technology. Our twenty-first-century scientific community feels the need to take on board the relevance of our spiritual aims as we are continually challenged when focusing our purposeful and moral ontological orientations. An example is how AI is being taught to compose music, in a combination of digital and analogical methods, and the question of whether we should also be offering critique according to general audiences, in respect to our functional use of music, might be important.

In *Problem of Christianity*, Royce makes a case for interpretive musement as an aspect of the religiosity of the Pauline Church, because there are integrated functional and aesthetic qualities of spirituality. Our interpretation of signs is a continuity of the community's spiritual beliefs, that is, each person's loyalty is a tool for increasing acceptance of other people's differences. I turn again to music while investigating the social problem-solving dynamic of this multifunctional interpretive aesthetic, as music often helps unify people with a sense of spiritual inclusiveness. Some songs of contemporary American Folk music are symbolic of ongoing values of inclusive communities, as they can be interpreted and reinterpreted globally as popular culture.

Folk music is noted as historically being sung by a family or community, rather than a lone voice distanced from their audience.[76] As well folk song is spotlighted for its many uses in everyday life, such as providing tempo and rhythm to work by, march by, and to make romance by. Folk songs also sometimes carry news of wars, floods, crimes, social injustices, and heroic deeds. Petr Bogatyrev distinguishes folk songs from other music because of such functionality, writing that musicality as a matter of excellence or difficulty of musical form is often not dominant. Bogatyrev also distinguishes folk songs in reference to a split of functionality between the differences of social orientations between town and country. An example Bogatyrev offers is the practical function over musicality of a national anthem. People sing an anthem to demonstrate nationalistic patriotism, not minding as much to the musical qualities of the song, so some people would not find meaning in the song because they are not carrying forward a particular nationalistic orientation.[77] We can think of how many national anthems sound alike, but for distinctive cultural elements and words, as they are all sung boldly, evoking collective memories with compassion.

We should note that Bogatyrev reinforces a historical view, in kind with many scholars of popular culture who hold that prior to the eighteenth century in Western culture separation of participation in folk music according to peasantry and aristocracy was insignificant.[78] So thinking of a folk song as unifying culture was evidential, but when social classes became increasingly separated by differentiated living conditions, folk music in Europe became romanticized, serving an "aesthetic function, reflecting, in addition, the moral and patriarchal life of honest peasants."[79] Folk song as a sign of protest also became associated with literary circles, and Bogatyrev finds examples of such cross over of song and literature for political reasons in the Russian Narodniki revolutionary movement.[80]

As a pragmatic semiotician, Royce could possibly add to Bogatyrev's study of the functionality of folk songs, adding thoughts about personally meaningful songs as being inspirational. I assume in difference to Bogatyrev's views, Royce would find it important to point out that while distinguishing what is individual versus Collective, we will always remain embodied in our social cultures. When a contemporary folk singer wails out from a stage to an audience below, there is often no straining of connection in relating the meanings of the song, because the singer "loves the community as a person."[81] For Royce, the individual's challenge is not to find social power through functionality but to find the compassionate essences of their community, thereby understanding loyalty as a value connecting all communities. Folk songs are expressive of such loyalty, to our own communities, but also signs of ethical values of loyalty to loyalty.

The American folk music genre includes, nonexhaustively, blue-grass, Appalachian ballads, country-western, blues, ragtime, rock-n-roll, beat poetry, and jazz, as well we can easily extend the genre contemporarily by including hip-hop, theatrical musicals, D.J. mixing, and sampling. An example of such diverse interpreting of popular folk music is Bob Dylan's music from the 1960s. In 2016 Bob Dylan was awarded the Nobel Prize for literature "for having created new poetic expressions within the great American song tradition."[82] His lyrics resonates with cultural signs from history, using reinterpretations of very old folk songs as social critique: such as imparity and poverty, pollution/disregard for animals and our natural environments, unjust incarceration, world hunger. In one of his songs, "A Hard Rain's Gonna Fall," Dylan voiced his objections to war, religious intolerance, racism/slavery. Yet he also gave voice to a universal community of peace activists, through a reinterpretation of a European folk song.[83]

When listening to the song, we take in the profound spiritual and ethical messages, while focusing on the cadence and sequences, which remain memorable, as repeated and reinterpreted. Dylan's poetry and music are often singled out because of Dylan's use of pastiche and trans historical sentiment, but what makes it more than a sign of past communities is that his songs remain as means for communities to be self-reflective.

Historically, "Lord Randall," the ballad from which Dylan took his inspiration and melody for "A Hard Rain's Gonna Fall," is a sign of a long since past community's value-*making*. Professor Francis James Child traces the ballad's lyrical composition to an Italian ditty, approximately 250 years old. The lyrics and melody are similar to Dylan's, as well the form of answer/question as refrain remains intact as a rhythmic conversation.

When thinking of the interpretation and reinterpretation of this song, we should consider that it was originally passed by singer to singer aurally, another important aspect of folk music, so it was not subjected to formalized composition in terms of specialized harmonies of specific instruments. With a minstrel ballad, originally composed and passed on with purposes of remaining memorable and socially meaningful, language and music are meshed in musical technologies of rhythm and timing, pushing us from the past to the present and preparing the future. But along with the musical structure, there is a theme, which is purposeful for the community, taking on new meanings as they are sung and resung. The past versions of this ballad were about lost love and death by poisoning, as well as possibly an Adam and Eve morality tale, as the interlocutors are a prince, his mother, and a murderous women lover. As for the patriarchal meanings in the original ditty, we could use that older version as a matter of disclosure to investigate feminist critique in contemporary folk songs. Putting the sexual psychological context aside for the moment, the ballad is about fear of poisoning one's relationships with one's community and one's connection with nature. These themes recur in Dylan's version, as a matter of a global existential crisis in respect to war and poisoning our environments through pollutants. Yet, Dylan's song is a sign of our self-consciousness of the power of hope that our relationships are redemptive and hopeful. As an activist, he holds on to loyalty in respect to all people having an interrelational nature, both personally and environmentally.

Dylan's version is interesting in respect to world ethics, alerting us to problems that cannot be solved by community in isolation of one another. In this regard his reinterpreted ballad, "A Hard Rain's Gonna Fall," is an example of an extension of time and symbolic truth. Royce can help us understand how intertwined aspects of poetry and music break from merely theoretical explanations of universality. Some aesthetic theories put forward theories of art based on either sense-based perceptions or a priori imagination, but Royce explains poetry and music as passing on "time-filled" cultural values in respect to ethics.[84] Through reinterpretation, I might add that the mixing of histories, places, and actions, through many interpretations traversing many communities, breaks aesthetics from formal codes of good taste, and the music and participants in song become involved with an interplay of cultural traditions.

Peter Burke, in his text *Popular Culture in Early Modern Europe*, offers insight into differences between the European cultural schism, happening throughout the fifteenth to eighteenth centuries, as "popular culture" becomes more and more distanced from elite culture.[85] In the early modern era there can be no definitive line drawn between two aesthetic classes in terms of education between town and country, yet later there is a difference in work and education. A philosophical understanding of aesthetics, specifically in respect to Western societies, also draws a line between urban and rural, between people who are nature bound or intellectually inspired.[86] The philosophical divisions ventured into areas of metaphysics, as aestheticians such as Joann Christophe Gottsched and Alexander Gottlieb Baumgarten offered differing aesthetic theories in terms of conception or perception, and subsequently in terms of the symmetry of time, place, and the contents of "art" or of the dissymmetry of nature and expression. For example, Burke tells us that reformers of culture during the eighteenth century attacked what was singled out as particularly "profane" art on the grounds of "breaking the rules laid down by reason and good taste, in other words the unities of time, place and action."[87]

For Royce, such aesthetic rules, or in another theoretical sense, the romanticization of popular culture in terms of unbridled natures, become nonimportant when thinking in terms of community loyalty. All aesthetic concerns begin and are active in the context of a person's loyalty, which is intertwined with one's community's values. Royce points out his new direction for values in aesthetic terms in *Problem of Christianity*:

> For his social enthusiasm is awakened by the love of his kind; and he glories in his service, as the player in his team, or the soldier in his flag, or the martyr in his church. If his religion comes into touch with his loyalty, then his gods are the leaders of his community, and both the majesty and the harmony of the loyal life are thus increased. The loyal motives are thus not only moral, but also aesthetic. The community may be to the individual both beautiful and sublime.[88]

Regarding the technical aspects of poetry/music, we have learned Royce thought in terms of "time inclusiveness," as time is unified by relationships, loyalties, and cultural interpretations, so to apply aesthetic rules rather than new circumstances and social/community conditions is not what Royce understands as an artistic sensibility.

Was the Noble Prize committee wrong to award a folk musician and rock star a sonorous literary award? There have been debates about this issue on several fronts, as some aestheticians disapprove of thinking of folk songs as literature, and some music lovers think of Dylan's music as mostly derivative. Other people are critical of Dylan in a more general sense as an artist who was a political opportunist, relying on a capitalistic neoliberal popular culture, rather than a true loyalty to social/political reforms.

I admit I am not able to resolve these cultural riffs, by thinking in terms of Royce's philosophy, but I do understand by our review of semiotics and value theory that interpretive processes assist us in crossing many boundaries between aesthetic codes and semiotic cultural markers, as well as value orientations. I think Royce's aesthetics goes as far to think that signs assist intelligent beings in crossing existential boundaries of loneliness and hopelessness, promoting more actively relational ways of life. Royce explains interpreting our relationships with others through the arts as the very essence of our human condition, as our cultural processes are expansive and ongoing, as all semiotic relationships have transformative qualities. A Community of Interpretation is a culture that is authentic by way of commitments to transform boundaries of cultures.

If there are metaphysical positions in Royce's value theory, it is his ideas on the doings and strivings of what is culturally realistic in terms of one's loyalty to the integrity of their environment. Our human reality depends on our interpretations of such relationships. Such an existential orientation requires every individual thing to realize their community, as mediated by another. Royce explains:

> In brief, then, the real world is the Community if Interpretation which is constituted by the two antithetic ideas, and their mediator or interpreter, whatever or whoever that interpreter may be. If then interpretation is a reality, and if it truly interprets the whole of reality, then the community reaches its goal, and the real world includes its own interpreter. Unless both the interpreter and the community are real, there is no real world.[89]

If our advance technologies are able to help us solve existential crises, such as nuclear war, overpopulation, and climate change, will we have to trust in each other's abilities to imagine ourselves as part of a better future, living alongside one another in new circumstances? If folk songs can help us continue our interpretive musement, we should try to sing along with all valuing beings.

4

Art and Soul: James and Scheler on Pragmatic Aesthetics

Max Scheler read pragmatic philosophy in the context of William James,[1] and there is controversial scholarship on his use of pragmatic notions in relation to the sociology of knowledge and philosophical anthropology, but his aesthetics has not been previously looked at from a pragmatic approach.[2] My understanding is that Scheler describes a process aesthetics, of the sort developed later in the twentieth century, which echoes James's views on pragmatism as including a valuation of lived experience.[3] This investigation serves to further the conversation of virtues, in aesthetics, and more specifically, in relation to art practice and reception. I bring forward Scheler's thoughts on the artist as a free agent who creates by way of working through an aesthetic struggle to signify values in a world of domineering striving for power and perfection. Aesthetics, for Scheler, is a matter of the practical and axiological; I conclude that there is a moral dimension to art, which can be addressed through a deeper realization of actualized values amid artistic and community practices.

Although neither thinker wrote protracted texts on art, I have found that both combine art and soul (in my synthetic reading of James and Scheler soul means human lived experience), thereby assimilating the material effects of aesthetics with creative beliefs for the betterment of culture. To introduce Scheler's idea's into discussions on pragmatic aesthetics, I investigate how his ideas look toward artistic production and reception by studying philosophical discourse and looking at paintings.

Perception, Ideation, and Pragmatic Aesthetics

To begin, Richard Shusterman investigates James's writings so as to bring forward the aesthetic aspect of his philosophy in relation to embodiment and perception, thereby revealing the entwinement of aesthetics and art with lived experience. Shusterman sees a prominent dynamic of pragmatist aesthetics as

> The continuity and combination of the aesthetic with the practical, a theme expressed in the integration of art and life, the recognition that bodily appetites and desires can also be aesthetic, and the appreciation of the functionality of art and aesthetic experience.[4]

I surmise that there needs to be additional inclusion, in the discussions on James' aesthetics, of ideas and imagination. Moreover, I put forth that Scheler's writings on aesthetics expand current notions in this regard. I look at three main comparisons between James and Scheler's aesthetics, thereupon explicating a synthesis and disclosing a main axiom of Scheleian aesthetics, which is that ideas are embodied with things through reflection and materiality. For Scheler aesthetics is not a matter of either perception or representation but of creativity, which involves an ongoing process of construction and manifestation.[5] I will explain this process throughout the chapter.

Subsequently, I draw out a pragmatic connection between Scheler and John Dewey (in that the latter's aesthetics is influenced by James), by paying particular attention to Thomas Alexander's writings on the moral imagination and community. Throughout this chapter I think about aesthetics through paradigms of art and artistic making that can have a moral dimension. The social critique of the painter Otto Dix is especially relevant, in that his work raises moral issues, such as questions surrounding the virtues that are called for in living as an individual and as a member of a community—such as respect, dignity, and benevolence. I focus my interpretations through Scheler's understanding of art as self-contained in its own aesthetic structures yet imbued with imminent connections to the essential drives of life and the possible virtues of communal living.

If we think of pragmatism, as James did, as a method that finds meaning in notions and actions by tracing their practical effects, we can understand Scheler's views on art and aesthetics in a similar light. Although Scheler rejects the idea that meaning is found in consequences, his thinking does not conflict with

James. James found meaning in relationships (as effectual) not consequences. For Scheler, active virtues, which are given in experience (as meaningful approaches to life), engage and build aesthetic structures (ways that we feel and interpret things) that structure our experience. This phenomenological approach can be seen as pragmatic in that meaningful relationships of virtues to creative experience are an active, practical experience. Scheler finds meaning in art through the influence of aesthetic intuition interacting with materials or mediums, and this process engages a "working out" of sense values; for example, "the painter 'sees' with the point of his brush, a drawer 'sees' with the point where his pen touches the paper he draws on."[6] Through the creative making of art, the active medium participates with us bodily, telling us something about ourselves and opening up new possibilities of self-reflexivity so as to make value-laden insights into the world. This is a phenomenology of art and culture that folds into pragmatist aesthetics.

As said, Shusterman concentrates on James's perceptual orientation when referring to experiences that please or displease, and he quotes James as recognizing such experiences as far ranging, from the aesthetic pleasures of philosophy and wonderment to the pleasure of movement and consummated action. However, Shusterman leaves open the door for a phenomenological approach to aesthetic experience in regard to an intuitive sense of value. He recognizes in James's writing a reticence against "aesthetics" in the abstract, schematic, cognitive sense while at the same time tracing James's theory of a unity of consciousness to its influence on Dewey's "seminal theory that aesthetic experience is essentially constituted by a nameless, unifying quality."[7] Shusterman notes that James finds that the "nameless qualities of aesthetic experience make works of art so different in value and spirit."[8] Such "nameless" qualities are explained indirectly through highlighting the perceptual aspects of embodied cultural habits. I find it clear that James's attention to the originality and culturation of embodiment goes further than the recognizably perceptual, and of what is presently evident in experience, by recognizing creative, imaginary qualities of the unity of commonly lived experience (pure experience). These qualities are unifying as well as being *in the making*, and this a possible reason James talks of such qualities as unidentifiable.[9] Scheler's insights into metaphysics, aesthetics, and art can be read as answering James's "namelessness" in this respect. Hereafter, I describe this phenomenological creative opening of aesthetics as an artistic valuation of soulful action, and I explain how each thinker approaches this valuation.

Art and Imaginative Value-Making

Scheler and James bring forward a cultural dynamic with their views on aesthetics and lived experience in respect to creating what is ideal, and because of an aesthetic quality in art's presentation, art helps trace a cultural dynamic.[10] Throughout this discourse, I find helpful some hermeneutic disclosures made through cultural history. To begin, it is interesting to interpret the curious similarity of both philosophers having been close friends with famous painters. John LaFarge was James's long-time friend and painting companion, and Otto Dix enjoyed the company of Scheler.

The painting of George Inness, which reflected the spiritual monism of Swedenborg's followers, surely influenced LaFarge and James. Swedenborgism is at the heart of the spiritualism James was taught by his father, Henry James Sr., and while he reacted against these teachings, they still influenced his concepts of "pure experience" and the "fringe" of experience.[11] James thought of all experience, physical and mental, as interconnected and pluralistic, in that what is not paid attention continues to exist in relation to one's sense of the world. Psychologically James formulates a map of unchartered territory into the unknown influences that play on a consciousness rooted in a unity of experience. In a similar deportment, at the turn of the twentieth century, American painters explored what it meant "to have soul"[12] in relation to a unity of nature and spiritualism, and the Tonalist styles of Inness and LaFarge exemplify such queries. By way of a like-minded quest, Tonalism resembles the German Magic Realism painting of the fin de siecle.[13] In turn, German Post-expressionism and surrealism were partly influenced by these painting movements in the early twentieth century.[14]

While, I am unable to fully describe these cross-influences in this introductory exploration, I can make visual reference to Inness's late painting *Sunset in the Woods* (1891) as a metaphor for James's aesthetics.[15] The painting is of the last light of a late afternoon in a New England wood, and it was completed in the artist's studio many years after its first conception.[16] The oil on canvas emphasizes Inness's skill of employing chiaroscuro and sfumato to capture photographic-like passages of atmosphere, while capturing a mood of a natural phenomenon. The sunlit area in the picture presents a clearing of verdure foliage, as it also presents the conscious attention of the artist and viewer. At the same time, the darkened forest shows what surrounds one's focused attention and what continues to spur the imagination. In similitude to the depiction, the Jamesian notion of a unity of consciousness, which includes unknown aspects of consciousness, can be seen through his concept of *the fringe*, as a deepening or enrichment of lived, experiential, phenomenon. Metaphorically the painting portends both the attention and curiosity of the artist and viewer, along with embodying a feeling of how one's mood is actively disposed through the art experience.

Although by way of a different style, there is an evocation of such phenomenological aesthetics to be experienced by viewing the paintings of Otto Dix. Dix lived and painted in Berlin during the Weimar Republic. Along with George Grosz, he was named a *Verist* in that their work from that time was often social critique and included elements of graphic realism, revealing the hard truths and hypocrisies of postwar society. Yet, along with employing techniques influenced by journalism and caricature such as reportage and animation, Dix and Grosz drew with a hyper-naturalism of form, often immersing the viewer in a hyper-realistic narrative. However, they both had a penchant for painting landscapes. Dix painted and drew as a social critic, utilizing drama and techniques of magic realism. During their time, the romanticism of German paintings, the emergence of popular culture, and the urgency of social critique fused, thereby resulting in the outspoken socio/political/aesthetic movements of Dadaism and surrealism.

Culturally, prior to Hitler's rise, Americanism was a key theme of the Weimar milieu, as the artists, intellectuals, and citizens welcomed America's music and movies and its innovative spirit and progressive directions for society. Dix was a reader of philosophy, and he knew Scheler well, even doing a famous portrait of him in the late twenties.[17] As active members of the intellectual movement of the Weimar Republic, the Nazis considered both to be undesirables. Americanism also spread through philosophy and Scheler intently thought about pragmatism. However, both Scheler and Dix were critical of the calculating, competitive side of American culture, and they were skeptical of an emphasis on domination by wealth, mass production, and manipulation of the status quo. An interpretation of Dix's work, throughout this chapter, brings Scheler's pragmatic aesthetics to light in relation to such paradoxes, specifically with regard to culture and human nature.

Scheler's treatise *Cognition and Work* exposes a love-hate relationship with pragmatism.[18] On the one hand he criticizes the general pragmatic perspective as being too utilitarian and consequential, and on the other, he champions James's thinking on embodied knowledge gained through action and work.[19] In his essay on aesthetics, "Metaphysics and Art," he critically aligns general pragmatism with empiricism and a latent, passive subjectivity, while conversely going on to outline an aesthetics that echoes James's approach.[20]

I surmise that Scheler misunderstood pragmaticism in relation to autonomy and James's notion of one's creative stream of consciousness.

Scheler's general use of the term "pragmatism" does not fit with James's method of understanding meaningful cognitive particulars cojoined with practical experience. James distinguishes contextual ideas from the kind of redundancy of thought and action Scheler infers by asserting that we select and focus on particular relationships that our ideas have with things through testing those relationships.[21] Scheler would be wrong if he suggests that pragmatic aesthetics focuses on either a theoretical or an associative stance that would measure art merely by its representative value or social capital, in that James recognizes all aspects of cognitive *and* practical experience that stands out as significant as a matter of chosen meaningful relationships.[22]

Soulful Pragmatic Values

Regardless of Scheler's objections to what he terms general pragmaticism, he understands aesthetics (feelings and emotions, which are enlivened in experience specifically through artistic practice and reception), as pragmatically constitutive of embodied meanings and collective values.[23] Even though Scheler posits aesthetics as a relation to the seminal reality and meaning of the world, which is theoretical contrasting with James's pluralism, there is a constructivist side to Scheler's philosophy. Scheler's aesthetic philosophy is pragmatic and alike to James's on three interconnected accounts. Initially, there is the vital connection between the functionalization of values through objects, which can be compared to James's notion of *ideas cum rebus* or ideas with things. Furthermore, Scheler puts forward a top-down valuation that explains the artistic embodiment of value and a materiality of value-making. This is an active yet cognitive aesthetic, akin to James's preferring of one way to look at our experience over another as a means to better the world. Finally, Scheler's notions on the *vital soul* (what is meaningful to a living being), and *phantasy* (as a vital act of imagination) have curious connections to James's belief in the possibilities of experience.[24] While James and Scheler have nuanced views on imagination, they both agree that the unifying aspects of aesthetic structures and art are creative, directional, and real.

All three comparisons imply virtues or meanings that interweave with values of community. Despite the emphasis on individualism throughout James's mostly psychologically oriented writings, acknowledging the self as a character built on active, productive relationships necessarily understands the individual and culture in a community-minded respect.[25] Similarly, Scheler's personalism is built on individual dignity and responsibility to all persons (collective persons). Aesthetically, for James and Scheler, art and soul (once again as what is meaningful to human beings in lived experience) are pragmatic in both an individual and a communal regard.

Stikkers explains the connection between Scheler's thinking and James's notion of *ideas cum rebus*, saying that both realize that unless ideas are "with things" they are idle and nonhistorical. There is no object/subject divide in that ideas are "with things" rather than coming before the physical world, as with Platonic Forms, or after, as with a positivist bias.[26] In this respect, James understands the agent as creatively sketching her world. James also describes an ongoing process of meaning making that has a place in the world because of the world's state of affairs.[27] In such an aesthetic process, practice and ideas evolve with the making and using of objects to bring forward contrasts, critiques, and similitude from the flux of experience, not merely as practice as a utilitarian implementation of the *homo faber*. In relation to art, such ideas and habits are not a matter of stored knowledge but of directional action or making, that is done to explore the effects of what is preferred in cognition and brought into focus creatively from the absolutely real or what James terms *the fringe*. *The fringe* is a description of the "giveness" of the world where we find the acting, emotional person already in experience. This Jamesian view seems to echo through Scheler's mode of phenomenology, which is attitudinal rather than eidetic.

Although Scheler states that art "with ideas" is a falsification, because art symbolically represents or points to an ideal realm "through concrete contents of intuition," he does take up a concept similar to *ideas cum rebus*, by explaining the functionalization of essences/values in the making of art.[28] Scheler understands an apriority that is functional through individual's dispositions revealing a hierarchy of values, which are the personal and the ethical responsibility of the person. This hierarchy is axiological in that it is based on a formal, very real apriori, but it is relative to lived experience and action. Each person has a value disposition coming from the core values of utility, pleasure, life and nobility, spirit and the divine. However, I must stress that Scheler's axiology is revealed through democratic, free actions within lived experience. His notion of art as *poiein*, meaning an activity of embodied making, stands at the center of his process aesthetics as an ongoing, embodied yet constructive functioning of such existential values. Scheler's understanding of artistic making is as follows:

> Art is "poiein" building, the producing of a sense structure out of material, a structure that at least cannot be matched for its correspondence with the "fortuitous reality" of the world.[29]

Scheler sees the artist as both an idealist *and* a realist who realizes experimental ideas that posit values, or "aesthetically worthy meanings," that are conscious.[30] Moreover, art objectifies ideas and/or values through an aesthetizing process that is *telic*, as art changes reality by directing dispositions to a goal of understanding and appreciation. Scheler sees art as more than experimental and as truly creative. Art is more intelligent than the descriptive exercises of metaphysics or science, since those discursive structures are based on the "fortuitous reality" of the world, whereas art is based on the perfecting of a new world made with virtuous insights into the meaning of the world.

For example a landscape painting does not describe or symbolize nature as geographical data; it signifies the ideas, factors, or virtues of nature of a particular time and place through its medium and aesthetic structure, leaving an indication of an aesthetic/value structure to be acted upon by its reception. For Scheler, the *vital-soul* and *phantasy* are living forces presenting the values and challenges of culture and community through creative, aesthetic productive imagination, and such value-laden aesthetic structures can be seen in the landscape paintings of the German Magic Realists.[31] Dix's "Randegg in the Snow with Ravens" (1935) makes clear a contrast between the virtues of the ideal *Gemeinschaft* and the society of ravens that feign the fire and warmth for life outside of community.[32] When he painted this landscape-portrait, Dix was separating himself from the Nazi regime while living with his family in the Swiss borderlands. His painting immerses the viewer in the scene with the mood of a foreboding, snow-laden sky and a somewhat shallow perspective of distance that reflects on itself, continually returning the viewer to the action in the foreground. Here the ravens dive bomb for a patch of food in the snow. Yet, at the center of the picture are the village's hearth and a wagon with winter reserves, depicting a feeling of community virtues alongside the life of the ravens. Unlike a geographical map, the viewer experiences direction toward the existential significance of the ideal world. Are the virtues of community eternal that are shown in the picture's contrast? One could say so for this picture, not in the sense of being detached from the physical existential world but through an ongoing relationship of feelings about a perfected world, in contrast to a society where *phantasy* does not serve what is good in forming what is good for substantiating the virtues of benevolence and caring. Scheler veers away from a moralism of normative standards; instead, he envisions a creative existence constructed with aesthetic values in mind.

This brings us to the second major aspect of comparison: both James and Scheler think of aesthetics as relative to a world more valued than the present world. Scheler explains a top-down aesthetics that is "a building of what is not there, but what would be worthy to be there according to aesthetic ideas of value,"[33] and this is comparable to James's notions on meliorism. The major crux of the comparison here returns the discussion to Scheler's thinking on art as funding and being founded on primordial essences of virtues that are soulful or driven by meaning in lived experience, and James has a very different take on essences and essential values. In Scheler's *Formalism in Ethics and Non-Formal Ethics of Values*, the value essences are ranked in an *ordo amoris*, which is a nonrational order that is in accordance with a love of all that exists. Preferring certain values to others exemplifies the advancement of a person's disposition through the apriori that the ideal points to, yet the practical realm remains unintentional until it is affected by art and action. However, as said these values do not present an abstracted reality; they are embodied through persons in lived experience and are signified and built upon by art. These values can direct the free *vital soul* and *phantasy*.

Scheler finds that art has its own aesthetic values that bind value-laden autonomous worlds. The process of creating these worlds is a matter of presentation by which we add value to the real world. The aesthetic values of art serve as "leading and guiding factors of selection and composition."[34] Proceeding with the primal values each artist is best able to work with, the artist works through conscious intuitions which through sensation take on forms, such as language and signs, to create a new world in which primordial essences are vital and active. The artist is never "disinterested" in setting the actual world aside, and the process of lived experience has its effects in the art's "immediacy of giveness" of its essence of value.[35] This ontology develops an aesthetic anthropology of sorts, not a judgment of taste. In the same respect, art history is a matter of revealing the wonderings of our hearts and souls as being involved with the "variations of creative feelings of style—and not variations of the 'taste' which forms itself only on the basis of the works of art created and enjoyed."[36] So artists create worlds free of judgment, yet more aesthetically valued than the present world. Yet, such freedom from normative moral prescription does not seem to me to exclude, but rather refer to, an ethical and community-minded ontology of art. I am using ethical here, with a creative connotation, and in the context of a "good" sense of place, where a stability of relationships among living beings remains a matter of openness to what is practical, spiritual, and valuable.

Pure experience is the complete flux of life and world, and according to James, someone's disposition is made through relating to certain aspects of this flux. Essences, if there are any, are valued properties that are selected psychosomatically from among the relationships of experience, and they differ from situation to situation and person to person. Therefore, trust and belief in the possibilities of experience and an interconnected community of human affairs are foundational to the values of a meaningful reality.[37] James also points out that these relational properties or essences are not associative or static but able to be analyzed and they are directional to the course of the state of affairs.[38] Likewise his notion of *ideas cum rebus* includes a notion of an ideal world alongside an absolute world that can be perceived by many people knowing the same value of the meaning of a thing in a myriad of reflections. In relation to art making and reception, there is a preferencing out of this common sense that can be understood as a striving for what Shusterman explains as "better worlds of experience."[39] Shusterman references James from *The Principles of Psychology* on this point:

> The world of aesthetics is an ideal world, a Utopia, a world which the outer relations persist in contradicting, but which we as stubbornly persist in striving to make actual. (pp. 123–5)[40]

The upshot of the comparison here, in light of their differences concerning aproiri essences and common meanings, is that both James and Scheler find utopian worlds of art not abstracted from the real but made of the real, in respect to an ideal.

A third aspect of Scheler's philosophy of art that relates to pragmatist aesthetics is his thinking on the creative autonomy of *phantasy*. *Phantasy* is the activity of the imagination, yet *phantasy* and imagination can hardly be separated in that conative action is Scheler's ground of aesthetics. *Phantasy* is active as a matter of consciousness partly based on memory in order to reproduce feelings or sensations; it is a sense and a way of being. Furthermore, it is a source of creativity funded from the *vital soul* of life, and through *phantasy* we "can feel what we never experienced, and wish what we never encountered."[41] Values imbued with drives are given to experience and can be the working out of *phantasy*. It is what one is driven to act on from the utopias of phantasy that persists against chance events of the world, which are often not experienced artistically.

This view might seem to be in contrast with James's concept of imagination in his early writings in *The Principles of Psychology*, wherein imagination is based on memories that are rearranged in novel ways. Yet, James was consistently opposed to associationism, and he comes to add value to imagination by way of the creative agent finding new directions in the continuity of experience that is valuable. For James's radical empiricism, the imagination is praxial as it finds the world a phenomenon to be acted upon creatively. The difference between a thinker like Hume (who searches for sources of value in a reconstructive imagination) and James is that the latter finds the reconstruction of imagination to be valuable in an experimental sense, since we invest our actions not only through the actual but also through the possible. James's core aesthetic value is how persons look toward a ground of belief for our ideas, experiments, and dreams within lived experience. In *The Principle of Psychology* this is what James calls *Soul*.[42] For James *Soul* is a relational aesthetic ground of belief in the possibilities of actuality. James describes his meaning of *Soul* in the *Principles of Psychology*:

> But what positive meaning has the Soul, when scrutinized, but the *ground of possibility* of the thought? And what is the 'knocking' but the *determining of the possibility to actuality*? And what is this after all but giving a sort of concreted form to one's belief that the coming of the thought, when the brain-processes occur, has *some* sort of ground in the nature of things? If the world Soul be understood merely to express that claim, it is a good word to use.[43]

James's *Soul* is the source of imaginative action, just as the *vital soul* is the drive behind *phantasy* for Scheler.

Thomas Alexander credits James with producing one of the most, if not the most rational understanding of thinking as aesthetic imagination. Alexander reflects on James's impact on epistemological theories:

> Our rationality is a process then, which is driven by an aesthetic eros. For James this includes a banishment of uncertainty towards the future, a harmonious anticipation of the world acting "congruously with our spontaneous powers."
> (In quotation William James, *Will to Believe*, 75-6/66).[44]

But this certainty of belief is not unconnected with the real world of situational flux, and as Alexander rightly points out, James was not putting forward a "voluntaristic nihilism." Instead James is explaining that people's creative thinking on life's problems matters in realizing possible worlds of experience. Alexander looks toward John Dewey to extend James's notions of the possibilities of experience to a moral community.[45] Dewey brings the imagination into the matter of choosing possibilities because we have learned how to make choices in relation to others. According to Alexander, Dewey's realm of imagination is primarily a matter of community.[46] In fact Alexander views all three of the classical pragmatic thinkers, Peirce, James and Dewey, as finding community building as necessarily indebted to imagination and aesthetics. For these thinkers, inquiry into perceptions of experience and the testing of new innovations through experience are a matter of creative action as learned with others.

Alexander explains:

> To acquire sensitivity to the developmental meanings of events, which define the significance of the situations in which we find ourselves and the values they possess, is what I have called here the moral imagination.[47]

Values for Dewey are the qualities of continued practice that persist, as the past takes on the expectations of the future in the present moment. Dewey's aesthetic experience involves a unity of meaningful value-laden habits that allow for improvised projections into an innovative future. Dewey conceived imagination as a source of social and moral growth, in that it is an artful approach to life. This is a democratic ontology in that creativity factors in practical qualities of experience as recurring because they are consistent with communities' active values and conditions. Alexander makes Dewey's intentions clear: "The democratic community for Dewey is the community which understands itself as actively pursuing life as art."[48]

Scheler also saw an artful existence as the most imaginative approach to bettering the moral and social fibers of communities. In his axiology, Scheler locates cultural values of the *life-community* as the second-highest tier of virtues. Without belief in virtues of providence there is a diminished social ground, that stagnates cultural solidarity of belief in the betterment of community, so there is no moral progress or creative artistic culture. However, communities must constantly reflect on what their world "ought" to be and are responsible for making that belief a reality. Art is virtuous reality and can be understood as a pathway to understanding and comprehending the possible virtues imbued in the existential activities of life. Scheler exclaims:

> A work of art says, as it were: "This, You Eternal Ground of all Things is what You just wanted to tell me—be it without quite being able to do so, or, being able to do so in Your rational and Impenetrable 'Fiat' of Your willing." Or it addresses us by saying: "This also You could have told us without violating the idea of a possible world of essence."[49]

By recognizing Scheler's aesthetics as a positing of qualities that are embodied forms, which function as they are conceived intuitively through belief and imagination, we can deem a close relationship between his aesthetics and James's sense of melorism and Dewey's moral imagination. For James and Dewey the aesthetic experience is the forward-looking aspect of life, and for Scheler "art creates a *new* world added to the real one."[50] Aesthetics and pragmatism take on a unique voice through such views on *phantasy* and imagination, as art and soul work together through the creative, directional, and experimental actions of the artist. How does this experimental yet value-laden aesthetics play out in practice? Let us turn to another example in the painting of Dix to disclose the directional qualities of artistic valuation.

In Scheler's and Dix's era, human drives were played out through a full-throttle madness, as two World Wars and a cultural disintegration ended in a kind of mass suicide of the Nazi regime. In Dix's "Lustmord" of 1929,[51] we find the fascination of the Weimar culture with the procreative and destructive, mixed with Dix's method of painting that he claims unleashes a Dionysian spirit. Maria Tatar's interpretation informs the viewer that Dix, like his Weimar milieu, associates "woman" with the unruliness of biology and earth, while the bourgeois setting of the room and architecture outside of the window depicts the opposite, showing the *Geist* of spirit and mind. Tatar thinks the murderer is victimized by what is perceived as the woman's disruptive and disorderly dead presence. This is a probing and complex interpretation, and it deserves mention in light of the rationalization of murder that is a cultural phenomenon during war, and in respect to feminist concerns. However, in relation to an aesthetic that looks to purge such drives, thereby acting as a deterrent, as Dix proposed, one can think of the murder scene as a contra-ideal world.[52] In an interpretation that reflects Scheler's aesthetics, which is not necessarily completely contrary to Tatar's, Dix acts as a surrealist and social critic. It is clear that the overturned chair to the left of the gashed and violated victim shows that the viewer flees from the scene of the crime, both from the reality of the cultural sleaze that surrounds it and from the false solutions that serve only to devastate all virtues of the heart. There is a subversion of love and togetherness, both with the macabre murder and the vacant urban setting. Talking about Dix's painting, the Weimar art critic Ilse Fischer wrote:

> And he attacks everything, though without any sort of system. With persistent brooding he strives to scrutinize all things chance pushes to the forefront of his restlessly groping mind, searching for their true reasons. He pounces violently and impulsively on his object—never mind whether person or thing—brutally eliminates all decorative trimmings, rummages cruelly and critically around the exposed strands, disintegrates, dismembers, dissects everything he encounters with the ecstatic thrill of the sex killer. But like the latter, who horribly sobered walks empty from the crime, he too stands, in the end, before things and

people, before himself, sobered, hopeless. Do you now understand the dreadful truthfulness of his sex killing pictures, you who think a bit contemptuously of the choice of such a motif, a motif that seems dishonest to you, unnecessary, because you know very well that this good-natured fellow will never murder a woman?[53]

Dix's art makes such a terrible and pointless crime meaningful and despicable. Dix does not depend on a psychic distance in order to create a facsimile of activism to cure social evils; he critiques in the strong terms of an ideal world, by revealing the problems of the real world. He creates a morality tale based on the possibilities of a particular act and shows the destructive side of aesthetic experience in terms of virtues, which are by contrast good and beautiful. The painting presents a view of aesthetics based solely on egoistic desires, in that there is no understanding here of the values that make life possible for the *life-community*.[54] Scheler and Dix imagine the implications of the Dionysian woman/man in that a realization of the anti-rationalistic life force can push woman/man to revalue its values. In this regard Dix asks here a question that Scheler answers pragmatically: namely, if one separates spirit from the forces that drive the *vital soul*, is there a lesser valuation of lived experience? And importantly, Scheler answers, the drives of the *vital soul* thrive in a spiritual manner on valued feelings and shared actions in respect to community. Therefore, we are all responsible for addressing and answering this question of existential angst.

Community as a cultural space of human dignity and self-respect must be constructed on respect for the otherness of others, and on the foundations of trust and belief in one another, as well as a love of life that gives persons a disposition to assume such mutual respect. This is a big order if there are no aesthetic values that signify our loving relationships. Scheler and James practiced a pragmatic aesthetic that finds such creative values "in the making" through art, as an embodiment of people's ideas about community and a life well spent together. Art and soul work together to actualize such a creative realization and participation in life.

5

The Icon Moves: Diversity Through Pragmatic/Religious Aesthetics

Ukraine's minister of education Serhiy Kvit wrote in the Spring of 2014 about the EuroMaidan revolution: "Not only political differences but also social and national barriers became secondary on the Maidan Nezalezhnost. Ethnic Ukrainians waving their flags were joined by Crimean Tatars, Jews, Poles, Belarusians, Georgians, Armenians and others."[1] He goes on to report, "'*Glory to Ukraine!—Glory to Heroes*!' became the Maidan's slogan. It's repeated constantly by representatives of different political ideologies in all regions of Ukraine." Unfortunately, despite his hopes for tolerance, the Maidan revolution has spawned a civil war, resulting in thousands of Ukrainians being killed over nationalistic allegiances and geopolitical divisions, and afterwards an ongoing war with Russia.

However, I am interested in ideas and actions rooted in peace, as Ukraine has been able to continue to retain its democracy and association with socially progressive Europe. The cultural artifacts of the 2014 Maidan remain as reminders of the ethos of the sharing and inclusive sense of community practiced in Independence Square that year: the flags, slogans, and the icons, the later, which we will focus on throughout this discussion.

Artifacts rely on participant's feelings and people's communications about those feelings with one another, as members of collective, forward-looking communities. People's feelings are focused by cultural values, symbolized by cultural artifacts. In this regard, the Maidan revolution was significantly influenced by religious art, creating a spiritual context for the revolution. What might cultural dynamics continue to resonate, from the efficacy of such religious

Originally published in "Pragmatism Today." *The Journal of the Central European Pragmatist Forum*, 6(2) (Winter 2015): 21–37.

aesthetic symbolism, which intended peace and social progress? I contend we can find answers to these matters in the writings of two American pragmatists, as they looked to pragmatic aesthetics to provide solutions to war and social injustice.

William James and John Dewey's discussions of religious attitudes offer a philosophical understanding of such attitudes as a means of emancipation. My overarching thesis is that religious attitudes and art, as human resources of imaginative feeling, thinking and acting, have a strong aesthetic valence in terms of peaceful agency. Also when used as cultural tools, these sensibilities help to counter measures of revolutionary violence and social injustice. This is a controversial topic considering that religion and politics can be a violent mix spawning fanatical movements, including an anti-Russian, jihad-like movement in Kiev.[2] But I describe a peaceful, inclusive sense of religious agency in terms of James's investigations into mystical religious experience and Dewey's understanding of human nature as creatively moral and artistic.[3] Although these two philosophers have differing approaches to religious experiences, as will be noted, explaining their views on religious attitudes combined with artistic practices in a setting of community helps us understand more about civil inclusiveness, nonviolent activism, and productive, progressive collective political action.[4] I highlight the events in Kiev during February 2014, to give an example of a political revolution, in our new Millennium, which was influenced by religious culture and art. I look specifically at Byzantine icons as hermeneutic examples, which although used by many political factions during the conflict, they were symbols of peaceful resistance for a commonplace ethos.

Pragmatic Aesthetics, Tradition, and Religiousness

To advance my point that religious attitudes and artifacts can inspire sociopolitical change in terms of social justice, I compare Dewey and James's ideas on religious experience with Hannah Arendt's thoughts on political praxis based on her interpretation of Kantian aesthetics.[5] I contend that Arendt does not take on board a full range of revolutionary ethos for she does not place any emphasis on value-making through artistic practices.[6] Arendt understands revolution as a form of thoughtful, critical action, but Kantian aesthetics limits her project because transcendental *sensus communis* leaves us with an abstract approach to God and creativity in relation to everyday life.[7] Let us come to Arendt's problems with aesthetic agency after discussing the strong sense of pragmatic aesthetic agency James and Dewey afford to religious experiences, art, and culture.

Some political theorists refer to ethnic, cultural, and religious differences as pretexts for geopolitical agendas pointing to those as major causes for revolutions. Yet, we should take seriously religious aesthetics as being inspired by a collective spirit that is concerned with ongoing meanings of life. Aesthetics as a study of what Dewey investigated how unifying diverse religious beliefs work with attitudes of democracy is helpful.[8] Both Dewey and James place emphasis on religious attitudes as a matter of our personal and cultural purposes in life. I find that they share views of religious feelings and political agency through two interrelated axioms in this respect: (1) religious/aesthetic experiences are an aspect of our awareness of how we are connected to each other and to our environments, yet they also make clear there are community tensions involved that help us to continually reflect on our future purposes. (2) Also, such awareness effects people's expansive sense of imagination and creativity. Although Dewey writes explicitly on the social progressive aspects of religious experience, both he and James look toward people's liberation from fear and alienation, thereby becoming more open to creative possibilities for freer, shared lives and a more empowered sense of culture.

Throughout this chapter, I use the term "religiousness" in the same pragmatic sense that Dewey used "religious" in *A Common Faith*. Dewey sought to emancipate our collective feelings and actions from being thought of as supernatural or institutionally dictated or defined.[9] For Dewey, being religious is a creative process and as such is a matter of feeling, thinking, and acting imaginatively, as an integral part of larger, cultural environments.[10] Obviously, people are productive in their communities through artistic practices while relying on their religious beliefs; concurrently they are often decidedly focused on cultural and political changes.[11] Dewey extends our understanding of artistic religious production, explaining our traditions as long-standing cultural artifacts, which do not necessaryly involve static dogmatic beliefs. For Dewey traditions necessarily involve progressive attitudes and new contemporary art forms, as tools to facilitate aesthetic agency and cultural change.

For James, existential tension is a private feeling that something is wrong with one's life, and this can lead to a person adapting more optimistic and religious attitude toward life in general. He thinks individuals, through realizing they can feel and express a sense of having an intimate connection to a vaster field of relationships other than their own private circumstances, can resolve their anxieties. In searching for what is better than failed experiences in revealing ultimate truthfulness through abstract thinking, an individual becomes more engaged with the interconnected relationships of life. James admits that philosophy is hopeless in fully describing this aesthetic connections, while he finds that religions often record these feelings as "a fact of experience."[12] He goes on to explain that "the divine is actually present, religion says, and between it and our relations of give and take are actual."[13] This sense of divinity or interconnected wholeness, although largely ineffable and unexplainable through fortuitous consequences, has a quality of "*plus*, a *thisness*," which "feeling alone can answer for."[14] Religious experience, according to James, is not like Kant's "Transcendental Ego of Apperception" as religious experiences are not abstracted from our feelings, interpersonal relationships, or understanding. A religious attitude is felt as relationships between people, environments, and even things or objects, in that religious experience is not transcendental because it never leaves human experience.[15] Religiousness as an attitude is a matter of orienting our minds to the grand scope of relationships in our life's circumstances. James finds through personal testimonies that religious experiences offer people a sense of shared purpose and intention, but—unlike Kant—this unity of purpose is not presented to us prior to our lived experiences. Through a religious attitude, a person takes up a way of living James thinks of as "healthy mindedness," and this condition affords an empowered sense of personal moral agency and freedom.[16]

Sounding much like James's description of the anxieties of people's existential crises, Dewey thinks that people experience enhanced perceptions through wrestling with what is stable and precarious, leading to a sense of consummation and the completeness of life's processes. Yet people are also conscious of their own personalities, failures, and well-being as we sometimes discern our abilities to increase our connectivity with such tensions, and sometimes bypass our involvement with natural processes.[17] Art helps us connect, perceptually and conceptually, with the natural processes of our experiences. Dewey writes that "the religious experience that accompanies intense aesthetic perception" is a moral pursuit, in that not only do we bring our existential situations, and fears, into focus but also holistic religious feelings help us envision our future goals, as look forward to consummation and completion.[18] Religiousness, as an artistic sensibility, begins for Dewey with an imaginative or experimental attitude, as the artist sets up the existential rhythms of our perceptual and conceptual awareness and the religious-minded person looks faithfully toward a consummative experience. Dewey explains that this aesthetics attitude is creative and holistic in terms of art, science, and community involvement,

> The religious attitude signifies something that is bound through imagination to a *general* attitude. This comprehensive attitude, moreover, is much broader than anything indicated by "moral" in its usual sense. The quality of attitude is displayed in art, science and good citizenship.[19]

James also gives a great deal of thought to the practical effects of religious experience, finding people can feel and act with a greater sense of involvement and purpose. Religiousness is tied with creativity by building our personal sense of character and individual freedoms. He writes,

> Religious feeling is thus an absolute addition to the Subject's range of life. It gives him a new sphere of power. When the outward battle is lost, and the outer world disowns him, it redeems and vivifies an interior world which otherwise would be an empty waste. If religion is to mean anything definite for us, it seems to me that we ought to take it as meaning this added dimension of emotion, this enthusiastic temper of espousal, in regions where morality strictly so called can at best but bow its head and acquiesce. It ought to mean nothing short of this new reach of freedom for us, with the struggle over, the keynote of the universe sounding in our ears, and ever-lasting possession spread before our eyes.[20]

Moreover, people's religious experiences have real effects in terms of political revolutions, as evidenced by my second point of comparison; that people can affect real and positive changes through religiousness by means of cultural value-making.

Tradition may seem like an archaic, useless, and even a destructive word when discussing the challenges of turning over powerful governments and economic systems, because traditions seem to offer a false sense of security. But just as religious attitudes are personal methods of change as aesthetic processes through which beliefs are felt while acting upon them, traditions as creative cultural mediums help us realize communal values as developed by our living histories. James explains constructive aspects of cultural religiousness and value-making:

> The world interpreted religiously is not the materialistic world over again, with an altered expression; it must have, over and above the altered expression; a *natural constitution* different at some point from that which a materialistic world would have. It must be such that different events can be expected in it, different conduct must be required.[21]

James contends that moments of truthfulness, trust, shared sacrifice, and pleasure are creative and mystical points of invention in a boundless universe of relationships.[22]

Dewey also thought of religious experience as creative and he wanted to emancipate religiousness from religion, breaking with traditions that restricted growth and static ideals presented as universal dogma. Again, sounding like James, Dewey thinks of religious "factors of experience" that can never be abstracted from everyday situations and should not be "drafted into supernatural channels."[23] However he goes further in describing how people use religious traditions and cultural artifacts as technologies for value-making, inculcating positive habits and creative practices which embody ongoing meanings. The effects of religious experiences can be traditional and artifactual while continually reproducing transformative changes, offering new moral possibilities and deepening shared values. As ontological experiences a community's religious traditions have enduring felt qualities through which people change themselves and their environments. Constructing a world through aesthetic means such as religiousness, artistic practice, and scientific inquiry is often a matter of history as imbued with aesthetic meanings. Dewey explains,

> There are transient and there are enduring elements in a civilization.—The enduring forces are not separate; they are functions of a multitude of passing incidents as the latter are organized in to the meanings that form minds. Art is the great force in effecting this consolidation. The individuals who have minds pass away one by one. The works in which meanings have received objective expressions endure. They become part of the environment, and interaction with this phase of the environment is the axis of continuity in the life of civilization. The ordinances of religion and the power of law are efficacious as they are clothed with a pomp, a dignity and majesty that are the work of imagination. If social customs are more than uniform external modes of action, it is because they are saturated with story and transmitted meaning. Every art in some manner is a medium of this transmission while its products are no inconsiderable part of the saturating matter.[24]

Habits and traditions can be followed without much thought or social-critique, but Dewey describes a transformation of these experiences when traditions become "funded" by meaning.[25] When there is a problem to be worked out in our environments, we use our imaginations to connect our past histories with changing environments as we discern the consequences of our experiences. Religious beliefs and traditions are relevant because religious attitudes do not necessarily shackle people to static dogmas or to a political sense of nationalistic exclusivity. As value-laden artifacts, traditions can be practiced artistically and they can be conduits for assimilating history and memories to the present and as a means for revaluation. Such revaluation includes thinking about more expansive fields of civil inclusion as people envision about their integrated yet on-going futures.

Hannah Arendt also thought about aesthetics and citizenship as catalysts for social change and revolution. In difference to James and Dewey, she thought of aesthetics in direct relation to Kantian phenomenology.[26] Her approach to aesthetics is that a person develops their thoughtfulness and autonomy as a spectator using one's imagination, which is a faculty of the mind, thereby able to judge social situations in consideration of other perspectives (i.e. disinterestedness is integrated with sensus communis).[27] Aesthetics for Arendt and Kant is the rationalizing of feelings non-determinately and imaginatively, yet they both leave out an active sense of religious culture.

In terms of democracy and revolution, Arendt's idea of praxis is that political actions are motivated by creative and reflective thoughts, and these thoughts have their foundation in the workings of the imagination and communicability.[28] Culturally for Arendt, individuals realize values, or human rights, in light of the historical epochs they are born into. Yet, Modernity is devoid of the most natural states of being, unlike when people were doers and makers and intuitively social or political. How to reconnect people as *homo-faber* and *zoonpolitikan* was Arendt's moral project.[29] She saw the answer as being concerned with political discussions by communities in times and spaces cleared from the inequalities and prejudices of everyday life. Unbiased dialog is for Arendt, the most effective form of political action.

So we can see some connection here with art, democracy, and social change, as with the pragmatists, but aesthetically Arendt does not really contribute to solving the problem of a modern disconnect of judging our world and being involved in its ongoing development. Because of her Kantian aesthetics, she thinks of a person as coming to think imaginatively and therefore democratically through self-conscious reflection, and their conceptual *disinterestedness* leaves a gap between them and everyday cultural practices.[30] Therefore, a person's imagination is blocked from the ongoing traditions of collectively funded, emotional experiences. Theoretically this gap would mean positing an individual subject and an outside object, which they reflect about, even though Arendt insists that Kant was dedicated to "interplay and cooperation of sensibility and intellect."[31] However, to bridge this gap creatively Kant allows for special genius talents, while Arendt posits that people's political orientations are a matter of rational discussion.[32] Kant's program to find *sensus communis* as a priori reflective thinking is also part of Arendt's political theory, in that an orator should be an interpretative and imaginative judge, who marks history.

However, my view is that an orator could not have the creative experience of an artist, who is embedded in their community. Arendt's orator cannot possibly be an effective aesthetic agent as she is not directly emotionally involved with the traditions and histories of her community. Arendt's philosophy presents us with a conceptual gap between spokesperson and culture, so we can surmise there is a distance between such orators and the activists in revolutions.[33] So when employing Arendt's social tools of praxis and political debate, there is a theoretical distance of intellectuals from the hearts and minds of people protesting and calling from the commonplace for social change. As well, when considering the diversity of political and religious feelings and traditions among people, any theoretical universal rule of law is doomed to being over-ridden by differing personal and cultural perspectives, even when "non-judgmental" discussion is possible. But through people's attitudes of religiousness, social changes carry understandings of interconnected values, which are vehicles for broadening cultures' norms. We will look at an example from the Maidan revolution, of these values in action in the following section of this chapter.

Imaginative and Political Artifacts

James emphasizes social transformations as a matter of ideals and value-making through using one's imagination. In his 1892 lecture *What Makes a Life Significant*, James clarifies that allowing a person or community to understand another perspective is a matter of feelings and values and paramount to a religious experience.[34] James said:

> And, when you ask how much sympathy you ought to bestow, although the amount is, truly enough, a matter of ideal on your own part, yet in this notion of the combination of ideals with active virtues you have a rough standard for shaping your decision. In any case, your imagination is extended. You divine in the world about you matter for a little more humility on your own part, and tolerance, reverence, and love for others; and you gain a certain inner joyfulness at the increased importance of our common life. Such joyfulness is a religious inspiration and an element of spiritual health, and worth more than large amounts of that sort of technical and accurate information, which we professors are supposed to be able to impart.[35]

Knowledge becomes a more aesthetic field when thinking through James's understanding of religiousness. Dewey adds art, traditions, and habits as the very medium of our imaginations, vital to our interrelational natures. He clarifies that by viewing religion and traditions as closed systems, we can misunderstand some qualities of cultures as nonprogressive and mundane. Dewey thinks of religious feelings and traditions as powerful tools for community building as well as instrumental for broad social exchanges.[36]

Kant's concepts of the imagination are nonexistent in respect to Dewey's understanding of religious traditions, because even as a person *imagines* political freedom through a critical space of reflection such thoughts would have to be recognized as having been, through some manner of relationships, established among one's culture.[37] Moreover, "thinking without a banister"—which for Arendt is thinking, imagining, and communicating without static traditions, religions, or public opinions—cannot come to a just way of judgment without people's value-making attitudes, which can be traditional as well as civilly inclusive and progressive.[38]

My point is that thinking of our imaginations as a form of universal subjectivity separated from real-time traditions, habits, religious feelings, and events is a dangerous philosophy, by which we place political decision making into limited and often elitist positions. Such a noneffectual praxis is actually antithetical to Arendt's own project of eradicating totalitarianism through concerted political action. By contrast, Dewey thinks of imagination as an aspect of religious faith and as a real contributing factor to the wholeness of experience that people strive for in order to solve social problems. Imagining in regard to thinking about multiperspectives is beyond people's capabilities if they are separated from others in respect to moral and political decision-making, and traditions provide such connections and continuity. Traditions and religious beliefs can harbor a strong sense of aesthetic agency if people avoid using traditions as ends, rather than methods of communication and acculturation. To ignore self-reflective value-making as embodied in people's emotive traditions and expressive cultural artifacts cuts people off from truly communicating with others who hold different values and who offer new and possibly challenging aesthetic experiences.

Thus far, we have discussed a distinction of differing views of aesthetics, made clear by understanding James and Dewey's ideas on religious and artistic experiences. The distinction is basically between concepts that are abstracted from imaginative ideas and meaningful beliefs that are felt and *in the making*, that is, religious traditions. Now we can think more clearly about connections between religiousness and democracy. It is this point that I want to take a hermeneutic approach, so as to consider historical and cultural factors as important to our discussion.

Fighting in the Maidan, citizens used their religious traditions and collectively funded histories as means for revolution and community building without demanding static sets of rules, institutional Church doctrines, or exclusive nationalist political boundaries. The Maidan ethos in 2014 was also one of cultural diversity. Amid harsh winter days and nights, the people struggled through a raging conflict. Orthodox Christian priests of many denominations, wearing sacramental robes, stood within range of gunfire and Molotov cocktails, shoulder to shoulder, forming a line between the antigovernment protesters and security police, while praying for peace.[39] They raised crosses and held rosary beads in demonstration against governmental corruption and oppression. Many of the older women of Kiev brought icons from their homes, holding them like shields against aggression on either side of the barricades.[40] They pointed to their Saints, so that their fellow citizens might use their faith of the Christian Holy Spirit as a means for acting with beatitude. This was one of the most radical uses of traditional art in recent history, and it was part of the Maidan's art explosion that also included contemporary art projects.

Eastern Orthodox icons have brought people together in prayer, tradition, and revolution throughout history. Icons are symbolic of the fates of communities, carried along with the stories of the tumultuous events of people standing against oppressive authoritative governments. Through the reverence of icons individuals share a sense of importance and equality with priests, who are elevated by the hierarchical institution of the Church.[41] An example is the Russian peasant revolution when icons were used to try to secure basic human rights. On "Bloody Sunday" January 22, 1905, Father Georgi Gapon, who was born into a peasant family in a region that is now Ukraine, led thousands of workers and their families to petition the Tsar in St. Petersburg for equal rights and better working conditions. The people held icons at the frontlines of their protest to present the Tsar with the power of common faith. Despite their show of peace many were shot and killed that day by the Tsar's Imperial Guard. Stories of Gapon's bravery as a revolutionary are told alongside accounts of Nicholas Tsar's struggle to retain ultimate authority over his empire and his elitist attitude in regard to the struggles of the Russian people. Nicholas thought of his family supremely blessed as he was an extremely devote Christian with a renowned collection of icons. Gapon and Nicholas used the same means for binding people together, religion and art, yet they present us with very different approaches to their faith. Their paradoxical use of icons can be thought of as an example of the differences Dewey spoke of between *being religious* as an attitude of creative personal and communal development and religion as a source of elitist authority.

The Tsar's hopes for unity under supreme authority were forever dashed by the 1917 October revolution, and a restrictive form of communist ideology replaced Gapon's hopes for human rights. The communist revolution sought to replace religion with political and social bureaucracy and laws, but people in Ukraine regained personal and political freedom, declaring their liberated country a democracy on August 24, 1991.

But what was the nature of their icon tradition that remains as a productive source of religiousness, revolution, and liberation? Leonid Oupensky was a Russian icon painter and historian, who wrote, along with his colleague Vladimir Lossky, about the making and theology of icons. Oupensky explains revering icons is not a transcendental supernatural experience but a catalyst for an attitude, helping viewers focus on a visionary world, authentically felt, making it present. He writes in *The Theology of Icons*, "The icon does not represent the divinity. Rather, it indicates man's participation in the divine life."[42]

According to Ouspensky, human nature takes part in divine life through those reverent imagining and praying as part of an inclusive and freely felt spiritual world. This phenomenon happens as a person experiences a sense of acute perception, as their complete bodily feelings, when praying to an icon, are more vital than their sight. Theologically there is a paradox in both the Orthodox and Catholic religions in that they hold that Christ, whose presence on earth is made clear through viewing the icon, has two natures: divine and human. But the Holy Spirit, as an earthly ethos or cultural attitude, is communicated through icons by uniting those natures. In Eastern Orthodox religion there is no division between the material and the spiritual, so a material object can be divinely endowed with spirituality. Ouspensky writes: "All reality, including the physical, has the potential to be sacred." So, what does *sacred* mean for the zoographer (an icon maker)? Icons express the divine wisdom of God instead of the wills of the artists or viewers. As well, icon viewing is meant to be a means for personal transformation from being and acting from an individual perspective to having a broader understanding through feelings and thoughts of divine love and charity for all people.

When viewing the icon, it is not the icon that is venerated but the relationship of being engaged with, feeling while thinking, the meanings of the ideas that Christ or the depicted Saint carried forward by their experiences. Unlike portraits, icons depict figures for the purpose of presenting a living ideation, not in the manner of homage. The icon is a receptacle for veneration, as the divinity of God is presented by a direct engagement with the viewer.[43] Through the veneration of icons, a person utilizes the material object as a catalyst for an experience centered on their beliefs, thereby uniting feelings with practical aims for a more shared experience of life. What is important politically about the icon's appearance is that it emphasizes the collective beliefs of the Christian community.

In the modern era icons have been painted with layers of tempura and plaster, while ancient icons were modeled with a wax technique, called encaustic painting. The features of the icon's figures, however, have remained the same, as they are vital to the meanings of the paintings. The eyes, ears, and mouths of the image are idealized so as to downplay specific traits of beauty. As artifacts of worship, the icon presents a prayer, which manifests for the faithful as an actualized working belief, as well as valuing ideas which transverse pre-set cultural boundaries.[44]

Human Nature and Religious/Political Value-Making

Intriguingly, Dewey draws from the art traditions of the Byzantine churches to expand his notions about freedom in *Art as Experience*, leaving open an area for further hermeneutic study. Dewey did not think in terms of two natures of experience, particularly in respect to a separation of what is human and the ongoing process of one's environment. He explains "Nature" as our physical environment in direct correspondence with the developmental nature of human feelings, thoughts, and actions.[45] While explaining his use of the term "Nature" with a capital "N," Dewey contributes to our understanding icons by explaining that engaging with ideas concerning cultural diversity and inclusiveness are integral to the purpose of an icon because, while viewing icons, we perceive our interpersonal natures as expansive and as part of natural processes toward greater diversity. Dewey illuminates the connection between art theory and theology explaining that Byzantine art inspires a meaningful experience of the wholeness of varied perspectives.[46] Dewey explains:

> In reference to Byzantine art, I put the term nature in quotation marks. I did so because the word "nature" has a special meaning in esthetic literature, indicated especially by the use of the adjective "naturalistic." But "Nature" also has a meaning in which it includes the whole scheme of things—in which it has the force of the imaginative and emotional word "universe." In experience, human relations, institutions, and traditions are as much a part of the nature in which and by which we live as is the physical world. Nature in this meaning

is not "outside." It is in us and we are in and of it. But there are multitudes of ways of participating in it and these ways are characteristic not only of various experiences of the same individual, but of attitudes of inspiration, need and achievement that belong to civilizations in their collective aspect. Works of art are means, by which we enter, through imagination and the emotions they evoke, into other forms of relationship and participation than our own.[47]

Icons are inspirational by a sense of our integrated natures and through inspiring openness to new relationships. Icons are not made to transport people out of reality but to bring into view our aesthetic involvement with the universe.[48] Human relationships communicated with such religious feelings inspire empathetic understanding and equality through value making. When praying in front of the icon, the individual comes to experience the divine as present with oneself and so experiences a sense of compassion. Oupensky talks about such compassion as the language of Orthodox theology inspired by divine grace. This transformative emotional quality of icon worship does not get lost in relation to people's attitudes toward each other and our hopes for a better future but is part of the communicative aesthetic process.

Icons are living artifacts because of the revaluation they inspire throughout communities. There are three major Orthodox churches in Ukraine; together they make up the majority of religious people in Ukraine. The Ukrainian Greek Catholic Church and the Roman Catholic Church comprise the minority of Christians, and there is also a religious minority of Sunni Muslims, Protestants, and Jews. The Moscow Patriarchate has declared itself the Orthodox mother church, and as the only true successor to the ancient Kievan See, which was established in the tenth century. Moscow's recent movements to unify all Orthodox Christian followers in Eastern Europe have been talked about as being a deterrent to Ukrainian nationalistic movements. What this has meant in the past is both an intensification of political religious tensions and a general distraction from the unifying aesthetics that are inherent in religious experiences. Yet, with the current political crisis, many of the various leaders of the Orthodox churches have come together in their opposition to all forms of violence.[49]

Although religion is often immersed with national identity—despite the initial geopolitical basis of conflicts—religiousness, once evoked, can take precedence. Being religious is not a matter of race, and it is not commanded nationalistically by birth or privilege as religious feelings and thoughts often supersede political agendas, money, power, or the ownership of land. James remarks, "Among the buildings-out of religion which the mind spontaneously indulges in, the aesthetic motive must never be forgotten."⁵⁰ Accordingly, churches are not miracle factories, religious artifacts are not talisman, and violent revolutions are not a replacement for constructive community action. To build progressive values, religions, art, and revolution must be participated in cooperatively.

In this respect, the icons carried into the Maidan Square were beliefs in action. They were not the priceless icons housed in the Khanenko National Museum of Arts in Kiev. However, the icons used on the frontlines of the conflict had been encoded artistically to evoke the history of older icons, and they are comparable to the museum antiques that date back to the seventh century. Made in the late antique Christian era, the Khanenko relics are from a time when people extended their material reality into what they believed spiritually through their commonplace objects and modern distinctions between materiality and spirituality did not apply. The presence of the divine on earth was spread through the physical qualities of icons.

An example of this is an icon—which has been prayed to since those times—of *Saint Sergius and Saint Bacchus*. It dates from the sixth century, and being a small panel, approximately 28 by 42 cm, it was probably a lid for a reliquary box.⁵¹ The figures are painted and sculpted by encaustic wax, and contemporarily it has been immaculately restored. Its visual qualities are reflective—the gold leaf of the halos, the ashen whites of the robes, and cornelian reds of the honorary sashes—giving off light to the objects around it. The Saint's divine images are depicted in head and shoulders posture, together filling the complete picture field. The two figures sit side by side, and as soldier Saints, they have donned their military costumes. They wear Roman toques as necklaces, denoting their honor and bravery. Each toque bears three large painted jewels, symbolizing the Trinity of Christ. Their countenances are humble and compassionate, as the two soldiers have characteristically iconic features of closed mouths and luminescent eyes. In the upper register of the panel, between the two saints, a much smaller circular icon of Jesus Christ intersects their halos. The relic is comparable to marriage portraits of its time, with the icon of Christ taking the place of the *pronubus* or best man. However, both the two Saints are men, for this is an early example of same-sex friendships within church iconography. Sergius and Bacchus were comrades, but their own army martyred them—persecuted because they would not make cultic sacrifices to pagan Gods. Contemporarily the icon has become a symbol of tolerance toward homosexuality, although as Saints they were asexual and divine in life as in death.⁵²

The faithful are called to meditate on the icon's presentation of spiritual rewards after persecution. As well, the icon's symbolism brings into stark reality the contemporary cultural struggles in Ukraine, as there is a deeper aesthetic dimension to its revolutionary semiotics, through which the viewer has visual proof of a world where tolerance, and acceptance of difference, is a better way forward for communities.

Coming from a critical perspective, Slavoj Žižek wonders how Ukraine can become successful if it joins the EU, because of the grip of global neoliberal agendas and inauthentic political motivations on the part of Ukraine's institutional churches. As well, the European Union, according to Žižek, needs to be saved from itself, as it continues to ignore the plights of immigrant's worldwide and of disadvantaged communities that are all but forgotten by global financiers and religious leaders.[53] He asks how churches can continually turn a blind eye to diversity and immigration problems, while setting up distractions from religiousness by struggling for political power among themselves. He thinks Eastern European churches are forsaking the very religious aesthetic/values of inclusiveness, on which they have been founded.[54] He finds that under the current conditions, Europe and Ukraine are lost until they disengage from "The New World Order," which continually propagates a human nature that is money and power rich for some, yet spiritually and resource wise impoverishing for many more. Žižek thinks that answers lie in breaching ethnic and nationalistic lines of authority and division.

Žižek fears not that Ukraine doesn't know what it is getting into by emancipating itself so as to join Europe but that Europeans in general remain hesitant to continue to develop and engage with an inclusive culture of equality. In regard to politics, this is disappointing in that Europeans fought hard for humanistic rights over the centuries. The spirit of liberté that helped drive the revolutionaries of the Maidan was reminiscent of the eighteenth-century French Revolution. But as the situation slips back into one of continued conflict, one realizes that political ideals and dialog are not enough, as is evident with the philosophy of Arendt. At the current Ukrainian impasse with Russian separatists, I think Europeans should think more about Žižek's criticism and continue to emphasize the interrelational aspects of their communities and by using religiousness as an intercultural tool to avoid further violence.

In *Art as Experience*, Dewey explains that the aesthetics of worshipping icons changed after the 787 AD Second Council of Nicea. It was then that Christian churches begin to censor the symbolization of icons, and consequently the liberal Christian culture entered a more politicized and elitist aesthetic era.[55]

Dewey's main thesis in *Art as Experience* is that art motivates people's embodied feelings of religiousness through the everyday relationships of culture and community, which have been in modern times denigrated as mundane. Dewey placed great emphasis on everyday experiences, not only calling us to act more politically, in relation to values and community building, but to be more artistic. Compatibly to his ideas, commonplace icons are not considered by the faithful as being any less genuinely inspirational or aesthetically motivating than their rarified museum counterparts.

During the heyday of the Maidan revolution, artists working with a myriad of mediums immersed themselves into the revolutionary ethos. Jon Lee Anderson, a journalist for the *New York Times*, arrived on the scene after the fall of Yanukovych's government. The photographer Monteleone, who documented the everyday iconography of the revolution, accompanied him.[56] Anderson describes how Monteleone's pictures—which feature objects from the camp, in high relief, shot with a single reflex camera, and using an intense color sensitive film—represent the co-passionate, collective spirit of the camp. Although he titles his article "Revolutionary Relic," Anderson does not talk about Monteleone's photographs of icons found among the camp's artifacts as religious; instead, he presents the photos as material culture, a hand-painted helmet, a book, a glove, bullets, a pillow.

One of the photos is of a miniature icon that carries an immense collective cultural history, although it is in its humble, commonplace presence that it seems exceptionally inspirational. The small icon is a *Theotokos*, Birth-Giver of God, and it is rendered in cross-stitch embroidery, on a piece of cloth that is lined on its upper and lower edges by tiny seed pearls. This cloth is mounted on muslin-covered foam board behind its 2 ½-by-3 ½-inch gold-painted frame. The image is familiar, as it is a duplicate of a well-known icon of The Holy Mother. Her figure is always bordered in purple, the color of Creation, and stars that in the Maidan-embroidered icon have been stitched over a lapis blue ground surround her. Her body is robed in red, the color of human vigor, and her gold halo is outlined in white, the color of divine light, which is symbolic of her immaculate holiness and closeness to God. Her poised frontal figure seems understated as it blends into the blue field, but her slim face is detailed with finely stitched golden threads. Her head is tilted in reverence, though her expression is not downcast but direct, with focused and enthralling eyes. Her hands are crossed in supplication, and from her fingers emanate the seven rays of wisdom, which are the symbolic tools of the Holy Spirit. In Monteleone's photograph the icon is suspended on a black ground, as are all the other common-place objects from the Maidan camp. Yet all of the objects, including the gaze of the *Theotokos*, reach out to the viewer visually across the layers of representation and mediums—the computer screen, the photograph, the framed icon, the embroidered cloth, the designed configuration of the portrayal—to meet the onlooker's gaze.

This tiny, personal icon would have been carried in someone's coat or purse throughout the difficult days in the Square, but Monteleone employs it as a public call to arms, not only for contemplation but also for interpretation. If a person is devotedly Orthodox or Catholic, they would know that the little piece of stitch work is the same image as its more illustrious sister icon, *Our Lady of the Gate of Dawn*, housed in the morning chapel at the Medieval Gate of the Vilnius Cathedral in Lithuania. The Cathedral is both a holy site that draws pilgrims from all over the world and a symbol of Lithuania's centuries-old struggle for independence, which was finally achieved in 1990. The Cathedral's and the icon's history and their part in Europe's history are too complex to recount here, but there is one aspect that is particularly relevant. The icon is for Lithuanians and Poles a reminder of their joint uprising to free their Commonwealth from Russian rule in 1795. A Polish revolutionary from that uprising, General Tadeuze Kosciuszko, who was also a general and military engineer in the American Revolution, led the Commonwealth's insurrection. Kosciuszko initiated the campaign by writing a landmark proclamation (the Proclamation of Potaniec), which was circulated throughout the Commonwealth and Europe. It abolished serfdom and granted civil liberties to all peasants. This was the first official manifesto of its kind in Eastern European history.[57] However, Maksym Zalizniak, a Ukrainian hero of the people who fought against the Polish aristocracy and the Russian government in 1768, had first put forward ideas for equal humanitarian rights. The Ukrainian and Polish/Lithuanian revolutions failed at that time, but the uprisings are considered the beginning of the spread of Modern Political thought throughout Eastern Europe. The Vilnius icon is thought of as a source of strength in the face of unbeatable odds for these cultures. The icon is replicated in Catholic and Greek Orthodox churches alike, in many countries around the world from Ukraine, Poland, Belarus, Turkey, Brazil, the United Kingdom, and the United States. As well as being symbolic of previous revolutions and humanitarian theories, *Our Lady of the Gate of Dawn* is also distinct because the image of the Holy Mother is without child, and this icon stands out as a strong feminine statement. The icon can be thought of as inspirational in relation to more dynamic roles for women in Orthodox and Catholic churches.

Égaliberté in Europe meant freedom-in-equality, and that idea stands out in the passages of history as a unique and great contribution of Europe to the global political imagination.[58] But a political nationalistic idea of freedom is not enough to create just and safe states. To be more fully effective in our belief in democracy, we must realize values of inclusiveness that are made every day through our common relationships with each other. Liberty is better realized as a religious feeling of personal and cultural inclusiveness and wholeness than as a preconceptualized scheme or an idealized theme for discussion. Likewise, people around the world deserve better than a limited, static freedom based on consumerism and inauthentic images of our communities. We all deserve to be valued, as we are all boundless and free as participants in divine experiences.

Yet, it is true that political and religious institutions have separated religiousness from aesthetics modes of action. Many religious leaders remain caught in static and immobile public positions, and just as many continue to vie for power through statehood. Religion, not religiousness, is often used as an institutional structure of control to embody immovable, intractable positions of power. It is no wonder that prayerful communion is often thought of just a continuation of the forces of politics and economics. But through understanding religious aesthetics as *presenting* us with a better, more equal, and just world, which we can feel and act on, our values and motivations can change, moving us closer to forging peaceful and community-minded solutions to political problems.

For in the coat pocket of an activist fighting for freedom, on the frontline, the icon image is not a stand-in for a political ideology, nor a conceptualized critical theory. The icon is not a strategic weapon, nor a work of art that will soon be put up for auction, but it is, as Dewey said, a saturated image of who we are culturally. For our feelings and perceptions radically transfigure our values, and those values are re-presented through our collective traditions and histories, hopefully allowing our compassion and openness for a diverse world, including many people's hopes and beliefs for the future, to win over violence and separatism time and time again.

6

Dewey and Kahlo: Cosmopolitanism Midst Crisis

Focused by John Dewey's naturalistic approach to aesthetics, we can discern solutions to ongoing immigration and emigration problems, particularly in regard to his thinking about art, education, and cosmopolitanism. Accordingly, I think many answers to contemporary problems of forced immigration and social injustice lie with increasing restoration efforts for indigenous communities, not in a postcolonial militant manner but through propagating individual and community well-being, as people enliven the cultural dynamics of community-oriented education.

Throughout this chapter we will investigate such an approach, focused by Dewey's thinking about aesthetics as a field of experience, which is constituted by making evermore meaningful the fruitful relationships of individuals with their environments. Aesthetics, according to Dewey, is built on the practices of communities, inspiring people's purposes in life, while building interrelational values. We will unpack this philosophy, turning our attention to Dewey's recommendations for the practices of education. Dewey thinks communities are empowered by progressive educational programs, in which students learn to share cultural arts.[1] Along these lines, we can explore how individuals and communities reach out across ethnic, gender, cultural, national boundaries, as a matter of artistic endeavors. Accordingly, we will discuss how art education propagates an interrelational human nature, as a matter of cultural cosmopolitanism.[2]

Investigating hermeneutically, we can turn to the self-portraiture of Frida Kahlo, helping disclose naturalistic interpretations of Mesoamerican culture, presenting us with some of the intercultural values at play in the situation of Mexicans and Central Americans, as they continue to be plagued by immigration problems with the United States. Kahlo's mythical self-portraits open our abilities to relate to one another multiculturally. Her paintings are inspiring artifacts, communicating to many people across cultural divides. We will come to find that Kahlo, alike to Dewey, thought of selfhood and culture as bound with nature, including our self-reflections as a matter of realizing that one's purposes in life are inspired by and integrated with our shared environments. Also, both thought of teaching/learning as an integral value of cultural strength. So, we will discuss culture as an educational and culturally cosmopolitan practice, following Dewey and Kahlo's thinking on pedagogy as naturalistically, practically, and politically oriented. As well, both the philosopher and the artist thought education is a matter of learning to communicate and act across diverse groups, often resisting separatist controlling interests, and such praxis enriches everyone's cultural practices.

Immigration problems with the United States could improve by developing naturalistic and cosmopolitan aesthetics, and we will discuss how we can change authoritatively established Eurocentric anthropological views of culture. Comparing Dewey's ideas with Enrique Dussel's ontological mythology of indigenous Americans, we can analyze the significance of a change in Mesoamerican's cultural aesthetics. By connecting the philosophies and art work of Dussel, Dewey, and Kahlo, in respect to their views on "cosmopolitanism," we are on firm ground when suggesting progressive educational solutions for people caught in a destructive cycle of migration and subjugation.

Our search for answers to immigration problems in relation to a cosmopolitan aesthetic field of culture is somewhat historical, as Dewey wrote specifically on immigration problems several times throughout the early twentieth century. Especially significant are his writings from the early 1920s, when he was traveling in Mexico researching pedagogical practices. He thought of community-oriented schools as a source of intercultural cosmopolitan progress, highlighting how people can develop high regard for societal diversity.[3] Education should not attempt enculturation, according to Dewey, in the sense of employing methods of assimilation or coercion, nor should education include attempts to order one's culture or environment with exclusive interests of privilege. In his book on aesthetics, *Art as Experience*, he warns against threatening our well-being with passive, noncommunicative methods of education:

> However, the verb "to civilize" is defined as "to instruct in the arts of life and thus to raise in the scale of civilization." Instruction in the arts of life is something other than conveying information about them. It is a matter of communication and participating in values of life by means of the imagination, and works of art are the most intimate and energetic means of aiding individuals to share in the

arts of living. Civilization is uncivil because human beings are divided into non-communicating sects, races, nations, classes and cliques.[4]

Thinking in terms of how art aids a communities' shared, progressive imagination, Kahlo and Dewey combine art practices with political resources. Although, when thinking along these lines, we should remember that they held different views on communism and American democracy. However, I think their engagement with education and art clears a cross-cultural path, by which we create stronger intercultural values, so as to benefit our shared futures.

In 1945 Dewey turned his attention to global concerns, writing an introduction to the then new edition of Jane Addams' book *Peace and Bread in Time of War*, describing immigration in the United States as an educational value building practice. He stressed greater reciprocity among people worldwide by trading cultural artifacts and practices. He also puts forwards ideas about a democratic solution to war, in terms of fostering democracy worldwide, as a form of civil organization that includes cultural reciprocity.[5]

Although he stresses intercultural sharing and engagement, he warns against the displacement of people's indigenousness, in terms of their cultural orientations. Culture, materially and value-wise, helps us combat social problems caused by people being displaced from their communities and thereby being destabilized in terms of their identities. Dewey suggests we look to reinterpreting relational ties, which continue to be funded by our cultural and natural environmental resources, often ameliorating our social circumstances. For Dewey, answers arise by paying close attention to the meanings of our patterns of human relationships, as our varied emotive interpretations and expressions of those relationships are fruitful to our collective purposes. Our curiosity and interests in other people's circumstances thereby constitute our political methods and endeavors, clearing a more inclusive path for social progress.[6]

We will keep in mind throughout this chapter that progressive political attitudes and policies coming from such intercultural experiences are part of organic, aesthetic processes. Gregory Pappas thoughts on Dewey's aesthetics are relevant here in terms of putting a stop to systemic racism:

> Dewey did not simply uncover multiple causes and factors in racial prejudice. He pointed out their mutually reinforcing "organic" relation. A complex "organic" problem requires an intelligent organic approach. That is, the approach requires not only that we ameliorate the problem from all sides but that we are alert as to how one-sidedness effects, sustains, and nourishes the other sides.[7]

Dewey thinks of human relations as involving imagination, creativity, and innovation, hoping to expand human horizons, while warning us of supplementing static institutions instead of relying on a diverse interchange of meaningful relationships. Dewey explains his sense of cultural reciprocity in *Art as Experience*:

> Nevertheless, when the art of another culture enters into attitudes that determine our experience genuine continuity is affected. Our own experience does not thereby lose its individuality but it takes unto itself and weds elements that expand its significance. A community and continuity that do not exist physically are created. The attempt to establish continuity by methods which resolve one set of events as one of institutions into those which preceded it in time is doomed to defeat. Only an expansion of experience that absorbs into itself the values experienced because of life-attitudes, other than those resulting from our own human environment, dissolves the effect of discontinuity.[8]

Value-making can be diverse and pluralistic, thereby overshadowing institutional cultural restrictions. Meaningful shared cultural artifacts are necessary aspects of our community identities, marking the value of our personal relationships, as well as being dynamic instruments assisting us in making new relationships with different cultures. We will now turn our attention to many examples and further explications of these ideas.

Dewey's Naturalistic Aesthetics, Communicative Art, and Pragmatic Cosmopolitanism

Cultural activities, including political and artistic ones, are most meaningful when embedded in our everyday events and practices. Edgar Holger Cahill, working as the national director of the WAP/FAP in the Unites States during the 1930s and 1940s, thought of Dewey's aesthetics as connected with a multipronged cultural approach to education. Speaking at the dedication of a wall mural at a public school in Bronx, New York, 1938, Cahill describes a three-pronged approach to Dewey's naturalistic aesthetics:

> If art is defined, as John Dewey defines it, as a mode of interaction between man and his environment, then we may say that our art resources will fall into three categories: the resources in man himself, the resources in the environment, and the resources which come about through the methods and techniques developed in this particular type of interaction between man and his environment.[9]

Finding this naturalistic approach as democratic, in that our artistic methods should help us create social solutions out of our differences of opinions and interests, Cahill goes on to remark:

> Our resources in the environment will consist not only in what artists call "nature" which includes the elemental environments of earth and sea and sky and the visual and spatial aspects of the environments which have been created by human society. It will include also the stored-up environment of the past, the tradition of art which is the result of prolonged and cumulative interaction between man as artist and his environment, and which, in the form of works of art, has become part of our aesthetic environment today.[10]

Cahill's broad view of nature, as including culture, is for Dewey a matter of imaginative, creative practices being integrated with holistic experiences. The communicative qualities of an art work can be inherent to the artist's and viewer's attentive experiences, carried forward by skilled, yet often spontaneous, practices. An individual's heightened senses are transformed to be ever-more active by one's more intimately realized connections with both one's environment and an artistic medium. An artistic experience is consummated by feelings, perceptions, and emotions, and when combined, they become more easily expressed and communicated through a person's attitudes, actions, and values. Such communicative praxis carries on the artistic process, as these experiences involve "imaginative vision" by which one brings to their relationships insights needed when constructing a better future. Dewey explains:

> Only imaginative vision elicits the possibilities that are interwoven within the texture of the actual. The first stirrings of dissatisfaction and the first intimations of a better future are always found in works of art.[11]

Likewise, Dewey's aesthetics offers a philosophy of culture, including innovative disclosures about political thinking. Democratically, people's thinking can become part of the cultural process of making a more progressive culture, while ideas are put into practice experimentally. Fallibilism is a matter of being open to people altering their visionary ends, in respect to changing conditions, and such is a quality of artistic processes, as well. For example a painter continually changes her stance while viewing her work in progress, altering her medium and reconfiguring her images. Culturally important ideas and practices are never merely instrumental, in the sense that they are creatively mutable, in the head and hands of politicians, artists, and/or critics. New ideas for the benefit of our communities are a matter of our greater awareness of the interconnections of our environments in respect to our practices, emotions, imaginings, and values. Such aesthetic ideas and practices are made meaningful by being openly shared as inclusive communication.[12]

Dewey thinks of aesthetic processes as communicative, as people and cultures pursue desires and interests, constituting values, which we validate by ongoing community-oriented habits. Making art can be thought of as a value-driven habit, akin to attending town square meetings, working for a charity, or voting. Investing our energies with our direct and emotive communication is also what Dewey means when he claims that "aesthetics" and "having an experience" are a matter of expanding one's selfhood, as we continually engage our world with intensity and conviction. Our identities become integrated with broadly based interests when our personal experiences are made more meaningful by realizing the interrelational and environmental connections and cultural similarities and differences of others. In accord with such an inquisitive-based aesthetic, our self-interests are always connected with the interests of others, rather than self-interestedness. People's self-hood and meaningful communications are constituted by expansive, value-laden relationships with other people and our shared environments. Dewey emphasizes the importance of naturalistic, community-oriented values in respect to our personal identities:

> The ultimate significance of this appeal is, however, to make us realize the fact that regard for self and regard for others are both of them secondary phases of a more normal and complete interest: regard for the welfare and integrity of the social groups of which we form a part.[13]

Dewey thinks creating art marks our participation with our communities, making evident our values. Cultural artifacts are not static by-products of unmindful production, nor are they, as ideas, aimless concepts of one's subjective imagination. For Dewey, we can know "a thing," but it is never "in itself" as the rhythm and dynamic of one's environment is embodied with our artistic mediums. As an example, one might be directing a film, using the camera as one's eye, while embodying the images with meanings in respect to novel ways of viewing a scene. These perspectives can be common to an audience because they are participants in the human and/or environmental relationships of the film. But the process does not stop there; by experiencing the participatory aspects of artifacts, we find our participation is novel and experimental, thereby realizing what might be possible in the actual, and culturally such imagining can clear a way for new social directions. Dewey explains:

> While perception of the union of the possible with the actual in a work of art is itself a great good, the good does not terminate with the immediate and

particular occasion in which it is had. The union that is presented in perception persists in the remaking of impulsion and thought. The first intimations of wide and large redirections of desire and purpose are of necessity imaginative. Art is a mode of prediction not found in charts and statistics, and it insinuates possibilities of human relations not to be found in rule and precept, admonition and administration.[14]

This creative cultural process involves self-hood, artistic medium, environment, and human relationships. The process also portends to cosmopolitan attitudes, as people experience value-laden moments of reflection, while continually exploring and sharing varied relationships, as a matter of their culture's "concrete affairs." Once again Dewey explains:

Regard for self and regard for others should not, in other words, be direct motives to overt action. They should be forces, which lead us to think of objects and consequences that would otherwise escape notice. These objects as consequences then constitute the interest, which is the proper motive of action. Their stuff and material are composed of the relations which mean actually sustaining culture to one another in concrete affairs.[15]

John Ryder aids our understanding of cultural creativity by framing the relationship between naturalism and cosmopolitanism. He also describes pragmatic naturalism as connected to Dewey's thinking on democracy. Ryder understands naturalism as indicating a porous view of the human condition, which we can think of in terms of aesthetic/perceptual interrelationships, eliminating boundaries between the broad environments of Nature and human nature. Human nature, including our reflective problem-solving reasoning, is interdependently social, while sometimes protectively autonomous, so we constantly experiment with revelatory possibilities for meaningful experiences, as we have discussed. Ryder thinks in terms of democracy as an equalitarian and value-laden social form, which harbors our natural cosmopolitan sensibilities, as we continually reach out to what is new through sharing and caring for our communities and interrelated social environments. Our sense of security is based on shared, yet culturally endowed, joint endeavors. Ryder concludes that cosmopolitanism is the evolutionary ground of both pragmatism and democracy, as such an approach to human ontology broadens one's positive effects on the world (a sensibility of meliorism). In line with Ryder's thinking we can return our discussion to problems surrounding contemporary culture clashes because of immigration. Ryder addresses immigration in respect to his views:

The principle of cosmopolitanism calls on us to take to heart, what is to take seriously the interests we share with those beyond our own ethnic, national and cultural borders. It is internationalism, though it is more than that. If internationalism means to value international interaction and cooperation, then cosmopolitanism goes further and asks of us that we interact with others in ways that allow us to identify, and where necessary to create, common interests that enable us to work together in their pursuit.[16]

Ryder understands Dewey as realizing that relationships are able to arbitrate between selfhood, community, and an enlarged community, as part of an aesthetic cosmopolitan process, which is, as said, useful yet experimental and creative. Such pragmatic cosmopolitanism works as a matter of progressive intercultural values, as our investigations of the horizons of our experiences become more and more a matter of shared pursuits.

Dewey and Kahlo's Cosmopolitan Naturalism

Examples of aesthetic reciprocity between selfhood and cultural practices are found in Kahlo's self-portraits. Kahlo was an internationally known art figure during the politically charged era of the early twentieth century. When young she thrived in the cosmopolitan atmosphere of Mexico City of the 1920s, following the Mexican Revolution.[17] Mexico's urban culture, during the years after the Revolution and leading up to the Second World War, was influenced by influx of international artists, who were inspired by ideas about social progress.[18] As participants with this cosmopolitanism, Kahlo and her husband Diego Rivera lived for short periods in Europe and the United States; however, they both remained community minded, as permanent residents of Coyoacán outside of Mexico City. There and abroad they associated themselves with a milieu of communist-minded artists who held to Marxist principles. Kahlo compared what she saw as the favorable communist direction of the Soviet Union with the oppressive capitalist direction of the United States. However, she eventually lost her admiration for Joseph Stalin, although it is unclear through my research if she understood the reach of Stalin's violent, authoritative regime in the then newly formed Soviet Union. That said, Rivera and Kahlo voiced strong objections to violence of all kinds and to political totalitarianism.[19]

Dewey was associated with Rivera and Kahlo, through friends, and in the spring of 1939, he spent over a week at the couple's Blue House. Dewey chaired the Trotsky Commission, organized because Stalin had exiled Leon Trotsky. Finding temporary refuge in Mexico, Trotsky wanted to reclaim his Russian identity, so the Commission enacted a mock trail, then discerning that he was innocent of sedition.[20] After the trial, Trotsky went on to live two more years in Mexico before his brutal assignation, ordered by Stalin. Dewey disagreed with Trotsky's political ideology because of his militant approach to Marxist communism but participated with the Commission as a proponent of humanist values, standing firm with the committee when they found Trotsky had been falsely accused and persecuted.

One aspect of Marx's philosophy that Trotsky, Dewey, and Kahlo would have agreed upon is realizing workers should be involved with all aspects of their labors, benefiting by being cooperating partners, while having the opportunities to be educated and knowledgably about all the processes of production. Such theories of co-production are echoed in Dewey's aesthetics, as an artistic medium is part of a consummate experience, constituting an artist's thoughtful purposes through skilled making. Just as an artist anticipates a completed art project, she envisions or feels shared emotions and/or values to come from others participating in the art's reception. Kahlo was one such emotive value maker, as she was an activist for better futures for the people of Mexico. Although her paintings depict suffering and pain, she finds new meaning in her physical pain by using her experiences to inspire cultural unity. She does this by developing a characteristic iconography throughout her paintings, depicting growth and spiritual transformation, as will be discussed.

Besides Dewey and Kahlo's divergent political views, there are significant interconnections between their views on naturalistic aesthetics, art, and culture. When Dewey visited Kahlo's home, *Art as Experience* had been published two years earlier, and it is possible Kahlo read the book and/or discussed it with friends. Regardless of whether Dewey and Kahlo talked about their views on art, they certainly shared a love for Mexican artesania and a naturalistic approach to art. Dewey had a deep appreciation of Mexican arts and crafts, first writing about that material culture as value-laden and transformative to communities, when researching Mexico's educational practices in 1926, which we have noted previously as informative to his views on cosmopolitanism. Dewey wrote for the *New Republic*:

> As a rule, if what we saw may be depended upon as evidence, the designs in the small rural schools were much better, even though the work was crude, than in the industrial schools of the city, where department store art has made a lamentable invasion. If the schools can succeed in preserving the native arts, aesthetic

traditions and patterns, protecting from the influence of machine-made industry, they will in that respect alone render a great service to civilization.[21]

Kahlo's fascination with artesania is more well known, in that the Blue House, which is now a popular museum, is filled with the couple's collection of ancient Mayan fetish ceramic figures, pottery, and Mexican Christian ex-votos or retablos. Rivera and Kahlo had over 2,000 retablos in their collection, and both painters incorporated symbols from their collection in their art.[22] They kept an anthropological codex, noting the symbolic meanings for many Aztec and pre-Aztec artifacts, in their library. Undoubtedly, Dewey would have found their collection stimulating and possibly was impressed with Kahlo's use of symbols in her paintings, which also decorated the Blue House.

During this era, particularly in New York and Chicago, there existed a network of avant-garde artists, socially minded philosophers, and liberal political activists who were loosely connected socially. Some were involved in what we can now talk about as cultural anthropology of material culture. Miguel Covarrubias, who was an active agent of the cosmopolitan art and intelligentsia, traveled and worked both in the United States and Mexico, at that time, and was particularly interested in the cross currents of cultural identity.[23] Covarrubias's art is an example of a cosmopolitan artist and human scientist, in that he was not only an internationally influential illustrator and portrait artist but also a curator, ethnologist, archaeologist, as well as being instrumental in introducing contemporary dance to Mexico. His art and books on ethnology serve our purposes here, helping us realize how an engagement with the practices and habits of indigenous communities, without colonial assimilation, can expand pluralistic attitudes.[24] Being that he was a portrait artist, he depicts individuals and indigenous cultures as having complex histories and unique cultural practices, not merely cultural stereotypes. His work moves us away from stereotypical views of indigenous cultures and is important to a new conception of cosmopolitanism, as each community serves as a unique participant, sharing common values of their communities with others.

Mentioning such associations, I want to emphasize, in respect to Kahlo's painting and Dewey's philosophy, a cultural perspective they shared, that being their appreciation of art's agency. I think of their approaches to cosmopolitanism as unlike the cursory meaning of the word used when people enjoy traveling as tourists to foreign lands feeling comfortable anywhere they find themselves, or as a description of economic advantage for privileged individuals, enjoying profits wherever they locate businesses. Those kinds of aesthetic orientations are limited only to wealthy people or are afforded to people who work from a privileged or falsely superior Euro-Western cultural foundation, so such attitudes have no real pluralistic value for social change. For Dewy and Kahlo, meaningful cosmopolitan endeavors are realized by people who come to know their relationships with natural environments and personal circumstances as motivating forces and then finding new opportunities for sharing and trading their resources. Cosmopolitanism, in this respect, takes on a more profound intercultural meaning than those other, more vernacular, meanings. Such opportunities arose for Kahlo and Dewey, while they at the same time recognized the systemic abuse and symbolic violence suffered by many people who were indigenous to Mexico, because of the greed of many capitalists during the industrial era. In response to those injustices, they realized that there was opportunity for cosmopolitan value-making, especially in relation to artistic and pedagogical practices, as means for social activism.

Kahlo depicted cultural tensions between Mexico and the United States. In the montage paintings, *Self Portrait on the Border between Mexico and the United States*, 1932, and *My Dress Hangs There*, of 1933, she paints a cautionary tale for industrial society; the first portrait documents Detroit's industrial ambitions, while the second noted painting is a portrait absentia, criticizing New York City's air pollution, impersonal architecture, and overcrowding.[25] In both paintings she evokes collective/community memories of her organic and naturalistic Mexico. Later in her oeuvre, I think her portraits of the 1940s, painted while living permanently at the Blue House, present the viewer with a fuller awareness of naturalistic aspects of selfhood, community, and cosmopolitanism, as we will now discuss.[26]

During the 1940s Kahlo held classes with select students who were enrolled in the Public Education of Mexico School of Painting and Sculpture. Importantly, her students made political statements, participating in community collaborative mural projects. Kahlo remained artistically tied to such political projects; her own mid-career/late portraits were transformed through her iconography of visionary imagery. While it has been noted that Rivera seemed to lose confidence in collective imagination, turning to didactic pictorial narratives in his paintings, Kahlo seemed to become increasingly liberated in her use of symbolism and naturalist wisdom.[27] Kahlo portraits express a broad understanding of cultural anthropology through naturalism. In her mature art, Kahlo relates her personal experiences, to ancient Aztec and pre-Columbian symbiology, especially in relation to her inability to bear children and her health problems. Her work was distinct from what was then considered surreal, as she becomes increasing enthralled with a naturalistic iconography. She embodies her paintings with collective, mythical meanings, presenting natural, scientific/medical references and community-oriented values.

Kahlo's passions for a collective Mexican culture became infused with her sense of organic naturalism through her chosen genres of portraiture and still life.[28] Her historicity was not always exacting, in relation to indigenous cultural symbols, depending much more on her interpretations of the naturalism of the many ancient Mexican cultures. She paints as a way to honor life's cycles of birth and death, bringing to the surface of her canvases a common life energy between humans, plant life, and animals. Intimately she relates her self-identity to vast cosmic, creative energies, which transform life through organic growth.

In the self-portrait *Self-Portrait with a Thorn Necklace and Hummingbird* (1940), she relates naturalistic creative values, in relation to her personal struggles, with her country's strivings for social justice.[29] Stylistically we can discern references to icon painting, as she pushes her figure forward against the flat background, her closed mouth and stylized gaze emphatically anticipating the thoughts and feelings of the viewer, not merely her own thoughts. Yet, unlike a stylized icon, she sets herself amid an abundance of verdant tropical foliage. Her Indios clothing, her braided hair, the plants and insects of her garden, her pet monkey and cat, all take on quasi-religious mystical-like meanings, marking her iconography.[30] She depicts herself as emblematic of nature's transformative growth and as spiritually in communion with Mexico's indigenous people and their ways. She is a feminine Christ figure and a maternally oriented person born with a natural gift for creativity, as she also prophesies social change.

She incorporated the medium and practices of the Catholic *ex-voto* paintings, in her collection, in her portraiture. Working with oils on tin, she constructed many of her self-portraits in the stance of icons, as mentioned, scaling her painting down to the size of personal icons. Philosophically, Kahlo also invokes humanistic values, in that art historically she draws on the Old Master tradition of Western painting. I am thinking specifically here of the genre of *Ecce Homo*, as Christ is depicted prophetically marked by stigmata, reminding the viewer of his sacrifice of his suffering for the eternal life of faithful people. Pilate, who condemned Christ, exclaimed to the mob, "Behold the Man," thereby naming the *Ecce Homo* genre. Kahlo finds herself in Christ's situation, symbolized by her necklace of thorns. Referencing both Christianity and Aztec mysticism, she becomes a sacrificial believer in an ongoing Mexican spirit.

Kahlo's self-portrait in which she depicts herself as *Ecce Femina* is radical in respect to feminist art history, for Kahlo is referencing her entry into the

Renaissance Master's tradition of *Ecce Homo* self-portraits. Albert Durer painted *Ecce Homo*, circa 1500, which is often thought of as the first humanist self-portrait.[31] Portraying himself as Christ could be misinterpreted as self-conceit, yet an *Ecce Homo* can be experienced as "the moment of viewing presentation," eliciting spiritual and human values of reaching out and caring for all humanity. With such an interpretation of an *Ecce Homo*, a self-portrait transforms the image of the artist into a symbol for those oppressed and those who feel like, and are seen, as outsiders, so what is demonstrated most apparently are the humane effects of compassion and beneficence in the presence of an ordinary person.

However, such humanistic art possibly fails to protect the uniqueness of the organic nature of culture Kahlo sought to express. Intuitively, she discerns a difference, highlighting a mode of spirituality that is vital as a matter of variety of transformative qualities of nature, rather than a single source of universal spirit. Kahlo's portrait discloses her profound desire to embrace her own authenticity as well as her communion with nature and a political symbol of the oppression of indigenous, spiritual culture in Mexico. Regardless of the metaphysical source of such redemptive spirituality, her use of both Mexican votive paintings and the Western art tradition of *Ecco Homo* portraiture is expressive of a pragmatic, pluralistic, progressive valuation of culture.

She wrote in her diary, "Fruits are like flowers—they speak to us in a provocative language and teach us things that are hidden."[32] In her painting *Thorn-Necklace*, she becomes an ancient goddess, surrounded by flowers, yet, her headdress is an *ayatl* head cloth and her raiment is a *huipil* overblouse, which is traditional pre-Columbian everyday women's dress. She surrounds herself with the fauna of her garden, the animals living with her at the Blue House, conveying to the viewer the spirit of the people of her community.

The portrait is evocative of mythical Mexican culture, yet it also symbolizes the country's cultural/class divides at the time it was painted. In ancient Mesoamerica, monkeys were associated with the arts and the deities of fertility and dance. Kahlo would have known monkeys represented Ozomatli, a god of the Aztec calendar, symbolizing cleverness, craftiness, and unpredictability, while she also honors the animal's niche amid the ongoing processes of nature. The monkey, on Kahlo's shoulder, picks at a thorn on the necklace, uninterested in the drama occurring on Kahlo's opposite shoulder, as a clawed cat is ready to pounce on the hummingbird, hanging as a crucifix like pendant on Kahlo's necklace. Cats were thought of in Aztec iconography as embodying the power and aggressiveness of the jaguar, which was a god, second only to the god of the snake. Kahlo's black cat is stalking the hummingbird strung on her necklace of thorns. The hummingbird is also a potent Aztec symbol of a god, Huitzilopochtli, the god of war. She painted the portrait in 1940, so the lurching cat could have been an ominous reminder of the fear and death of the Second World War, which was felt throughout Mexico and internationally at that time.

These symbols can be seen as personal and poignant, remembering that Kahlo's father was a German immigrant to Mexico, so she surely identified with people fleeing Europe during the Second World War. Possibly because of her pluralistic cultural identity—as her mother was a native Mesoamerican—her portrait connects her personal approach to Mesoamerican culture, while linking her cross-cultural sensibilities with the indigenous natural resources of her environment. I think her foreignness is counterbalanced by her spiritual birthright as a source of self-identification as native Mesoamerican, so her portrait expresses both a need and a respect for cultural acceptance and diversity, while tying such values with spiritual and communal unity. She displaces class consciousness with a more profound presentation of women as visually articulate; however, unlike romantic or existential artists, she does not separate herself from the struggles of her community, revealing a more holistic connection with our world.

Huitzilopochtli, the god of war, is also the quintessence symbol of ancient Mexico's masculine virility and the dynamic of the warrior, and as previously mentioned, it hangs around Kahlo's neck. The symbol in the portrait can be seen as communicating a collective anxiety about the lives being lost in the global struggles of the time. Yet, simultaneously Kahlo depicts herself as the Mayan goddess Ixchel, mother of all and rainmaker of purifying change. Her headdress is made of snakes and butterflies, symbolizing an eternal, yet transformative and communicative, natural process of all life. Dragonflies, which are painted as hybrid flowers, guard Kahlo. These elements of her portrait mark her spiritual transformation as she is overcoming the pain of domestic violence, alike to *Ixchel*. The myth of *Ixchel*, a goddess who was raped by the sun god and a survivor of domestic violence, is a contemporarily relevant symbol, encouraging to many women who are hesitant to open up about their experience because of the shameful stigma of being injured by one's spouse. Such shame existing because praise and blame cultures still abounds, but possibly the shame also exists because our natural desires to give birth and to nurture others are crushed by violence and war. Kahlo empowers everyone to employ creative relationships in the face of emotional and physical violence, which can split asunder our organic sense of self.

Kahlo did not think of herself as a surrealist, and although she knew many influential surrealist artists, most notably Breton, she held a different view of the revolutionary dynamics of art.[33] André Breton, the international impresario of the surrealist art movement, was also a participant in the Trotsky Commission. He and Trotsky collaborated when writing "Manifesto for an Independent Revolutionary Art." In difference to basing her paintings solely on communist ideology, and surrealist imagery, designed to shock and baffle, thereby motivating people to think in a different way and thus motiving political action, Kahlo realistically uses symbols with intimacy to communicate a sense of community unity. She thought of herself as a craftsperson, using her engagement with the natural environment and the community's material culture, history, and social events as mediums for her art, as well as paint. Her self-acclaimed style of "revolutionary realism" was informed by her commitment to her personal self-discovery, expressing our communion with nature, as well as her political views.[34]

Kahlo's visionary realism communicates directly to viewers today, bringing forward feelings of beauty, abundance of procreation, as well as pain and suffering in terms of our social and environmental problems. Through her use of symbols, she reorients our shared perceptions, thereby altering our approaches to life, so in difference to competitiveness or overarching ideologies, we are engaged by her feminine creativity and strength, organic and symbolic interconnectedness, natural and self-transformation, and growth through diversity. These natural traits of reality can become values for our communities.

Embracing nature, Kahlo expresses a pluralistic cosmopolitan orientation to self-identity.[35] She understood natural environments as culturally profound, in that as we are integrally connected to our environments, people can find new values and in a sense transform our human natures.

Dewey's Cosmopolitan Aesthetics and Dussell's Ontology of Social Justice

Dewey also sought to reorient people's values, philosophizing about aesthetics and art. His approach to value theory in relation to self-identity is more than implicating subjective tools for personal expressive or social critique, and he thinks about personal growth as a matter of organic, cosmopolitan practices. The importance of one's self-identity, as a cohesive aspect of one's culture in respect to a transformative, transcultural approaches to life, he explains in *Art as Experience*:

> Just because art, speaking from the standpoint of the influence of collective culture upon creation and enjoyment of works of art, is expressive of a deep-seated attitude of adjustment, of an underlying idea and ideal of general human attitude, the art characteristic of a civilization is the means for entering sympathetically into the deepest elements of the experience of remote and foreign civilizations. By this fact is explained also the human import of their art for ourselves. They effect a broadening and deepening of our own experience, rendering it less local and provincial as far as we grasp, by their means, the basic attitudes of other forms of experience.[36]

At this junction of this discussion, as art, ontology, and social changes are found to be working together, it occurs to me that Enrique Dussel's philosophy of a transnational Central and South American ontology is sympathetic to many ideas involved with pragmatic cosmopolitanism.[37]

Dussel, who is very critical of colonial philosophies, thinks in terms of an indigenous naturalistic cosmopolitanism, understood by reconstructing ancient ontologies of Mesoamericans. He has not been silent on the issues of systemic cultural violence, which plagues contemporary life in both North and South America, recognizing the urgency of resolving migrant, immigration, and emigration problems, while calling for a far-reaching disclosure of Meso-Latin American political and socioeconomic histories. He hopes to help people change the world with his forceful liberation philosophy as a guide. He asserts a philosophy of self-empowering authenticity, tied to the indigenous and complex intercultural understandings of *Indios*/Latin cultural identity, so such cultural awareness becomes a resource for new global values.[38] Contemporary problems of immigration, according to Dussel, stem from colonial and postcolonial European appropriation of entitlement through culture and selfhood, and consequently people continue to depend on an Ancient Greek-European-American ontological mythology. He claims modern philosophy, with its academic structures, has helped erase the authentic heritage of indigenous American cultures, finding that an ancient lineage of civilization actually encompasses ancient Asian, Phoenician, Egyptian, Middle Eastern, Native American, and pre-Columbian philosophies. These ancient civilizations had ways of life that did not always value what is now considered rationally oriented thinking. An authentic Indios/Latin American ontology depends on communities living according to their interpersonal relationships, while marking transformative passages of selfhood, mythologically and symbolically, as part of the growth of those communities.

Such a philosophical anthropology differs from the Anglo/European philosophy of individual, who is not completely authentically ontologically oriented with Nature but pursues self-directed happiness. This Anglo/European has contemporarily embraced a Cowboy attitude of greedy competitiveness and control.

According to Dussell, the Hispanic chapter of the shared heritage of Central and South Americans must be acknowledged as a profoundly meaningful epoch of human history. However, Hispanics must assert themselves through a disclosure of their participation with an authentically ancient Ameri-Indian world. Dussel proposes that all people adapt a transmodern "world-hood," as people in North American can then realize indigenous communities as vitally important, as cultures that teach others how to replace economic and social oppression with genuine interests in reintegrating our human, relational natures with our environments. He thinks the lessons learned by the failures of Anglo-Saxon cultures will be immense. Dussel writes:

> We need them to make present an American culture, that of the south, in the great country of the north. This culture can show the North American citizen other continental horizons and impart an increased responsibility for the poverty of millions and for populations who are not just markets but dignified human beings.[39]

Surely, Dussel's critique of North American Anglo-Saxon culture is in itself a sign of needed transformation of everyone's human nature. His reconstruction of this global genealogical narrative, spotlighting indigenous ontologies, sparks criticism because it can be thought of as partial toward ancient forgone traditions, which stand as a kind of authority of history, instead of postmodern and/or progressive ideas. Yet, Dussel highlights the essential element of historicity as a reflective critique, helping us retain meanings and providing us with solutions. If communication and symbolic messages of liberation and change are to be widely effective, they must retain a sense of ongoing transformations through not only individual's perspectives but histories and overarching cultural philosophies. At this point, I do not want to imply that social change must come slowly, but it must have resonance that runs all the way through our identities and how we approach our arts and cultures. I think Dussel rejects the postmodern slogan "the most important thing is the spectacle you make out of an event, as opposed to the event itself," as such is mistaken in terms of understanding how people's identities are integral to their participation with their communities. Through our cultures we relate ourselves to the world, amid our ever-changing natural and social environments.

As Dussel rewrites the origins of being in the world, politically, the Neo-Zapatista movement continues to center its efforts in the region of Southern Mexico, Chipas. This political movement is known around the world as a movement of "radical democracy." The Neo-Zapatistas are committed to extreme social change and civil resistance, funded and supported globally by highly effective internet/communicative praxis. They respond to political acts of oppression, defending the autonomy of indigenous people and other natural resources, while the most contested of these resources is the use of land and water. Particularly they work to make enduring changes in Mexico's natural governing structure and class system, consequently reaching out internationally to advice liberation movements around the world. Hopes abound that indigenousness people around the world might reform global systems of health, education, human rights, and economic opportunity. Although some progress has been made in the Chiapas region and in other communities in Guatemala and Honduras, there has not been the needed political support for law reform, and there has not been an adequate rooting out of systemic corruption in law enforcement.

There is no doubt that the U.S. immigration policies are affected by a collective sense of fear of invasion, possibly in regards to the kind of transformative change of culture Dussell writes about. North American culture has been a force for exploitation, benefiting those who think first about profit, motivating less reflection about community and environmental sustainability, and promoting a very different future than Meso-Indian cultures.[40] The Mexican government remains tied to a colonial identity rather than a relational and symbolically aware ontology. In contrast, Dussel claims Neo-Zapanistas are building a world where many worlds fit. This is pragmatically a cosmopolitan world, where communities herald their dignity and natural modes of efficiency, while building relationships with others in terms of beneficence, charity, and hospitality.

Dewey calls for cosmopolitanism, and as importantly he calls for meaningful communication, not merely a critique or a siren alerting us to problems but as part and parcel of the solution. He is very clear on what we can call cosmopolitan communicative praxis based on pragmatic naturalism, which he bases on a contemporary idea of cosmopolitan *paidea*, a melding of culture and pedagogy. *Paidea* might sound to Dussel as again echoing ancient Greek philosophy, but with Dewey's ideas of pedagogy, we put emphasis on artistic, scientific, and agricultural and technological practices, as being value-making tools as well as technical skills. Citizenry, as community governing, is also an essential skill to be propagated in schools, and this is taught best by attending and participating in cultural events. To sum up this part of our discussion, we might be best served by re-reading Dewey's description of this view in his community-minded text *The Public and Its Problems*.

> A community thus presents an order of energies transmuted into meanings which are appreciated and mutually referred by each to every other on the part of those engaged in community action. "Force" is not eliminated but is transformed in use and direction by ideas and sentiments made possible by means of symbols.[41]

Here, I highlight the connection I am making between Dussel's shift to radical cultural ontology and Dewey's thinking on education, culture, and symbols.

Dewey goes to say:

> The case is the same with the interest of the self as with its realization. The final happiness of an individual resides in the supremacy of certain interest in the make-up of character, namely, alert, sincere, enduring interest in the objects in which all can share. It is found in such interests rather than in the accomplishment of definite external results because this kind of happiness alone is not at the mercy of circumstances.[42]

We must continue to allow indigenous communities to teach us about sharing interests through profound meaningful exchanges of their cultural spirit, just as we work with others to achieve our mutual goals. We will then be able to stop the economic and class violence prohibiting education, progress, and growth. By comparing Dewey's ideas with Enrique Dussel's ontological mythology of indigenous Americans, we can analyze people's self-identities as rooted in feelings of authenticity; thereby, we truly care about teaching and learning from others, as effectively progressive modes of collective agency. Through such an ontology of intercultural learning from each other, we can explore solving contemporary immigration problems in terms of a new cosmopolitanism, thereby enriching our home communities and global culture.

Dewey and Kahlo's Cosmopolitan Pedagogy

As mentioned, Dewey discussed and wrote about problems of immigration, emigration, and assimilation.[43] He thought as a culturally pluralist, speaking up against segregation, and his approach to multicultural societies can be understood in relation to his ideas on education. Traveling through Mexico, he developed a pedagogy based on learning practices, by which students are "doing and making," while learning. For example when music students push through scoring a composition they have heard by ear, they confront anew, and through their firsthand experience, the artistic problems solved by the original composer.[44] This re-creating process involves an intimate experience of the student with her present environment, allowing for creative reinterpretation. Such an experience of integrating one's creative skills with an artistic medium involves being enthralled with experimentation, while remaining connected with a history. Such a process is practical, while broad and expansive, and Dewey finds it evident in Mexico's village schools of that time.[45]

Dewey outlined the curriculum for lower-school students, as multifaceted. Part of the day was to be spent on reading, writing, and arithmetic, with some study of foreign languages, but the remainder of the time, the students concentrated their energies on creative activities and honing their skills in respect to practical making and doing. "Practiced" arts, such as weaving, pottery, painting, building, is essential, as well as agricultural and engineering skills. Taking a radical position against impersonal industrialization and automated production, which disallows first hand making and doing Dewey wrote:

> If the rural schools can succeed in preserving the native arts, aesthetic traditions and patterns, protecting them from the influence of machine-made industry, they will in that respect alone render a great service to civilization.[46]

Nathan Crick and David Tarvin, who have researched pedagogical methods specifically in the context of Dewey's experiences with Mexican rural schools, find that Dewey's hopes for creative education are inspiring in the respect that such practical methods allow for students and teachers finding themselves involved in collective agency. Teachers and students need to be supported nationally, but they are also empowered by acting in a self-supporting manner. Crick and Tarvin's research brings to light the importance of this community-oriented approach to an international cosmopolitan spirit of respect and progress. Referring directly to Dewey's pedagogy, they explain:

> This experience, however brief, left a lasting impression upon him and culminated in an insight that I believe has lasting significance for international educational development, particularly in the developing world. In short, Dewey caught a glimpse of the progressive potential of a communicatively networked system of rural schools that integrated, through experimental method, the practices and traditions of local culture with the aesthetic and scientific resources of global cooperative intelligence.[47]

Crick and Tarvin further their analysis by suggesting that advanced technologies be included in rural education, as a means for spreading their contributions to such a contemporarily relevant mode of education. Students in villages throughout rural Mexico and Central America can use demonstration events on the worldwide web to augment their practical community-oriented education. As a naturalistic orientation becomes more prevalent by reflective awareness, propagated through their personal and community practices and collective, symbolic knowledge, people use communicative means to spread more pluralistic yet collective meanings. Crick and Tarvin inform:

> To understand the relationship between the local and the global in experimental rural education, one can look to how Dewey understands the multiple layers of the "public" in contemporary political culture. Here we find Dewey recognizing both the importance of sustaining local oral traditions and communities while also acknowledging the necessity of connecting them, through electronic and print technologies, to a networked global society. In Dewey's ideal of democracy, the public is not a single monolithic entity, but is instead made up of many publics interacting through a flexible network of public spheres.[48]

I can add that a return to a governmental focus and investment in rural public schools would solve many economic and social problems, community wise and internationally. "Migration" could be redefined, possibly becoming a matter of cosmopolitan, reciprocal sharing of ideas and practices, rather than focusing on the humanitarian crisis immigration problems, which have recently become increasingly worse because of the ongoing violence and economic greed by those who hold on to nontransferrable wealth.

A comparison can be made with Kahlo's pedagogy. In 1942, Kahlo turned to teaching painting, guiding a small group of students who were known throughout Coyoacán and surrounding areas as "Los Fridos."[49] Taking cues from her political approach, Kahlo encouraged this close-knit group of students to work together collaboratively with community purposes in mind, while painting intimate but politically charged art. She continued to express symbolic naturalistic wisdom, with her own painting, and subsequently her students spread a profoundly engaging artistic ethos.

Thinking in terms of education, art, and naturalistic cosmopolitanism has been apparent in societies such as the Native Americans and Mesoamericans for thousands of years. These legacies were important to Dewey, as well as other culture makers of his time. In an introduction to a landmark anthology of essays by artists who participated in the WAP/FAP program, in the United States during the 1930s and 1940s, Francis V. O'Connor describes the general lack of appreciation for community-inspired artistic endeavor in North America, and the misadventure of not turning to Native American and Mesoamerican cultures for inspiration.

> I would like to suggest that the general weakness of American mural art during the 1930s, and its virtual disappearance as a viable means of expression after the second World Ward, is a function of that very rootlessness which prompted the search for "a usable past" in the first place. The Mexicans could draw from the deep wells of their primordial past and their experience of assimilating Spanish conquerors. The great power of their murals lies not only in the fusion of traditional techniques with modern forms and scales, but also in the incorporation of the ancient universal images of their "usable past" in the service of their social revolution. They had heroic images for heroic deeds.[50]

Looking at contemporary activist art, we find a resurgence of naturalism and cosmopolitanism as a sign of changing ontologies, shifting from being enslaved by technocratic enterprises to being rooted somewhere as part of an autonomous community with a righteous sense of cosmopolitanism. Joel Artista thinks of himself as a nomadic artist, while being known as an educator and advocate for social justice for Hispanic culture around the globe. He paints in the Mexican School style of Rivera, yet with a sense of naturalism and symbology attuned to Kahlo's art. He collaborated with Chris Soria, on his mural *IX Chel*, and here we find once again the Mayan goddess of Kahlo's self-portrait.[51] The mural spotlights the neighborhoods of Harman and Knickerbocker in Brooklyn. Artista brings forward the meaning of the *IxChel* legend, emphasizing perseverance through feminine struggle, strength of self in the face of abuse, and finally rebirth and growth. The pain, fear, and sacrifice of Kahlo's self-portrait are transformed, as we find a contemporary symbol of hope, vision, and creativity, along with the formidable force of the goddess of all living things.

The Obama administration in 2014 issued a statement that the problem of illegal immigration, specifically the orphaned children crossing illegally from Southern Mexico and Central America into the United States, had reached the level of an international humanitarian crisis. Thousands of boys and girls, along with others of varying ages, had sat atop the Beast, a freight train that barreled through the breadth of Mexico. If the riders did not fall, with serious injury or death, they arrived dispossessed in border towns. Most would then again risk their lives by attempting to illegally cross the Texas/Mexico border, which is alike a militarized zone. Then in 2016, despite an increase in border security, a US-Mexico collaborative deportation effort, and the termination of the Beast, the numbers of people attempting to make the perilous journey soared. Many of the children and adults making the journey were Mesoamericans from small communities where they had only spoken indigenous languages rather than Spanish or English, compounding their problems when migrating to the United States. Mesoamerica is multilayered culturally and historically, but its history as a place of ancient civilizations, and its communitarian strength, has been denigrated because of poverty, gang crime, lack of progressive economic opportunity, and violence to their self-identities and cultural integrity, that is, a kind of cultural racism. But the story cannot end here, because they also possess a perseverance for their common place, a force of community culture that continues today.

In 2018 people again trekked northward, migrating from Honduras along ancient roads that have connected Central America, Mexico, and the United States for millennium. Historically, we should remember, people have always traveled these routes, to and fro, migrating and emigrating, while trading and sharing goods and practices. The presidential administration in the United States had changed, but resistance to migrants remains popular, but international humanitarian laws provide valuable shields for Hondurans and others fleeing crime, poverty, and lack of education in their countries. Many of these people are from indigenous communities—some located in cities and others from more rural areas. Undoubtedly, their existential crisis is rooted in greed-informed political and economic policies of exclusion, because of misdirected governmental decisions and immoral international criminal practices. Surely solutions are to be realized through our creative efforts to contribute to and learn from community education and our natural cosmopolitan talents.

7

Jane Addams's Trajectory of Creative Memory Contra to Intersectional Violence

Jane Addams's "hands on" activism through community involvement and international diplomacy was intermittingly curtailed by events not wholly within her control, such as melancholy, illness, World War, and loss of public support. Yet those times gave her opportunity to reflect and write, furthering her philosophical reach into a subject mostly investigated during her era through literature: feminist values of cultural memory.[1] However, she did not separate philosophical disclosures from her writing or activism, resulting in a dynamic style that is insightful and kinetic in motivating others. My overarching thesis here is that she paved the way for a literary and journalistic form of activism, employing cultural memory.

"Our duties of the heart," as well as Addams's persistence in pointing out the problems with institutional thinking, continuing militarization of many cultures, and violence against women and children, connect us today to Addams's pragmatic and socially critical philosophy and to her innovative spirit.[2] I hope to further discussions about Addams's epistemology and her activism, highlighting her understanding of how our memories can produce productive, cultural events. Our memories afford us comprehensive understandings of our situations, as we become more integrated with our environments. Although memory is obviously personal, it can be thought of as a creative, caring, communicative cognitive process, and such ethical utility links memory to feminist values, which we act upon in terms of culture. Addams calls for everyone to remember how vital, restorative, and instructive our memories are to our futures, in her first book of 1902, *Democracy and Social Ethics*: "We want to remind her that pity, memory, and faithfulness are natural ties, to be prized as is the development of her own soul."[3]

Focusing on Addams's thinking about cultural memory, I explain how her ideas and methods continue to inform feminist values. Throughout this discussion we will see how popular culture, particularly in forms such as literature and journalism, ushers in more interrelational social policies, while carrying forward our creative cultural practices. As an example of progress being made through such an aesthetic process, we will look at how our collective memories present solutions in respect to our world's refugees and homeless. Today we can reappropriate her literary techniques, via social medias, thereby revaluing our voices and practices as vehicles for a more creative, productive, peaceful, and just world.

Let me introduce my chapter more closely in terms of feminist and pragmatic philosophy. Addams talks about memory as a platform for broad social reflection.[4] Marilyn Fischer and Charlene Haddock Seigfried relate everyday aesthetics and naturalistic epistemology to Addams's understanding of memory as a key to expanding people's community purposes, so we will review some of their research. To fully explore how memories better our world, we can disclose from Addams's writings aspects of George Herbert Mead's aesthetics.[5] Specifically in relation to Mead's thinking about memories as emergent events of time, which are individually and jointly created and which can be valued and traded as cultural artifacts, as he and Addams look toward the future in terms of present possibilities, we will come to understand how Mead and Addams used these ideas about time and culture to explain a collective sense of social activism. I draw a trajectory of such aesthetic agency to Elena Ferrante's contemporary literature, specifically her *Neapolitan Novels*, in which she describes a post–Second World War world in Italy, to our ongoing history of violence against women. Ferrante uses memory as a matter of thoughtful experiences and radical events, allowing her characters to alter their roles in their communities, which is disadvantaged and pulled apart by systemic violence. I find Ferrante's social critique comparable to Addams's pragmatic, feminist philosophy. Finally, we will look at other contemporary literature and journalism, which is helping us build better communities.

Addams's multifaceted writings correlate with her innovation in the history of ideas, as she was one of the first philosophers to explain an intersectionality of modern-day violence, oppression, militarism, and elitist capitalism. Contemporarily we must underscore the warnings she marks in respect to dangers to democratic freedoms when any industrial endeavor reproduces goods or uses resources for solely the gain of wealth with no respect for the shared, and necessarily inclusive, futures of people and their communities.[6] With what now seems forewarning, she describes problematic institutional social control. Arguing that some social groups remain oppressive because of "unrestricted commercialism," "governmental aggression," and problems stemming from a military-industrial complex, Addams's philosophy becomes social critique.[7] In her often-quoted book, *Newer Ideals of Peace*, written in 1907, she explains:

> The nation which is accustomed to condone the questionable business methods of a rich man because of his success, will find no difficulty in obscuring the moral issues involved in any undertaking that is successful. It becomes easy to deny the moral basis of self-government and to substitute militarism.[8]

Specifically, Addams contrasts feminist values to militarism, the latter being how some people choose to prosper by appropriating violent means for their own privilege, amassing what they think of as superiority and power. She attempts to answer how we can change our militarized institutions, and our ways of hierarchical thinking, especially when financial and natural resources seem stretched. Addams also asks how we can retain community values amid our diverse cultural backgrounds and varied critiques. She finds creative forms of activism for social justice as the binding agent for values. In her *Democracy and Social Ethics* of 1902, we discern Addams's view that we are continually reoriented to our communities through standing up for fair treatment and just policies.

> It is well to remind ourselves, from time to time, that "Ethics" is but another word for "righteousness," that for which many men and women of every generation have hungered and thirsted, and without which life becomes meaningless. Certain forms of personal righteousness have become to a majority of the community almost automatic.[9]

She continues to develop our understanding of how to orient ourselves toward acting against institutional violence without being destructive to our existing cultural norms. Collective memory and feminist epistemology can be thought of as human resources, which offer us skills to remodel our communities in respect to our ever-changing, yet fixed in social justice, values. Such processes do not gain traction through nihilist nor static cultures, but because we become more inclusive as we focus on common goals, we can develop common histories and cultures. Addams clarifies this matter:

> Yet in moments of industrial stress and strain the community is confronted by a moral perplexity which may arise from the mere fact that the good of yesterday is opposed to the good of today, and that which may appear as a choice between virtue and vice is really but a choice between virtue and virtue. In the disorder and confusion sometimes incident to growth and progress, the community may be unable to see anything but the unlovely struggle itself.[10]

By "virtue to virtue" she means working for the involvement of fair treatment and consideration for everyone, which should be inherent in all values. This reciprocity of values is a matter of acting with care, which becomes our collective strength in contrast to a struggle for an abstract "good" or for sole personal gain. Addams thinks of feminist values of care as built on our collective memories. How culture allows communities to self-reflect upon reparation and restoration will be investigated throughout this chapter.

Cultural Memory as an Alternative to Institutionalized Thinking

Katherine Joslin, author of *Jane Addams: A Writer's Life*, explains that through stories and testimonies, Addams offers a feminist epistemology, which is less restricted from intuitive emotions and interpersonal understanding than conventional thinking.

> Addams's first book, *Democracy and Social Ethics,* synthesizes masculine and feminine modes of thought and speech, blending rational and intuitive knowledge, intellectual and visceral experience, objective and subjective points of view into patterns or frontal associative logic.[11]

Addams suggests a method of honing our relational associative thinking, by recalling memories through narrative and testimony. By collecting, recording, and communicating our memories (often creatively through myths and storytelling), our thinking becomes an interpersonal, and often a communal, resource, allowing for information to be contextually embedded as meaningful events. Institutional thinking by contrast is normative, as a way of thinking directed by authoritative purposes.

One of my objectives in exploring Addams's views on collective memory is to spotlight the problems of controlled institutionalized thinking, as such contributes to the ongoing militarization of our world, as well as violence in our communities. Addams recalls stories exemplifying how war thrives because many people depend on their sense of superior power, separating themselves from other people's desires and purposes. By furthering our understanding of storytelling within our communities, we can more fully realize the integration of personal and communal experiences, including emotions and future purposes for the community—aspects of experience that are often left out of institutional thinking. Retelling testimonies, in terms of communicating narratives of those who are suffering because of being controlled by power-driven decision makers, promotes critical thinking among the community. Importantly critical thinking must never be abstracted from such interpersonal, communicative experiences, if communities are to retain their value-making dynamics. Stories that relate cultural memory are vehicles for collective agency, carrying hopes forward in relation to what people can do in their current circumstances with the resources available to them, rather than depending on meta-narratives of superior heroism. Moreover we can take on board ritual and myth, as being vehicles for collective hopes, aspirations, and feelings, thereby presenting a shared sense of creative possibilities.

Hero stories, as with Greek myths and legends, are rhetorically effective because they are based on reasoned choices and the hero's individualistically motivated actions. A hero in a traditional sense is someone who rises above a phenomenon beyond her control, yet with such stories, there is often set up a dichotomy between individual choices and fate (the complex events at play). Fate is problematic as it contrasts circumstances of nature and society as contra to our willed purposes. Also when thinking in terms of being fated, we separate of our reasoned solutions to problems from circumstances out of our direct intercession, and this is psychologically and socially ineffective. Thinking along these lines, the hero's act is thought of as embodying divinely inspired human powers, superseding circumstances. Circumstances and natural events are thought of as predetermined; subsequently, human resources of care and community are denigrated as unduly willful. We can think here of Odysseus's journey, in respect to the masculinized translations of Homer's ancient myth. Odysseus seems unable to change the course of his fate.[12] In contrast, with a relational approach, community habits and actions are not uninformed by community leaders, artists, and citizens, who add perspectives and resources, so situations can be altered. We will return to Addams's thinking on heroism later in this section.

We can also observe that during Addams's time, some ethicists and social scientists thought problematic social conditions followed upon universal laws of nature, which applied to everything consistently. Addams saw a change when evolutionary science offered a more developmental approach to social ethics. Beforehand any ethical standards and moral rules would be controlled with a singular viewpoint of history, or even a sense that morality was transcendently apart from historical reference.[13] Such moral universality does not allow for interrelational decisions, beyond praise and blame moral judgments. Addams puts this lack of democratic morality in stark terms, in *Newer Ideals of Peace*.

She offers an example of how such a moral code based on superior authority is bound with strife for the community, comparing two pictures exhibited at the Paris Exhibition of 1900.[14] One picture presents a medieval castle, where in that village the peasants are protected, and a modern factory, where the townspeople are dependent on the factory's management and their economic control. The secure village finds shelter and care as a matter of a common aesthetic. Addams advocates for a new humanism, suggesting a moral equivalence to war, through an interrelational, situational ethics. She writes:

> We care less each day for the heroism connected with warfare and destruction, and constantly admire more that which pertains to labor and the nourishing of human life. The new heroism manifests itself at the present moment in a universal determination to abolish poverty and disease, a manifestation so widespread that it may justly be called international.[15]

Addams focuses on an aesthetic view, which is formed through the emotional lives of people, as they engage with their communities. Marilyn Fischer points out that Addams takes seriously the nineteenth-century artist John Ruskin's statement that "labor without art brutalizes." However, Addams does not forego industry and social progress but advocates an aesthetic based on social justice ethics.[16] Likewise, Addams does not turn a blind eye to those who are dispossessed because moral laws have been declared and enforced authoritatively, as such moral codes are made based on privilege according to social hierarchies. Relationships based on such a moral high ground dissociate us from the full range of possibilities for social progress and "revert to the use of brute force—to methods of warfare."[17] As well, artistry in our work and our daily life opens our thinking to consider a fuller context of our environment and circumstances, and here is where a creative method to everyday work and life meets a pluralistic ethical approach to social transformation. Addams clarifies her approach:

> The situation demands the consciousness of participation and well-being which comes to the individual when he is able to see himself "in connection and cooperation with the whole"; it needs the solace of collective art inherent in collective labor.[18]

For Addams, storytelling offers us ways to think more collectively, while employing emotional aspects of our decision making. Recounting a testimony in her 1921 book, *The Long Road of Woman's Memory*, Addams tells the story of a grieving mother who lost her son in the First World War. The mother's story offers insights into how people employing creative collaborative solutions could have helped peace efforts. She regrets that scientists had been conscripted into the military in order to use their research for military purposes, as her deceased son was before the war an innovative chemical engineer. Recalling her son's time as a soldier, she discloses the missed opportunities of scientists to help society by opening more collaborate ways of thinking, because they were subsumed as part of a military hierarchy.[19]

The mother laments how she had to stop her work with disabled children because of the war. After the war, she remembers how she was notified six weeks after the death of her son's death because his body had to be left in a ditch in enemy territory. Both of these aspects of her experiences could have denigrated her strength of character, but she speaks out as an advocate for social change. This mother received a letter from her son, after his death, which he had written expressing his deep frustration with the warring countries' military industrial complexes. Posthumously, he expresses his thoughts, saying that in one day more money was given by these governments to further chemical weaponry than provided to improve cities over many years during peacetime. Alternatively, he talked about chemical engineering as a science that could directly benefit the sanitation, health, and progress of many communities around the globe, propagating peace worldwide.[20] Accordingly, he admitted that his reflective thinking was changing his previously held ideas about governments as being truly in the business of seeking societal progress for their people.[21] Subsequently, the bereaved mother connected the loss of her son with a loss of moral progress by governments and scientific communities. She recalled:

> At the very end of the letter he wrote, and they were doubtless the last words he ever penned, that he felt as if science herself in this mad world had also become cruel and malignant.[22]

The disillusioned mother went on to explain the creative thinking of the scientific community, which was at stake:

> The international mind, which really does exist in spite of the fact that it is not yet equipped with adequate organs for international government, has become firmly established, at least among scientists. They have known the daily stimulus of a wide and free range of contacts. They have become interpenetrated with the human consciousness of fellow scientists all over the world.[23]

The mother's testimony and Addams storytelling can be reinterpreted as relevant for our twentieth-first-century problems with war, the military industrial complex, and the militarization of our everyday practices. Today, many scientific communities are motivated by military purposes and commercial profit. That being so, it is not difficult to discern how scientific methods remain objectively abstracted from the health of their communities, as scientists often proceed with restrictions on the use of their research and inventions, because of their controlled institutional ties. Oftentimes scientists must work in secret conditions, thereby limiting their full exploratory and collaborative prowess.

The scientific community is vital to our health and well-being, because of their collaborative spirit, in terms of innovation but also in terms of offering a contrasting mode of social progress to restrictive institutional authority. But we should highlight the importance of storytelling in communicating this ethical matter in a manner which includes emotional gravity and interpersonal compassion, maintaining the vital relationships between the scientific community and communities at large. Science seems daunting and dry for the general public, because its communities' modes of communication are out of reach in terms of popular culture.

Hierarchical aspects of institutional thinking are evident when thinking about militarism and the commodification of resources by "victors." Militarism spreads controlling institutional thinking as an ethos, in part when the elite bestow honor only on their selected group. Even when commanders and soldiers involved in war harbor unselfish feelings and ideas, a skewed sense of patriotism can ensue, as a matter of self-sacrifice for the exclusivity of the group. Consequentially, such exclusivity fosters a narrow sense of value-making, leading to the separation of people along false lines of honor. Warriors who die for honor and country in today's world are surely not always men, yet Addams marked a dier problem of militaristic values that is spread through traditional gender roles, as the privilege of honor depends on one's strength to protect and control, excluding many people within communities. Addams connects militarism to feminism in the following manner:

> I have become conscious of unalterable cleavage between Militarism and Feminism. The Militarists believe that government finally rests upon a basis of physical force, and in a crisis such as this militarism in spite of the spiritual passion in war finds its expression in the crudest forms of violence. It would be absurd for women even to suggest equal rights in a world governed solely by physical force and feminism must necessarily assert the ultimate supremacy of moral agencies. Inevitably the two are in opposition.

Women, children, the disabled, immigrants, and others who do not fit into restricted norms may be afforded a false sense of honor, but the ultimate privileges belong to those seen as physically, economically, educationally superior, and who are best able to support, and be presented emblematically as protecting, the elite or select group. People who are less important are not seen as fully honorable or fundamentally valuable in a militaristic culture, and they are in turn oppressed, discriminated against, dispossessed, abused, and—oftentimes—murdered.[24]

Some events and rituals we consider patriotic are associated with memories of sacrificial heroes, as we model our sense of respect on soldiers' bravery and honor. But is this a socially progressive attitude? A militaristic way of remembering often entails our de-personalized sense of duty, and we can distance ourselves from our relationships. A traditional heroic aesthetic presents a problem in relation to a community's future, in that war-filled stories often depend on values based on a soldier's death. Wartime heroes are traditionally associated with an eternal fate, but in contrast, pragmatic values promote a transformative approach to death and change.

Actually, it is one's hopes and trust in future purposes that affords honor to our deceased community members, so those stories should present the future possibilities of our personal and community relationships.

Even death becomes revelatory of ethical progress with Addams's method of storytelling. She collected eulogies, which she had given at funerals, in her book *The Excellent Becomes the Permanent* (1932).[25] In the final chapter, she describes deceased loved ones, as memorable because of the concerted, future-oriented actions of their communities.[26] Charlene Haddock Seigfried describes the book in pragmatic terms, as a forward-looking philosophical project. She notes how Addams binds our existential temporality with our beliefs in eternity, referring to our emotions for those we love as "values which pass the test of time."[27] I extend Seigfried's analysis in respect to our discussion, rethinking militaristic legacies, as one's honor becomes not so much a virtue that one will be remembered for in terms of their singular self-sacrifice, but their honor is actually a matter of bettering our ongoing relationships and plans for the future. We are then able to admit that our homage to soldiers is not so much concerned with them as heroes of war but more about our future plans in terms of bringing about and maintaining peace.

In the final chapter of the above-mentioned text, "Early Reactions to Death," Addams philosophizes about life, death, and myth. She presents her thoughts in a similar approach to other American transcendentalist philosophers such as Ralph Waldo Emerson and Margaret Fuller. Alike to them, she assumes human thinking as natural, not a mode of systematic cognition setting us apart from our interpersonal relationships and communities. Addams binds childhood memories with ancient Egyptian eternity myths, condensing historical time through her self-reflections. She unfolds her story, drawing from a tacit, collective kind of knowledge:

> Whether it is that the long days and magical nights on the Nile lend themselves to a revival of former states of consciousness, or that I had fallen into a profoundly reminiscent mood, I am unable to state; but certainly as the Nile boat approached nearer to him "who sleeps in Philae," something of the Egyptian feeling for Osiris, the god to whom was attributed the romance of hero and the character of a benefactor and redeemer came to me through long forgotten sensations.[28]

Describing her voyage along the Nile, she muses about Osiris, the Egyptian god of the underworld and judge of the dead. Osiris symbolically ushers in the dawn, marking time as a matter of nature's cycles of rebirth and transformation.[29] By retelling her experiences, she completes her past, orienting herself progressively by looking forward to the future in relation to her sense of personal and collective agency. She describes to her readers a sense of the comprehensive memory-filled present. Describing her feelings as integrated with her connectedness with nature, she offers her readers an account of heroism and myth as informative to future value-building.

Addams's autobiographical musings lead us into discussing how she spoke of women as naturally intelligent and heroic, especially in regard to their abilities to care for others. Mothers and caregivers sometimes challenge traditional norms of patriotism and institutional thinking by caring for "those at the bottom of society who, irrespective of the victory or defeat of any army, are ever oppressed or overburdened."[30] She goes on to explain that militarism and feminism are two opposing worldviews:

> It would be absurd for women even to suggest equal rights in a world governed solely by physical force, and Feminism must necessarily assert the ultimate supremacy of moral agencies. Inevitably the two are in eternal opposition.[31]

Military thinking calls for collective action in terms of rules of control and restrictions, rather than the practices of a communicative community. As well, thinking in terms of securing restrictive laws and equal rights for a populace was not enough for Addams, in that she argues feminist values are informed and spread by our *creative* collective actions. Humanist ideas, such as freedom and equality, can only be influential if they are informed by people's "daily knowledge and constant companionship."[32] So the vulnerable, oppressed, and those in need require special attention by the community, and new policies for caring should be a constant occupation.

Politically, Addams proposes global solutions to militarization, by thinking in terms of *cosmic patriotism*, which is a creative, collective, aesthetic mode of agency by people who orient themselves politically in respect to the needs of inclusive communities, while working toward productive fellowships.[33] Addams lays out her understanding of cosmopolitanism as a buffer to industrial and commercial greed. She examines what can happen if our collective memory is "overshadowed," by financial concerns. People with financial priorities might give charitably to the community but continue to make overarching policies authoritatively. Ideals for democratic industriousness are only useful when they are born out of the needs and desires of communities, thereby, leaders and organizations need to remain integrated with, and part of, their communities.

Communicating by telling stories with a relational aesthetic approach can be an alternative process of problem solving, as we participate in this story by integrating our present practices with our future-oriented values. Addams talks about changing our intellectual processes that propagate war in *Newer Ideals of Peace*:

> The first step toward their real solution must be made upon a past experience common to the citizens as a whole and connected with their daily living. As moral problems become more and more associated with our civic and industrial organizations, the demand for enlarged activity is more exigent.[34]

Social amelioration is accomplished in a facilitated manner when members of the community employ creative, collective, thinking and collective activism. The thoughts and actions of individuals are not effective if kept, as Addams's tell us, "in the realm of individual action," and we can note that she means individual values and purposes as well. Women, who traditionally have been isolated by authoritarian relationships, can find a more pronounced and productive social identity by acting on the values of their common experiences of caring and sharing.

Feminist epistemology, as referred to in our discussion, is surely a visionary area of philosophy, as written about by Addams and others.[35] Naturalistic thinking enhances our theoretical fields of analytic thinking and philosophy of science. Feministic epistemology pushes beyond any kind of objectification of nature (as well as people), to approach problem solving in difference to oppression and enforced compliance. Analyzing by remembering, in terms of relational situations, is naturally melioristic, rather than objectifying matters for controlling schematic reasoning. Such "memory thinking" includes storytelling as an inclusive democratic technology, as stories are passed freely for reinterpretation from person to person. As importantly the process can integrate us to an ethics of caring with our real-time activism. Literature and history can now be realized as a value-oriented dynamic of our thinking, which people can act and plan on effectively. Let us once again look toward Addams's writings for examples of this dynamic.

Aesthetics, for Addams, is developed creatively, as personal feelings are oriented ethically through participating in cultural events. In the first passages of *Long Road*, she clarifies that memory *and* art are transformative vehicles for our communities. Reflecting on stories of elderly people who had experienced hardship and struggle throughout their lives, Addams references Gilbert Murray's interpretation of *Euripides*:

> He writes that the aged poet when he was officially made one of the old men of Athens, declared that he could transmute into song traditional tales of sorrow and wrong doing because being long past, they had already became part mystery and part music. "Memory, that memory who is the Mother of Muses, having done her work upon them."[36]

Going further she draws upon her feminist approach while recognizing the symbolic reference of the Protean Mother, referencing James George Frazier's study of maternal societies and fertility cults.[37] Joslin marks these passages as a point where evolution by war and male aggression are usurped by an "older place in mythology and evolution."[38] Addams, recalling her travels to ancient monuments in Egypt, looks back, incorporating her feelings that connect her with nature, birth, and nurturing in the stream of time. Her memories become symbolic beacons, motivating and lighting her way as she continued her global advocacy for peace.

Addams's connections with myth are not so much concerned with uncovering "subconscious and semiconscious memories" but as a more instrumental aspect of our moral imagination, as artistic, vehicles for eventful change. Myth, for her, reveals growth, creative feelings, and mutual understanding in the sense of our transgenerational, shared experiences offer us renewed human resources.[39] I see Addams's reinterpretation of creation myths as feminist-inspired histories, by which people situate themselves in the world with more inclusive and nurturing moral attitudes, challenging and breaking with many problematic entanglements of the past.[40] But to understand myth making/telling as a forward-looking art, we need to realize such stories as arising from communities, as a matter of common experiences, not as stories or moral codes dictated by a god outside of nature, an idol, or a solitary genius poet.

In this respect we might also consider Addams's views of mythic aesthetic agency as alike to Jane Harrison's theories on ritual, who was one of the first women to investigate ancient art and culture.[41] Harrison regards the socially influential aspects of myth (storytelling, which is important to our communities) as born out of ritual (noting we can consider ritual as events of collective engagement with each other and with nature) and as culturally transformative. Harrison was influenced by William James's ideas on belief, as she theorized about the evolution and influence of ritual and art on our psychologies and cultures.[42] Harrison notes that ritual is key to community progress. Art and ritual are different, for Harrison, in that art does not preclude direct action, but ritual "makes, as it were, a bridge between real life and art, a bridge over which in primitive times it would seem man must pass."[43] We can understand ritual events as expressing people's beliefs in what is not yet *there, but is implicated by our experiences*, and such is a source of ideas and innovation. Addams is interested in people's engagement with art, as she is concerned with how art benefits communities in a forward-looking manner.

Harrison describes ritual in regard to leadership and our personification of ideas (leaders who are symbolic of the hopes of the community), and her thoughts on leadership are also helpful in relation to Addams's views on heroism. Harrison makes clear that the leader of a ritual, who is involved with her community through engaging events, begets "conceived" ideas by the group, while also relying on what has already been said, acted on, or known.[44] Harrison wrote about this artistic/cultural process in relation to ritual in *Ancient Art and Ritual*:

> At the back, then, of the fact of personification lies the fact that the emotion is felt collectively, the rite is performed by a band or chorus who dance together *with a common leader*. Round that leader the emotion centres. When there is an act of Carrying-out or Bringing-in he either is himself the puppet or he carries it. Emotion is of the whole band; drama—doing—tends to focus on the leader. This leader, this focus, is then remembered, thought of, imaged; from being *perceived* year by year, he is finally *conceived*; but his basis is always in actual fact of which he is but the reflection.[45]

How an artist, as a creative person, might not feel the need to make their ideas "real" in terms of their community, or understand how a critical chorus becomes a community of activists, is beyond the scope of my research here, but we can say that the leader of a ritual, or a storyteller, was a communicator who orients the community toward a mutually beneficial future.

Addams's investigations and use of myth became intertwined with her work as a social progressive and a pragmatic philosopher, most effectively when she collaborated with George Herbert Mead.[46] Mead wrote an illuminating short essay, noting his relevant theory of myth. He explains how myth is exemplified in contemporary life through people's imaginations, stressing the social, active dynamic of imagination.[47]

For Addams storytelling involves a social imagination, reinterpreting the past in respect to being both individualistic and collective. What is most important for my thesis is that this aesthetic process involves collective thinking and emotions, communicative praxis, and progressive motivations. In terms of feminist epistemology, my emphasis here has been on understanding how such collective thinking involves bettering our societies, through a peaceful, charitable aesthetic. We will now turn to investigating more closely how memory is creative, as part of our social events.

Part Two: Mead and Addams: Memory as a Social Event

The cross influence between Addams's feminist epistemology and the sociologist George Herbert Mead's cultural philosophy is worthy of a full-fledged study; however, we will here look only to one aspect of their shared views, that being their similar views about memory and community agency for social change. These two activists collaborated on many social projects, while familiarizing each other with their respective writings and research. They were close friends, and Addams presented a eulogy in homage of Mead's wife, Helen Castle Mead, at her funeral.[48] We are again reminded that memory and the ritual of funerals are aspects of a community event:

> Let us arise, therefore, and make for the departed a memorial in our lives. Let us re-member that only the discharge of the duties of the heart can really console the heart. Also that we are not singled out for a special judgment when we give up our dead; we but enter into a common sorrow, a sorrow that visits the proudest and humblest, that has entered into unnumbered hearts before us, a sorrow that should make the world one, and dissolve all other feelings into sympathy and love.[49]

Mead, alike to Addams, researched how memory allows us to take on collective emotions while realizing the perspectives of others. Such interrelationality is a necessary aspect of self-identity, as well as cultural identity, and subsequently we are better able to unlock our individual resources for making and doing when our activities include pluralistic aspects of our environments. According to Addams and Mead, individuals are never separate from our social presence.

Mead metaphysically understood memory as an aspect of time, as well as an active facet of our personal and cultural identities. In *Philosophy of the Present*, he explains how we realize changing facets of time/memory as cultural. Mead terms the present as an *emergent event* in time, marked by our social orientations as normative of culture.[50] Yet, the specious present is seamlessly the past and future; as we take on passing events in their aesthetic (perceptive/cognitive, personal/social) entirety, recalling our past prepares a larger context of experience for the future.[51] Sociality, according to Mead, is the adjustment of one's nature as we emerge from our past imbued with increased perspectival resources, for a prolific future.[52] In other words, the past is not repeated through memory, but by our recollecting, we create a context in the present for the future. The emergent aesthetic quality of the present is collective, reflective, and creative, as we stitch together our futures with our interrelational pasts.[53] Mead explains this emergent quality of time as eventful and momentous:

> Furthermore, the study of passage involves the discovery of events. These cannot be simply parts of passage. These events have always characters of uniqueness. Time can only arise through the ordering of passage by these unique events.[54]

Each emergent event has a unique, historic, funded quality, which cannot be completely resolved into the present conditions of one's environment, so we can infer the need for creative agency by collective memory.[55] Our awareness of time as a radical creative process exposes a multiplicity of perspectives in regard to these events, helping us move forward culturally, as we record our emergence into an ever-changing environment. As well, we trade memories symbolically, designating immense disclosures about our environments and situations at hand. Such memories are epic, as acts, which ensure our identity as we model our responses in the present because of meaningful responses to situations from the past. Moreover, in this process of communication, people are "an other before he is a self," so by becoming a *generalized other*, our memories of events carry with them the complexities of our relationships and social organizations.[56] Our social acts represent a consummation of our interrelationships and represent using our tools to forge our futures, such as collective memories, as we continue to orient ourselves among our environment.[57]

In his essay "Fragments on the Process of Reflection," Mead describes history as an interpretive, predictive art, focused by the problems of one's community. Worth restating, his innovative approach to history makes it clear that memory can be a kind of collective agency for social change:

> History serves a community in the same way as the memory does the individual. A person has to bring up a certain portion of the past to determine what is present, and in the same way the community wants to bring up the past so it can state the present situation and bring out what the actual issues themselves are. I think that is what history uniformly is. It is always prejudiced in one sense, that is, determined by the problem before the community.[58]

Mead is clear that memories are but vague images through language and other symbolic tools until we interpret them as part of what is present.[59] Communities work with such interpretations as emergent events, according to Mead. Public welfare is based on how we value these funded events, as these events are integral to the perspectives of people among varied institutions.[60] However, our revaluation of values is in accord with our awareness of passing time. We should understand that static values are restrictive of who succeeds in a community, and such values should be made more inclusive by renegotiating the situations by which these values arose. Mead uses the example of eugenics and birth control to exemplify situations that have undergone revaluation. Our takeaway from that discussion here is that revaluation is situational, requiring a change of social hierarchical positioning and controlling institutional social organization.[61]

We should note, Addams also thinks of memory as potently progressive and pragmatically melioristic, concentrating on our purposes in light of our historic disclosures. Interpreted memories propel us toward our futures, culturally binding unique individuals together with common ends in view. She remarks:

> I found that the two functions of Memory—first, its important role in interpreting and appeasing life for the individual, and second its activity as a selective agency in social reorganization—were not mutually exclusive, and at moments seemed to support each other.[62]

Furthermore, Addams furthers our analysis of time as a community experience, finding memory as melioristic by expanding our sense of fellowship. She explains her profound understanding of memory when writing in *Long Road*:

> The deduction was obvious that mutual reminiscences perform a valuable function in determining analogous conduct for large bodies of people who have no other basis for mindedness.[63]

So as she finds memories are binding agents for communities, as we realize them as novel, revalued situations, as a prudential when and where, in that previous to remembering there might not have been a dynamic community bond. As well, the novel emergence of memories carries with it healing and acceptance, rather than dead-end practices, which only mirror values replicating noncollective, noninclusive mindedness.[64] Mead qualifies this synthesis, explaining that some unique memories mark emergent events of time by which we reconstruct our situational value-making.[65] We can think here of the activism of Martin Luther King as value-changing events, specifically in relation to race relationships. Such events represent themselves symbolically amid our current conditions, as formative, symbolic, and instrumental to our revaluation. Our recollections of our challenging situations serve us as memorable events, as grounding for our critiques of the past and ideas for the future. These memorable events are the very social technologies of revaluations.

Marilyn Fischer points out that both Addams and Mead understood social problems as necessitating our understanding of ethical decisions as being based on varied perspectives and interests. She goes on to point out that both Addams and Mead think of memory as vital to our social conscience in that we remain engaged with memories in the context of the present so our confluence of views retains a resonance of personal feelings, while at the same time, we relate easily to general, public situations. Our memories are part of a collective moral process as we conflate moments of a situation, so many views *can be considered* as one meaningful event.[66] We are then more able to come to balanced and fair ethical decisions.

Collective memory is an especially valuable process to people who have been dispossessed or marginalized in that they then have a historical platform for more inclusive practices, as just mentioned in terms of Mead's *generalized other*. Through interpreting collective memory as a continually renewing and productive human technology; unifying, while broadening, our communities' practices in regard to our futures, we can discern the innovative dynamic of time as caring and nurturing.

So clearly, cultural memories are moral events. Although Addams's literary style is somewhat journalistic, she discusses the retelling of collective memories in relation to telling stories and listening for moral meanings in those stories. Myth engulfs Addams's ethics, born out of her experiences knowing women who had recently immigrated to the neighborhoods of Chicago. Addams helped found Hull House along with her long-time companion Ellen Gates Starr. It was a center where new immigrants not only could seek advice about their living situations or their job opportunities but could also live, attend classes, and trade cultural arts from their home countries.

At the turn of the twentieth century in Chicago, visitors to Hull House spread throughout their community a myth of a "Devil Baby." Women from the neighborhoods surrounding Hull House swore that a horned, deformed baby boy was born and living at the Settlement, scampering about the house shouting profanities and causing mischief. According to the tale, the baby had been born evil because of immoral actions by men. This urban myth threw light on the recurring physical and symbolic violence that infused throughout the immigrants' everyday worlds. Addams underscores the story because it became a social event.

> We had doubtless struck a case of what the psychologists call the "contagion of emotion" added to that "aesthetic sociability" which impels anyone of us to drag the entire household to the window when a procession comes to into the street or a rainbow appears in the sky.[67]

The elderly women of that community were first-generation immigrants, and they enlarged upon the myth, intermingling their own emotions and personal histories. Upon being told, by the Hull House staff, that the Devil Baby was not there, the women left disappointed as their claim to a morality, entailing signification of their oppression, was then disproven.

The men of the community were relieved that their transgressions against women might continue unchallenged. Yet, the myth continued as a strange collective memory, but rather than casting a black shadow on Hull House, Addams revealed the myth as a communicative social event and a source of critique and social progress.

A widow, who was part of the Hull House community, had been committed to an insane asylum, breaking under the stress of poverty and mind-numbing labor. Addams recorded her lament of losing her only son as he enlisted in the Army. Although her son had been a "vagabondish lad," she called for him to return, for that future event would represent an emergence from past suffering to a life with restored purpose. The woman cried:

> That wouldn't make any real difference to me—the work, the money, his behaving well and all that, if I could cook and wash for him. I don't need all the money I earn scrubbing that factory. I only take bread and tea for supper and I choke over that, thinking of him.[68]

Addams relates the mother's desperation to the overarching challenges to the community: "no one could understand the eternally unappeased idealism, which for her, surrounded her son's return."[69] She goes on to explain how the repeated Devil Baby myth was also a reminder of needed changes in those communities.

> The story of the Devil Baby many have made its appeal through its frank presentation of this very demoniac quality, to those who live under the iron

tyranny of that poverty which threatens starvation, and under the dread of a brutality which may any dark night bring them or their children to extinction; to those who have seen both virtue and vice go unrewarded and who have long ceased to explain.[70]

The Devil Baby was a metaphorical social event and a call for social justice. Despite these women's challenges, they remained caring and hopeful for a moral and cultural change, as they continued their tireless work of nurturing children and those in need. Addams thought of these women as modern-day Sybils, and not only did she give these women a more public profile in her day, but through retelling these stories, we as contemporary readers re-enliven their purposes.

Part Three: The Event of Memories as Radical to Social Change

The Devil Baby as an urban myth was evidential to real problems, and feminist literature carries forward cultural memory as a way of engaging communities, person to person, with their moral advocacy for social justice. Addams recalled that it was three Italian immigrant women who told stories of the Devil Baby, and I compare her description of their violent experiences with the cultural memories of Elena Ferrante. Ferrante writes fictional realism, capturing the global urgency of acting on feminist values.

Ferrante's Neapolitan Quartet offers readers an epic story of two best friends. Beginning when they are young girls in the early 1950s, the saga ends in contemporary times. The voice of Elena, whose memories of her singularly important lifelong friendship with Lila, the alternative voice of moral conscious in the novels, guides the story. Their neighborhood is Napoli, *Rioni*, where these two deeply bonded friends, their families, lovers, enemies, and husbands are entangled in cycles of illness, poverty, violence, and social change. *Rioni* is where their pathos plays out, but it is far from a fictional place, for in reality, it remains symbolic of systemic violence, which people still contend with today. Elena's memories are telling of her love/hate relationship for that neighborhood, as the community's hardship is tied to her love for her dear, unforgettable friend. This violence frames their portraits, as Elena tell us at the beginning of the saga:

> Our world was like that, full of words that killed: croup, tetanus, gas, war, lathe, rubble, work, bombardment, bomb, tuberculosis, infection. With these words and those years I bring back the many fears that accompanied me all my life.[71]

Throughout the four books, the characters, through their combined struggles, create community values of loyalty, but often these values are complicated by capitalistic greed, played out in terms of some people's criminality. But Elena and Lila find economic security through their intelligence and individual strength, as there is no support from politicians or aldermen. Lila becomes an expert in computer technologies for businesses, and Elena shines as an academic and author of fiction.

Yet, despite the intensity of their struggles, it is Elena's love for Lila that forms her purpose and success in life. Their sense of sisterhood goes beyond any of the male fellowships described in the books, although, in conclusion, they both release each other from their burden of care to each other, but not from their memories. What is most instrumental to them, in terms of values, which help direct their life choices, is not traditional societal roles or moral codes, but their love for each other and their communities.

In relation to Addams's philosophy, two main moral values relate to Elena and Lila's story; they value their love for each other and their abilities to help their community. How they go about acting on these values constitutes their freedom from the criminality others in their community fall prey to. Both women live creative lives, while showing moral courage to others, and they strive for justice in their community by helping and caring for others, including the men in their lives. They move forward into a new moral world, which includes strong socially active women, as they hold on to their relationships and community ties.

Addams explains such an ethics by emphasizing community welfare, which is built by people thinking deeply about social change, while continuing to acting with care for their community. Value changes are not a *fait accompli* because they express abstract ideas of inclusion and social justice, as new habits and practices must continue to support the stability and input from the community. Actually, such community strength is a sound basis of an individual's personal strength. For Addams value-making is a democratic process, led by people who strike out in novel, creative ways, but are supported by inspiring values.

> Such people, who form the bulk of contented society, demand that the radical, the reformer, shall be without stain or question in his personal and family relations, and judge most harshly any deviation from the established standards. There is a certain justice in this: it expresses the inherent conservatism of the mass of men, that none of the established virtues which have been so slowly and hardly acquired shall be sacrificed for the sake of making problematic advance; that the individual, in his attempt to develop and use the new and exalted virtue, shall not fall into the easy temptation of letting the ordinary ones slip through his fingers.[72]

Inspired individuals who help transform values often stand out as examples for the larger community and for government/community organizations, but their examples are not apart from community values already at play. Addams explains this ethical democratic process as in contrast with moral platitudes and institutional, regulated rules:

> The constant kindness of the poor to each other was pointed out in a previous chapter, and that they unfailingly respond to the need and distresses of their poorer neighbors even when in danger of bankruptcy themselves. The kindness which a poor man shows his distressed neighbor is doubtless heightened by the consciousness that he himself may be in distress next week; he therefore stands by his friend when he gets too drunk to take care of himself, when he loses his wife or child, when he is evicted for non-payment of rent, when he is arrested for a petty crime. It seems to such a man entirely fitting that his alderman should do the same thing on a larger scale—that he should help a constituent out of trouble, merely because he is in trouble, irrespective of the justice involved.[73]

Ferrante also looks to transvaluation, although she writes fictional accounts of cultural memory. However, Elena and Lila's story takes place in a very real community of today. Although she offers us a history of the city in the final novel of the series, it is a history of violence, and there are no shining passages describing the Baroque masterpieces in the museums and churches that Lila researches late in the series. Surely, Ferrante knows that memories are most potent when applied to personal relationships, as with Addams and Mead's relational aesthetics. Many contemporary social problems of the Nepolitan neighborhoods can be traced back to the Second World War, when the city was razed by the Nazi, as the Germans evacuated in 1943. The city's physical infrastructure was destroyed; afterward, neighborhoods on the outskirts were rebuilt as low-income public housing. *Riena* was established with little economic opportunity attached to its social existence, and the black market easily institutionalized itself during and after the war. This criminalization propagated a mistrust among community members, augmented by paranoia because of Italy's continuing authoritarian political outlook. Instead of an open sense of economic development, a closed sense of gangs and clans arose. These black-market-funded clans adopted warlike tactics to enforce their economic grip on the mercantile and factory working poor.

These interrelated problems were especially hard on the women who lived in the city.[74] There was an enforced, almost pervasive patriarchal social code, which often meant women were prohibited from pursuing their educational and/or career goals, while being subjected to domestic violence. In Ferrante's first book of the series, patriarchy irrevocably changes the life of Lila, who is not allowed to attend school past an elementary level. Her father dashes her hopes of continuing on with a formal education, beating her into submission. As said, Elena and Lila's neighborhood in the 1950s was not unlike the immigrant communities of Chicago at the turn of the century, as women found themselves situated in circumstances of poverty, criminality, distrust of lawful justice, and violence, all consequences of authoritative oppression. Addams was writing during the interwar period, and after the First World War, Addams had made education and economic self-sufficiency for women her central reform, as all was necessary for the social welfare of the community of Hull House.[75]

My Brilliant Friend readers are imparted to a world of women's memory, as subsequently through the following three novels, a historicity of the modern feminist movement is sketched. All of the characters are swept up in a shift of political persuasions, from national to global, yet the two main characters reenact women's long-standing, worldwide struggle to gain control over their private and professional lives. They rebel against forced conventional marital relationships and sexual taboos, and both engage with their communities as catalyst for social change. Lila, in book two, realizes the importance of a radical feminist pamphlet slipped to her by her husband's sister, who is an art historian. Elena read an article from the literature, silently, with her young daughters by her side, realizing that generational systemic sexism is apparent in politics, philosophy, education, and cultural values.[76]

Although Ferranti's character, Elena, does not react to this sexism nihilistically, she does realize the doctrines presented to her throughout her academic career were not valid as universal axioms of freedom. She remembers her inner voice echoing the wisdom of her friend and the latter's struggles in the community. It is then she realizes she must "unlearn" her conditioned education, if she will be able to write truthfully. Elena reflects about her alter-ego, Lila, while writing in terms of a revaluation of values. Her memories of her friend free her of static, authoritative morals. She begins to appreciate the radical nature of feminism, as she continues to search for how to change the culture of their home community. Memories become a tool for Elena, as her personal memories become inherent with her ideas on propagating feminist activism. Her memories mark a divergence from her past and a needed transformation of social values. Alike to Addams, Ferrante finds memory as a tool to reconstruct our futures.

Contemporarily another Neapolitan, Robert Saviano, as a journalist, records the present-day criminality of one of the world's most influential and brutal international crime organizations, the *Camorra*. The poverty, violence, and corruption remain rooted in this community under the evil auspices of this crime ring. The crime network falsely claims it upholds a code of family honor, when what they truly relate to are capitalistic greed and selfishness. Ferrante infamously writes under a pseudonym, for possibly reasons of personal privacy, but her fellow Neapolitan, Saviano, must live under the protection of the government, because of his 2006 book *Gomorrah*, which recounts the criminal truth about the Riona neighborhood.[77]

Riona is currently the home base for the Camorra's international trade of toxic waste, drugs, human trafficking/slavery, and money laundering. Although embedded in the society through political influence, the Camorra is motivated completely by economic gain. Capitalism as a competitive, immoral pursuit of luxury is their lethal weaponry, and this is the same model of institutionalism, which has left the Riona neighborhood with poor public educational resources and high unemployment. Saviano finds this state of affairs spreads as a corrupt ethos and as a brand of the neighborhood, advertising that the neighborhood is open for criminal business. The brash criminals refer to murders as if they were manufactured items.

Saviano immersed himself into the Camorra, discovering the cause of the violence as a participant, with no direct cover, although the Italian government now protects him. Addams's direct participation with the immigrant community on the Near West Side of Chicago, during her time, also uncovered violence. She related this violence to masculine values of pride, privilege, and wartime honor as character traits, which are foundational for sexist values, which include warlike military codes and mob crime familiarity. Saviano's writing also taps into the cultural memory of Naples, in a poetic sense, as being seminally rooted in that community, while reaching beyond that community in terms of his advocacy for a better, more fair society internationally.

The journalist Deborah Acosta also employs our sense of cultural memory. Leading a journalistic videography team, Acosta echoes Addams's methods of participatory and creative activism. Acosta contributes to our discussion on memory and symbolic praxis, with the video "Step into a Refugee Camp," *New York Times*, December 2016.[78] With her crew she visited the largest Syrian refugee camp, Zaatari, on the border with Jordan. Via live webcam coverage, she relays questions from people around the world through Twitter and Facetime to the people of Zaatari.

At one point during the web event, Acosta asks a young adult, Abud Habi Natur, what he misses most about his home, which was in Deraa, Syria. He answers: "What can one miss more than their own home and the tree they sit under?" A response then came from a woman in Columbus, Ohio: "When you feel blessed for just being alive and miss your home and the tree you use to sit under, you have much to teach the rest of the greed driven materialistic world." Acosta reports that the American women's great-grandfather lived in Syria, immigrating to the United States in 1902 and then opening a general store in Ohio. There then appears online an antiquated photo of the woman's great-grandfather shown alongside the ongoing report from the camp.

The art of relating symbols of peace is not an abstract semiotics for journalists such as Acosta and novelists such as Saviano and Ferrante. Their stories are living memories of wars that must be avoided in the future. Their efforts, and cultural memories, give people a different way of being in the world, with a sense of purpose knowing that resources for creativity and social progress will be made available by a global community.

In 2020 Zaatari remains a refugee camp, but in it is also an internationally engaged community. The people of Zaatari have opened 2,500 businesses since the establishment of their camp, and there are plans, put forward by nonprofit organizations that are collaborating with the United Nations, to create a special economic zone allowing the refugees to make their businesses profitable. As well there are international educational efforts to support teaching young Zaatari residents computer skills and robotics.[79] But will such efforts succeed if the present violent situations in places such as Napoli's *Rioni* or Chicago's West Side continue to reverberate throughout world culture?

I think we should continue to look to the pragmatic views of Addams and Mead when striving to solve the problems of violence and criminality, which are part of everyday life around the world. Mead's review of Addams's *Newer Ideals of Peace* remains relevant to such global problems. Mead confirms the intersectionality present in a militarization of immigrants as they are interred in refugee camps, rather than accepted into societies, which have the resources to give them opportunities to change cycles of revolution, war, and displacement. His statement of 1907 rings true today:

> The conflict between the doctrinaire eighteenth-century ideals of government and present conditions, and the consequent reversion to the repressive measure of a military community, is illustrated by the immigration problem.[80]

Mead's commentary is stunningly relevant to the global situation today, in that our current governments are run with principles of military regimes, often providing only abstract laws of human rights, rather than concentrating our resources on social welfare.

Our governments often have nothing to offer refugees culturally by way of protection but the doctrine of the abstract rights of man, a vote he cannot intelligently exercise, and the police to hold him in his place.[81]

Social activist movements have made some progress since Addams's era, but the neighborhoods Hull House helped are currently the most violent in the United States. Addams was a pacifist, and she constructed social practices of peace. But being against war was not only a political or legal position; it was a cultural attitude. To acculturate our peaceful attitudes to problem solving, Addams employed collective memory as a creative, practical tool. People sharing their memories is a creative effort toward diversity, and such sharing can further our peaceful relationships. Addams thought addressing violence and war is a matter of working toward more educated, collectively caring communities. She attempted to transform values, through allowing people to tell their stories and giving them the resources and freedoms to change their lives.

8

Science and Art Moon-lit by Values: Relativity of Epi-Genetics, Film, and Cultural Democracy

It is not incidental that Alain Locke's dedication to advancing both Black culture and a pluralistic American culture, as a rich and profound medium for individual expression, was fueled by his personal sense of difference from mainstream society, in that he was Black, gay, and artistically gifted during what is hauntingly remembered as the Jim Crow era. He understood prejudice and discrimination not only as an emotionally charged weapon used to gain power and social status but as stemming from individuals' ongoing feelings and attitudes, as our very sense of identity is integrated with cultural values. To counter prejudice, Locke initiated a progressive, unifying value theory, which he acted on by his leadership of artistic and educational organizations. His philosophy centers on his investigations into cultural relationships and self-identity, as he recommends value reciprocity, the later meaning the sharing and trading of one's cultural attitudes. Striving to put into practice "unity through diversity," Locke emphasizes the practices of value-making, as an aesthetic process, alike to art and science, by which people can develop mutual trust and loyalty to one another.[1] Acting as a cultural visionary, Locke attempted to take down boundaries of race and gender, so as to further people's happiness and well-being, and as beneficial to social democratic progress.

One of my central objectives in this chapter is to explain how artistic and scientific processes can be similar to value-making, focusing on Locke's insights into individual/cultural identity, value reciprocity, and cultural democracy. I discuss value-making as related to portraiture, epi-genetics, and examples from Black cinema, asking if disclosures from such examples can assist us in coming to terms with contemporary value clashes, specifically xenophobia and people's antipathy toward sexual difference. In conclusion, I find Locke's hope for solving such problems through value-making, as a liberating and culturally transforming process, which is as promising today as when he was writing:

> In my definition of culture I would include science as well as the arts. On that basis, then, all we should be sanely concerned about is freer participation and fuller collaboration in the varied activities of the cultural life and that with regard both to the consumer and the producer roles of cultural creation. Democracy in culture means equally wide-scale appreciation and production of the things of the spirit.[2]

Values, for Locke, are personal feelings and attitudes, which, once acted upon within the context of people's changing environments, can become culturally engrained. Cultural values can be historically analyzed and revised according to shared goals, while meaningfully expressed as part of people's personal, emotional lives, constitutive of their identities. Yet, Locke admitted to skepticism in the American values of his time, especially in light of his own personal experience.

> Small wonder, then, with this psychograph, that I project my personal history into its inevitable rationalization as cultural pluralism and value relativism, with a not too orthodox reaction to the American way of life.[3]

Clearly, while Locke's educated, artistic milieu, during and after the zenith of the Harlem Renaissance, crossed racial, sexual, and class barriers, in that they lived through a time plagued by the aftermath of chattel slavery and colonial imperialism. Such heinous practices formed as a postslavery culture, in the United States and elsewhere, beginning an era of widespread segregation and violence for native American people, Blacks, immigrants, and people of homosexual and bisexual orientations. Widespread segregation, citizen disenfranchisement, and continued persecution became acceptable throughout the United States.[4] Locke and his colleagues, as artists, scientists, and philosophers, sought to organize a radically different sense of morality, as a matter of a self-conscious popular culture, which was purposely diverse and, importantly, empowered each person to develop their unique talents and character. Global appreciation, and historical recognition, of the diverse American Black culture was one of Locke's specific goals, which he equated with moral progress.

From his early academic career, as an undergraduate at Harvard, studying under George Santayana and Joshua Royce, while reading the philosophy of William James, Locke was interested in the cross-references between aesthetics, value theory, and ethics. He chose to focus on value theory, when at Oxford as the first Black American Rhodes scholar, in 1907. It was then that he wrote a comparative thesis on French literature, "Concept of Value."[5] Locke's main challenge was to bridge the subject and object dimensions of experience as a matter of an author's expression of her attitudes toward life. With this early work, he begins to delve into some of the most compelling issues of his mature value theory, such as the worth of new values arising from appreciating an individual's artistic expressiveness, and what is universally ethical throughout different arts and cultures. His interests in values would lead him to study in Berlin with George Simmel and Hugo Münsterberg, both of who were interested in aesthetics as a matter of a person's sense of their participation in cultural experiences. Simmel stressed that each person attributes values freely amid their culturally structured personal relationships.[6] Locke learned from Simmel how values might be set free from a rigid normativity, by understanding how our systemization of the functioning of values influences our cultures.

While in Europe, Locke also studied the philosophies of aestheticians and value theorists who thought in terms of goodness and beauty as values stemming from an individual's appreciation, rather than being completely inherent in an object or event. This approach put forward an "ethics of self-realization," as an individual relates to what is beautiful, or good, for them, as part of their identity. For Locke, values should not be taken as ahistorical forms by which we used to set up rigid standards but part of self-reflective processes, contributing to a person's self-culture, embodied through her relationships.[7] Locke would find this approach inspirational to his theory of self-culture. During and after the Harlem Renaissance, he stressed in his writings a person's identity as tied to their culture, expressively. Defining culture, he explains:

> Rather is it the capacity for understanding the best and most representative forms of human expression, and of expressing oneself, if not in similar creativeness, at least in appreciative reactions and in progressively responsive refinement of tastes and interest. Culture proceeds from personality to personality.[8]

Furthering his interests in values, in terms of personality and self-expression, Locke heard Franz Boas speak on "The Instability of Human Types." Boas, who would come to study native American cultures in the United States, developed an anthropological argument for socio/philosophical development and evidencing racial categories as random and cultural.[9] Culture for Boas is a matter of values arising from community activities. Participants immersed as part of unique cultures can then outline their value genealogies. Locke would recognize the divisiveness of any façade of racial categories based on physical or mental attributes, pointing instead to individual expressiveness and the advantages of pluralism as more ethical.

Once back in the States, Locke finished his doctoral degree at Harvard, writing a dissertation on the building of structures and outlines of values, which is a forerunner to his influential 1935 essay "Values and Imperatives." As part of the dissertation he put forward a theory of the "Dynamic of a Genetic Theory of Value," claiming that values are prioritized and developed through changing contexts of culture, and although we can come to make value judgments on unique situations, or particular art objects, we do so with individual feelings and the ongoing histories and viable structures of our culture in mind. This meant that value judgments have a basis in feeling, and yet there are substantial cultural structures preventing them from being purely subjective.[10]

Leonard Harris points out that Locke clarifies, in the 1935 essay, that the epistemological challenge of categorizing values is not as important as "understanding our transposition of values."[11] Thereby, value pluralism becomes cultural relativism, as a matter of what Locke terms as value reciprocity. Values are developed through ongoing experiences and in relation to new environments; as our feelings and circumstances change, they are often replaced by new values. However, although values can become imperatives according to their functionality in accord with different individuals and cultures, such attitudes/practices can also be grounded in a universal, historical use of people's joint progress in culture building. So simply values are attitudes toward life, which we develop and use by continually renewing our mutually meaningful experiences, to the benefit of our shared relationships. Locke goes on to refer this transpositioning and transvaluation as cultural value reciprocity. This focus on the importance of relationships is alike to the value theory of his professor, Joshua Royce, specifically in terms of "loyalty to loyalty."[12] Locke embraces such a value reciprocity:

> Reverence for reverence, toleration between moral systems, reciprocity in art, and had so good a metaphysician been able to conceive it, relativism in philosophy.[13]

The word "genetics" appears in the title of Locke's PhD, as he seems to emphasize a turn toward cultural anthropology in terms of an evolution of values. I relate his thinking on value reciprocity to the scientific studies of genetics and race of his time, as Locke could have been aware of new developments in the field as a student at the University of Berlin. He was certainly aware of the groundbreaking cellular biology of his very close friend, the visionary scientist E.E. Just, while teaching at Howard University. In fact, in the early twentieth century, German scientists had observed a difference between a genotype, as an individual trait of sex and ethnicity, and the phenotype, as a trait impacting the outward appearance of the person, so perhaps Locke sought to understand what it might mean to realize a synthesis of these two physical structures while emphasizing the varieties of lived, interpersonal relationships.[14]

Actually, Locke's philosophy of culture has been considered influential to Just's breakthrough theories on growth and development, and I contend that such theoretical influence was mutual. We do know that Locke maintained a keen interest in science, as is evidenced in several passages in "Values and Imperatives," and I will locate more exactly, in an upcoming section, how his scientific interests figure into his value theory.

Before exploring the relationships between identity and expressiveness, art and science, and genetics and culture, let us revisit Locke's theory of values reciprocity in more detail, since this is at the heart of Locke's approach to culture, aesthetics, and ethics. Culture can be thought of as how people relate to one another through values and how they express and grow such mutuality through their arts and everyday practices. Such an ethics is dependent on social conditions, and Locke points out, values are not consistently functional over time. In democratic situations values and cultures are not best thought of in terms of institutionally rigid laws, nor abstract universal imperatives, but in respect to how well our values support our efforts in terms of education, self-expression, and active citizenry. Contemporarily, an example of values that function to serve our communities are the recently transformed cultural attitudes about same-sex and transgender relationships. We now value more openly and fully the love, respect, and dignity that such relationships bring to our communities. Accordingly, Locke thought of value-making as meaningful to our political situations.

Leonard Harris points to cultural democratization, in terms of Locke's achievements promoting Black culture:

> Thus, the Harlem Renaissance, under Locke's influence, represented the integration of the aesthetic into the arena of public consciousness as a political force.[15]

In turn we can say culture, which is propagated through shared values, is best developed pluralistically and inclusively. We can now put forward a working thesis, while continuing to investigate these matters, that when artists, scientists, and citizens express insightful aspects of their personalities, as embodied with our cultural values, there is an ethical parity, in terms of a cultural democracy being at play.

Art as a Relativistic Value-Making Process

Locke was an artful pianist, and a keen impresario of the arts, particularly intent on curating, researching, and collecting Black art. In his era, modern artists were breaking new ground with jazz and conceptual classical music; cubist, expressionistic, and nonrepresentational painting and sculpture; avant-garde theater and dance; photographic reportage; and the new mediums of radio and film. Artists broke art/technological ground with these new mediums while changing traditional, social, and political agendas.

Although such turns in culture, because of artistic inventiveness, are not unusual, during Locke's time, the stakes for social change were exceedingly high, as White people continued to use aesthetic standards to promote their sense of privilege. Segregation based on skin color was a particularly heinous example of their aesthetic privilege. Locke's view on aesthetic standards in terms of elitism can be misconstrued, in that although he advocated for "The Talented Tenth" in order to secure funding for Black Americans to universities, and he thought of some art as universally meaningful, he also thought everyone should propagate their self-expressiveness and artistic talents, thereby making a more diverse and meaningful cultural landscape.[16]

Locke crossed a threshold in the history of aesthetics, as he found meaningless judging what is beautiful and good according to social/moral codes. Historically, elite groups controlled other people's experiences and circumstances by setting rigid cultural standards, and these norms become barriers to self-expression and aesthetic transvaluation (a concept we will now discuss). An example of such privilege, in terms of restrictive artistic judgement and class privilege, would be feigning folk dancing because of a standard of precision in a ballet performance. In terms of a moral judgment, we can think of issuing a religious command against dancing because it incites sexual desires. Instead of such restrictive standards of art production and imperative moral judgments, Locke relates aesthetics to the process of how people's feelings take on meanings.

> For every value coupled by judgmental predication, thousands are linked by identities of feeling-mode; for every value transformed by change of logical pre-suppositions, scores are switched by a radical transformation of the feeling-attitude. We are forced to conclude that the feeling quality, irrespective of content, makes a value of a given kind, and that a transformation of attitude effects a change in the value situations.[17]

As is clear when people think of a painting depicting Christ being crucified as beautiful, an act by a selfless health care worker as miraculous, a natural phenomenon as a bad, ugly disaster, their attitudes change. He identifies "feeling-modes," as attitudes, that help develop one's approach to the world.[18] Feeling-modes (the content of values) are interchangeable in terms of fields of experience, and the examples Locke gives for such value transposing are clarifying:

> The awe-inspiring scene becomes, "holy," the logical proof, "beautiful," creative expression, a "duty," and in every case the appropriate new predicates follow the attitude and the attitude cancels out the traditionally appropriate predicates.[19]

A "feeling quality" stands out as a personal value, and while this quality is part of the context of one's experience, the feeling constitutes one's sense of self. Feeling modes can be directed to impact one's personal situation or toward one's wider relationships with others, respectively, as such personal values affect one's conscience and moral obligations of duty. Feelings can change in respect to circumstances and situations, and values can then transform. Cultural values of care and inclusivity becoming more pronounced in our societies, carried forward by openly gay, lesbian, and transsexual loving relationships, arts, sciences, as well as social activism, are examples of *how* values have been transformed.

Locke is clear in saying that once aesthetic feeling qualities become too subjective, as a person neglects intentions to share their feelings, the effects and purposes of values become limited. Locke explains how shared value-making is necessarily an ongoing process, such like art, science, and contemporary ethics:

> As a *quod erat demonstrandum*, the proof or demonstration is an enjoyed consummation of a process and is by that very fact aesthetic in quality. Likewise, the contemplation of an ethical deed, when the tension of the act is not shared, becomes a detached appreciation, though it needs only the sharing of the tension to revert to the moral type of valuation. In fact, moral behavior, when it becomes dispositional, with the smooth feeling-curve of habit and inner equilibrium, normally takes on a quasi-aesthetic quality, as reflected in the criterion of taste and noblesse oblige rather than the sterner criterion of "must" and of "duty."[20]

Values based completely on social structures do not prepare people and communities for such a beneficial functionality of values, which is most operative through aesthetic processes of transvaluation.[21] The artistic process, and reception, is similar in broadening people's range of feelings in terms of valuing new and different feelings, while associating those with their personal sense of self.[22] Giving an example Locke talks about learning to love Stravinsky, "The cacophony by repeated experience has become concordant, meaningful, and therefore 'beautiful.'[23] Old sensibilities of loving music are not replaced by hearing 'Firebird,' but first-time listeners find themselves part of a new expression, while retaining past sensibilities and their artistic orientation as someone who loves music." Describing this ongoing value-oriented artistic process, Locke writes:

> Now the illuminating aspect of this is that Stravinsky and Hindersmith have not to such a matured taste upset the approach to the appreciation of Mozart and Beethoven; nor for that matter has jazz upset the apprehension of classical musical forms and idioms, except temporarily. One hastens to add good jazz, which has developed for jazz idioms and forms more and more professionalized devotees, and rigidly normative criteria of taste and critical musical analysis.[24]

One's reception of art is augmented, not diminished, by accepting transformations as part of the process of our artistic engagements. Locke also makes clear that there is no hierarchy of artistic forms, although he considered fine art as what is most evocative of a universal feeling-quality of nature, being felt as authentic and truthful. Feeling-qualities of nature, however, can be experienced in popular arts without societal class distinction. The criterion for value-laden art is that art presents what is most transformative and identity building about human nature. Recognizing new mediums and art forms open avenues for progressive value-making, casting out the idea of beauty as a matter of a universal form in a timeless, unchanging sense.

Art reveals personal feelings and attitudes as bound with common experiences, eliciting our expressiveness and appreciation while we remain engaged with our cultural environments. As importantly, just as an artwork presents a feeling-quality, art provides people an opportunity to transvalue feeling-modes toward other's cultural values. Locke states his view in terms of art and transvaluation:

> Incidentally, this widening of the range of appreciation and participation is as good an example as we can find of what democratization can mean in a value field.[25]

The contemporary philosopher Richard Shusterman thinks of Locke's ideas on aesthetics as pragmatic, in respect to art being a process by which people, as expressive individuals, continually relate, progressively, to their shared environments. He informs us that Locke thought of Folk Art, or what was called Primitivism, in terms of pragmatic naturalism. By pragmatic naturalism, Shusterman means feelings and values expressed through art that are not biologically driven, as with an "instinct hardwired," but that which "emerge undeliberatively from our familiar natural *social* environment."[26] Shusterman emphasizes the cultural, and political, praxis that Locke affords to art and value-making.

Significantly, individual artistic expressions reconnect art to the grounds of present, common experiences. Whereas prescribed styles can be felt as aesthetically interesting during a certain time, but if abstracted from what is contemporarily meaningful in relation to shared emotions and feelings, those forms become trope-like. Likewise ethical prescriptions, as value-laden human technologies, alike to art, can become meaningless when distanced from one's feelings and the relationships of one's community.[27]

As the founder of the Harlem Renaissance, Locke wanted to elevate Black people's place in societies around the world, motivating artists' individual expressiveness, and more specifically thereby developing a more progressive American culture.[28] He was involved with music, film, and other visual arts, and while we will discuss his work in film and education later in this chapter, let us now turn to his collaborations with the visual artist Winhold Reiss. In regard to painting and drawing, specifically realism and portraiture, artists of Locke and Reiss's time became dedicated to breaking down racial injustice by turning away from depicting superficial, prejudicially coded stereotypes, such as subservient uncles, aunties, and mammies. Locke's approach was to impact such a change through an inclusive, pluralistic approach, as he did not advocate working exclusively with Black artists to break such symbolic violence. Sensitively rendered portraits by Reiss, who was a White German/American immigrant, serve as markers of Locke's inclusiveness. Reiss worked with Locke on several publications, including *The New Negro, Harlem Mecca of the New Negro*, and *The New Negro: An Interpretation*.[29] Interdisciplinary in nature, mixing art, social critique, philosophy, and poetry, these books are examples of how art spreads new values.

In *The New Negro*, Reiss's portraits include presentations of Black cultural leaders, such as Locke, W.E.B Dubois, and Mary McLeod Bethune, as well as people from Black communities in a more generalized fashion. The portraits of the latter, with titles such as *The Librarian* or *The School Teachers*, are depicted in the same sensitively rendered style as those who were well known, especially in respect to their uniqueness and dignity.[30] While some sitters are singled out by name, as they were considered at the time the most talented leaders of the cultural movement, those sitters are not rendered more monumentally, as if they were a superior class of "the Great and the Good." As a group the portraits in the book represent an educated and forward-looking community.

The art historian Frank Mehring interprets Reiss's portraits of the people of Harlem as marking a shift from depicting immigrants and people of color as stereotypical, relinquishing the reigns of aesthetic standards of White beauty and intellectual privilege. Reiss forgoes "white costumes" and paints skin color as a source of unique personality, beauty, and individual dignity. Mehring's observations find that Reiss's portraits are forms of activism for social justice.

> One might argue that the focus on skin colors and facial expressions on the portraits of Mexicans, Blackfeet Indians, German Americans, Japanese Americans, Chinese Americans, or African Americans challenges U.S.-American audiences to rethink issues of racial hatred, ethnic xenophobia, and to critically reassess the transnational dimension behind the motto e pluribus unum.[31]

Possibly, Reiss's sensitivity toward his sitters was due in part to his "shame of being white due to that race's cultural history of occupation, destruction, and insistence on racial superiority," as noted by Mehring.[32] Acting on values without critical thinking is not a viable option in our complex social landscapes, but understanding oneself as being moved by a composite of values allows for transvaluation toward what is more inclusive. Possibly along with Locke, Reiss understood how realizing one's distinct personality allows us to more readily recognize complex social mistakes. Clearly both men thought of American culture as a very different concept than that of assimilation, or a mere melting-pot; rather they hoped their efforts would support a democratic culture, composed of uniquely expressive individuals and communities.[33]

As Locke broke with aesthetic standards and brought down the façade of static moral judgments with his editing and publishing skills, Reiss strived for cultural change with his portraiture. He disposed of worn-out symbols of social coding, which, in the history of portraiture, had often symbolized prestige and authority, such as Roman columns, baroque swags of drapery, and honorific clothing. The three-quarter-length portraits of *The New Negro* present a realism that would have been important to Locke as a matter of people's individual self-cultures, which are not dependent on past legacies or authoritative approval. The community's values resonate through these portraits of teachers and librarians, who are role models and value bearers. The values expressed by the portraits are dignity and respect for each individual's personality, work ethic, and intellectual curiosity.

Setting the stage for the philosophical import of the book, Reiss's *Brown Madonna* is featured as the frontispiece of *The New Negro*.[34] Both a realist portrait of an unnamed mother and child and a religious symbol, the illustration is, however, atypical to Old Master religious paintings because the sitters are Black. Surely the drawing was seen, during the early twentieth century, as iconoclastic by racist viewers, but the portrait does not depend solely on skin color to carry its full meanings, as the delicate yet forthright figures carry a generational weight of social critique. Reiss attended carefully to the mother's pious, pensive expression, as her downcast gaze leads the viewer's eye out of the picture to the present world, which is often filled with uncertainty and misunderstanding. Yet the mother is stoic, while the baby is subdued and peaceful. As if the mother understands that the weight she feels is not the child in her arms but his impending struggle to grow up Black in America, she appears pensive and subdued. The child's forward gaze connects with the viewer, who is united with thoughts of a message of redemption from hatred and divisive feelings. There is a sense of sameness in difference in this portrait as the sitters' expressions can move the viewer's feelings no matter what their skin color. A viewer can feel the bond of the mother and child, realizing that we are all bound to the love of our families and communities.

The mother and child answer an unspoken question of whether there is racism and bigotry in Western cultures' most meaningful symbols, as Reiss embodied feelings of transvaluation in respect to a shared security, caring, and love for people of color and all others. Locke understood value reciprocity in relation to each individual's composed sense of self, in that "racial, national, and regional idioms" involve a distinctiveness of expression in terms of our values.[35] Yet, pluralism for Locke was about the multiple dynamics of our feelings, which blend our value orientations with our identities; being recognized as individual expressions, each part of our feelings, as we are caregivers and as we receive care from others, helps us find our security and purpose as part of our communities.

Race as a social construct involves "special emphasis from the general cultural heritage," which "in turn flows back into common culture."[36] It is then reasonable to think in terms of "cultural relativism" as expressing our particular values, as Locke explains:

> To be "Negro" in the cultural sense, then, is not to be radically different, but only to be distinctively composite and idiomatic, through basically American, as is to be expected, in the first instance.[37]

Yet, Locke's idea of value reciprocity also locates identity as a process of self-discovery, not merely composite blending or comparing oneself with others. Locke as the editor of books on Black culture was drawn to the mother-and-child theme in visual art, possibly as an homage to his own mother, or even as a vehicle to expand his own feelings. Enduring values of trust, protection of the most vulnerable, and unconditional love are also presented in the frontispiece of his edited text *The Negro in Art*, with a modernistic drawing of "Mother and Child" by Sargent Johnson.[38] Johnson's drawing is sculptural, rendered in a naïve style, portraying a Black woman sitting on the ground while locked into an embrace with her young son. Johnson drew the figures by shading, presenting sculptural, stonelike passages. The two rounded solid figures are drawn as one form, and the mother's protective embrace can be interpreted as anticipating possible violence and a subsequent sense of shame. The child wears no clothing, and as his back is to the viewer, he has no facial features.

Johnson offers the viewer a strong reference to art history, in that the portrait is clearly of the Christian "mother and son" genre, while the drawing can be seen as referencing both African wood carvings and European medieval renaissance paintings of the *Madonna of Humility*. Johnson is quoted as saying that he made art for Blacks not for White people, but no viewer could but help feel comforted in the warmth of this mother's eyes and wearied smile. The *Madonna of Humility* iconography always presents the Virgin with her head covered, an expression of piety, and she is always barefoot, seated on the ground. Johnson's Madonna is indeed barefoot and she wears a headscarf. The portrait documents the cultural reality of the Black struggle, and the expressiveness and embodied emotion take the imagery out of the realm of propaganda, creating moments of reciprocity of essential values, such as compassion, common need for family and security, and deliverance from shame and intolerance. According to Locke, these values can be developed through one's feelings and thoughts, and moral decisions, while being foundational to our communities.

Science as a Valuing Process: Epi-Genetics, Reciprocity, and Cultural Democracy

As progress in relation to social justice was being made through the arts during the first half of the twentieth century, tying together religious, ethical, and varied cultural approaches to values, a backlash against such progressive cultural development was gaining strength. People's more static views were supported through racist science and violent political regimes. The rise of the KKK during the Jim Crow era and Nazism in Europe were supported by propaganda in the arts and racialist science.[39] We will now discuss how the science of that time influenced Locke's theories.

Research in the area of the formation, growth, and development of cells, specifically the work of Locke's close friend E.E. Just, who was also African

American, is now thought of as a ray of light during that dark time. Meeting each other when both were teaching at Howard University, Locke and Just shared research interests concerning the development of personal and cultural identity. Just was at the forefront of research in the fields of cellular biology and embryology, while Locke philosophized in the areas of aesthetic valuation, philosophical anthropology, and cultural relativism. To the point of our ongoing discussion, both contributed to new understandings of identity and ethics. Similarly, Just and Locke drew inspiration from German theorists who were also inspired to work through questions of race and culture. Their European colleagues were also fighting intolerance and oppression fueled by false science and ideologies of racial superiority. Visionary research from that time, in disciplines we now recognize as bioethics and cultural anthropology, is especially poignant in retrospect because of the moral stain of the Holocaust, continued oppression and violence against African Americans, and homophobia.

Locke was forthright in voicing throughout his many publications the falsity of the term "race" as biological or tribal. "Race" is a term he sometimes used for social critique, other times finding it useful in understanding cultural distinctions. Locke explains race in terms of science, art, and social justice:

> According to such criteria, the critic has, like the chemist, the analytical job of breaking down compounds into their constituent culture elements. So far as characterization goes, this involves the task of assessing the accent of representativeness among the varying regional, racial and national elements. Theme and idiom would bulk more significantly than source of authorship, and important expressions of Negro material and idiom by white authors would belong as legitimately in a Negro as in a general anthology.[40]

Let us now look more closely at how Locke and Just fought against the racist violence of their times, by influencing each other's research into identity and ethics. Just put forth one of the first theories attributing the development and evolution of an organism to its cellular environment rather than centralized growth directed by the nucleus.[41] He found a living cell's cytoplasm creates a porous environment integral to forming and informing a nucleus. Biological processes are thereby connected to wider environments, than enclosed unites, and histories, so Just is now thought of as a pioneer of the fields of bio-ethics and epi-genetics. In contrast, some biologists at that time were orienting the science toward viewing the nucleus as controlling all cellular activities. Such an approach led the consensus of the scientific community to think of DNA codes as predetermining the organism's growth, appearance, and general character.

Eventually those theories constituted evidence that human DNA strands cause an individual's race, personality, and health. This view has now been replaced by a more environmentally responsive view of DNA expression, alike to Just's theories that the cytoplasm, and associated environmental factors, as integrated and functional, supplies triggers for expressing and changing coded genetic templates.[42] Just thought of live organisms, and humans, as holistic, so environmentally connected, as one's selfhood and progeny are influenced by community and broader relationships, rather than merely by parentage.

Insightfully, W. Malcom Byrnes lays out a convincing case for the influence of Locke's and W.E.B. DuBois's philosophies on Just's breakthroughs with cellular biology and embryology.[43] Byrnes notes that while Just was developing theories on the importance of a cell's environment, Locke and DuBois were arguing that culture is interrelational rather than inherited. DuBois wrote about the genius of Black scientists internationally, and Locke presented the beauty of Blacks as a matter of the individual creativity and intellect, and as contributions to universal culture. Writing about Locke's influence on Just, Byrnes writes about the philosopher's views of cultural relativism and reciprocity as being a matter of porous crossings of environments, similar to the scientist's understanding of the cell's cytoplasm as transformative. The cytoplasm is a vital part of the cell as culture is an inclusive dynamic of a community, and continually these agents work holistically, or interrelationally, in respect to diversifying the whole organism or community.[44]

Just thought about his scientific research as a relative ethical axiology, in that an organism facilitates mutual "co-operation and adjustment with their environment."[45] He suggests an environmental view of our existence, emphasizing that we should think of our very cellular makeup in terms of our cojoined histories and environments.[46]

Accordingly, his thinking on ethics pioneers scientific methods as value oriented, as scientists can and should take on board the desires and expectations for social progress embedded in their research. He explains:

> Man with his highly complex nervous system constitutes a species apart from the rest of the animal kingdom. Nevertheless, he maintains communion both with animate and inanimate nature. Still closer is his relationship with fellow man. These relationships rest upon a purely biological principle. ... Here, then, is indicated where we may seek the roots of man's ethical behaviour.[47]

Just presses further, recommending doing science as a matter of relating ethical ways of living to scientific processes. His approach to science is in accord with an artistic process, in contrast to an empirical data-based method used to give results that fit into a prescribed environment and social conditions, and he continues by explaining the need for a value-driven scientific processes:

> But be this as it may, life as an event lies in a combination of chemical stuffs exhibiting physical properties; and it is in this combination, i.e., its behaviour and activities, and in it alone that we can seek life. A living thing represents in its unity of structure and behaviour the highest order of complexity in nature. All this implies that the method employed in the investigation of a living thing cannot be identical with that used in physical sciences.[48]

His ethical biology clarifies that living things are specialized differently, by expressively, creatively, and purposefully presenting themselves as meaningful to others as part of historical time. Just remarks, "Life is exquisitely a time-thing, like music." In an investigation of the history of modern biology in terms of philosophies and methodological approaches, Maurizio Esposito finds common ground between Just's approach to research and Kant's purposiveness of the whole organism (a matter of determinate yet reflective synthesis) and Goethe's naturalistic, and poetic (and aesthetically symbolic) approach to life as interconnected and immanently meaningful. All of these thinkers' approaches, Esposito suggests, are ways to inquire about an organism's primary environment as a value-laden experience, unifying life's growth and potential.[49]

Yet, although Just highlighted an ethics based on naturalistic processes, he highlighted the complexity of human relationships, not as a universal purposiveness alike to Kant's ethics, which is grounded in a deterministic approach to science. On the contrary, for Just, a person has a complex organic ability to understand a more full dynamic of his engagement with histories and cultures. Just explains biology as functional activities substantiating an individual's unique makeup but also in respect to each person's position to influence each other and their environments.[50] Mutual influence is not a primary or secondary function but generative, stemming out of our cojoined historically diverse environments. Along these lines, I connect Just's theories to John Dewey's thoughts on value theory, as a practice, based on "the patterns of human relations."[51] Pragmatic value-making involves individuals and cultures benefiting each other, as our cooperative transfers of cultural values are sought after, through interpersonal relationships, while people's respective histories and cultures are in play.

Just furthered his ethical investigations by writing an unpublished essay on ethics and biology, in collaboration with his wife, Hedwig Anna Schnetzier

Just. Because of their interdisciplinary research, they are now thought of as forerunners in the field of bioethics.

Locke implies Just's research throughout his value theory, particularly in respect to cultural relativity and value reciprocity. Thinking in terms of evolving and developing organic life, distinct organisms locate and organize so as to effectively participate and transform their environments, and personal self-cultures and community cultures can be thought of as organisms in that respect. Locke's study of value-making is consistent with such science in that he takes on board environmental conditions and historical context of values, marking how values arise and revalue. As noted, values are emotionally meaningful forms of morality, embedded in cultural practices, yet the context and content of how such values are presented can change, as it is the emotional dynamic of the values that is continuous, but also changeable because of ongoing interrelationships. Locke suggests making objective studies of cultures, not comparing norms but recognizing and tracking each culture's value-specific utility, and then evaluating the emotional makeup of those values. His conclusion is that value-making, and a genealogy of values, is challenging if there is no reciprocity at play, as trading and sharing of moral norms is beneficial for a progressive, peaceful, fair world. So a biological version of value ethics can be thought of as similar, as long as it includes ethical progress in light of transformation and cooperation, not because of command or competition, and this was indeed Just's approach.

According to Locke, value analysis can give an account of values as marked by the ever-progressing histories and "relative permanencies" of people's cultural attitudes, which are necessarily in sync with their times (as people are usually socially cooperative). Value analysis can be thought of as an account of how values change and "transposition in a way that will not contradict one another."[52] Charting, describing, and using our values in order to engage more profoundly and resourcefully with one another does not have to be a matter of preconceptions and experimental probability, but nonetheless can be a scientific and practically oriented, as a creative process of ongoing analysis.[53]

Locke moves us forward in our understanding of ethics by likening value-making to the sciences and arts, while explaining transvaluation as a socially critical, yet conciliatory process. Locke compares valuation with a newer atomic theory, rather than mere cause and effect, as being added on to by theories of electronic valence. He explains that the older theory has been replaced, although the displaced theory might continue to be productive to what is now valued as true. Accordingly, people can readily acknowledge scientific truth as an ongoing process of values embedded in how cultures question and apply facts.[54] Art can also be understood as an expanding aesthetic transvaluation, through its plasticity of forms, as we change them to accommodate the layers and porousness of our cultural environments. An example of such plasticity of forms is American jazz music, which Locke was intimately involved with, as a promoter, during the Harlem Renaissance.

However, Locke and Just both realized that our moral frameworks have been stunted by racism, and philosophically. We have been unable to develop and evolve through natural mutable processes of transvaluation, thereby being able to respond to contemporary problems. Yet it is helpful for us to emphasize transvaluation as an ethical process of value reciprocity: "the process of reflective reconsideration of given values continually leads to changes in their status."[55] Interestingly, Locke quotes Dewey, illustrating the relative process of value-making. Dewey says:

> All valuation is in some degree a revaluation. Nietzsche would probably not have made so much a sensation, but he would have been within the limits of wisdom, if he confined himself to the assertion that all judgment, in the degree in which it is critically intelligent, is a trans-valuation of prior values.[56]

As well Locke states clearly, "stable values are exceptions rather than the rule."[57]

So values are factual but not as set principles but are instead markers of our emotions and feelings. We can realize these markers writ large as "cultural cognates," which hold progressive dynamics for communities.[58] Cultural cognates can be used as building blocks for global cooperation, as Locke explains in his essay "Cultural Relativism and Ideological Peace":

> If discoverable in any large number, they (cultural cognates) might well constitute a new base for a direct educational development of world-mindedness, a realistic scientific induction into world citizenship. Surely it would be a great gain if we could shift or even supplement our sentimental and moralistic efforts for world-mindedness, to an objective educational and scientific basis.[59]

We should note that Lockean value-making has been distinguished from an instrumental pragmatic view, such as with Dewey's understanding of values, which are used as *tools* for problem solving.[60] Leonard Harris points out, instead of describing a value theory as an "experimental science" then suggesting a "reasoning modality," Locke describes an ethical way of life based on values themselves, as we seek ever-more understanding of how our feelings and attitudes enrich and grow life through our various cultures.[61]

Yet, upon reflection, I find Dewey's interests in a scientific, yet process-oriented value-making may not be greatly different from Locke's. Art is the most transformative value-oriented practice for Dewey, as it is communicated by way of emotions and memories, which are meaningfully shared. Value-making, alike to making art, never leaves a person's personal or social mix of communication and action. Locke finds value analysis, in a similar way to Dewey's artistic communicative praxis, as a mode of social critique, as people relate to their values individually and expressively, thereby facilitating communication and cultural exchange.

Clearly, values are not abstract ideas of how we should live our lives, nor are our values cold objective immovable facts or mere catalysts for judgments, mainly because value-making cannot be separated from our everyday affairs.[62] But being tied to our environments and our practices in terms of our expressive, meaningful communications, our values are effective as ethical guides for political landscapes.

A poignant example of this tie between cultural values and politics is distinguished by Byrne, who points out that Just compared microscopic science with social sciences.[63] In our democratic political fields, values are processes of consensus, alike to cellular/environmental evolution, and Byrne points out that Just's breakthroughs can be thought of as "cellular federalism." As such, the nucleus of a cell acts as a reservoir of specialized materials, taken from the general, free stuff (population) of the cell, with the purpose of making a difference to the growth and reproduction of the cell and whole organism. The cell's chromosomes are thereby functional as infused with the cytoplasmic environment, while coded features of a consensual environment act as a democratic framework. Subsequently, social and physical environments contribute to an individual's physical identity, as well as imbibing self-identity, self-expressiveness, and citizenry. Thinking of cellular development as a democratic process, one can understand how important not merely making laws but reaching out to others by value reciprocity is to the health of our varied societies. Science, culture, and politics survive as vibrant fields of culture, through democratic participation. Science should be engaged with as a value-oriented cultural practice. As a matter of all three fields, by value reciprocity people retain their self-expressiveness and cultural identities while growing morally alongside others.

Promising to follow through on his ethics of biology, Just and his wife wrote pages of notes, never managing to publish a complete text. However, their thesis was clear: our human cooperation is constitutive of life. Cooperation of people within our respective environments is an ethical matter of expressing purposeful values found through our corelated experiences. Just's thinking applies not only to matters of bio-ethics but also to environmental ethics and matters of social justice.

Locke and Just did not struggle in vain, as both of their philosophies are contemporarily thought of as evidential and profoundly helpful to progressive efforts in multicultural ethics. Although they were clearly unable to vanquish racism, both in respect to the human sciences and in the field of biology, their research brings up contemporary questions by which we can disclose problems in our contemporary societies. Jonathan Marks writes about the polemics of scientists in respect to race in his book *Is Science Racist?* Marks asks if geneticists have acknowledged their parts in promoting scientific racism because of the widespread influence of their compliancy to the circulation of untruthful biological and genetic science. Marks writes:

> Indeed, the perseverance of scientific racism can be seen as a bioethical problem, combining the narrowness of scientific education, the arrogance of otherwise bright people, and the misappropriation of the authority of science.[64]

Just and Locke stand out in history as truth-tellers, by exposing the racist science and judgmental ethical standards of their time, particularly by pointing to inadequacies of some ethical and scientific methods as those are often disconnected from cultural values.

"Moonlight": Value-Making Through Film as Informative to Identities: Transgender Struggles as Transvaluation[65]

The arts also became political weapons during Locke's time, as we will come to investigate in this section. Fortunately physical scientists, artists, sociologists, anthropologist, philosophers, and others realized race is a concept only sustainable as a cultural construct. Speaking directly against racialist science, Locke wrote in 1942, "Contemporary racialism involves biological, sociological and anthropological misapprehensions not supported by the best knowledge and scientific theory in these several fields."[66] Aesthetic judgments were also weaponized as a matter of cultural superiority, using hierarchical authority and moralist maxims to exclude some people from full participation in society. Locke offers an example of Hindu priests, who held the most superior social position in their hierarchical culture yet in turn felt the brunt of class (and racial) exclusion when British colonialists displaced their power.[67] The priests then felt the pain and struggle of the outcasts they had for centuries excluded from cultural approval and acceptance. Racial prejudices are often fashioned as cultural prejudices. Locke refers to the medieval emphasis on Jewishness as racial rather than cultural, as an example of how such prejudices spread. Everyday codes of behavior, such as eating, dressing, and talking, become cloaked in biased ethical standards.

Locke points to the American South and the plight of oppressed women as examples of extreme cultural prejudice.[68] Locke is clear and upfront when decrying the intersectionality of discrimination by social codes and ethical judgments, writing:

> Thus, the prescribed social etiquette assumes practical importance beyond its superficial ceremonial meaning, for it reinforces the majority policy of dominance as expressed more realistically in economic exploitation, disfranchisement, group intimidation and social ostracism.[69]

Of course, racial, class, and sexual discrimination retain motivations and practices specific to the people and relationships involved, yet in general, prejudiced norms and racial bigotry often take a form of ethics involving praise and blame, and aesthetically shaming inhibits an individual's positive sense of self. Some people's false sense of superiority, supported by static aesthetic values, is sometimes acted out as interpersonal and institutional forms of bullying. Locke references Arnold Tynbee's writings in respect to scientific racialism, explaining that much prejudicial science is actually cultural biases that are engrained as aesthetic prejudices, such as body shaming. He explains:

> The opposite of the preferred or familiar in physical appearance, manners and behavior is then regarded as undesirable, and should any group antagonism arise, the contrasting traits will immediately become a focus of the dislike and the symbol of the other's inferiority.[70]

An example is selective population control based on a false science of eugenics, marked people as deviant, less intelligent, immoral, and dishonourable.[71]

Other examples include prejudicial views enshrined in Western culture, such as Grand Manner portraiture, as we have discussed, and by promoting the Great and the Good in conjunction with the false science of phrenology.

When people's ethics are a matter of shame and blame, values of parity, tolerance, and respect are shunned. It is then that minorities often suffer "outcast ostracism and pariah exclusions," and individuals suffer a repressed sense of self, feeling detached from community fellowship. Cultural democracy for Locke was not merely a political or international dialogue but a personal opening of oneself to the emotionally laden values, which move freely from person to person. To open these emotional, value-oriented aspects of our lives, Locke finds the arts necessary, so education in the arts is an imperative. Locke embraces popular culture, while hoping to make mass culture less prejudicial and more value oriented. He explains:

> But fortunately that issue is a matter of education and the general public taste rather than a mere question of racial condition or conditioning. There is, however, that special enemy ghetto-mindedness, which may well give us more than momentary concern. So we still have two arch enemies of mass culture to fight and conquer- Philistinism and prejudice-class bias and group bias.[72]

His solution to prejudice is rooted in our engagement with inclusive cultural practices and education in the arts.

Locke, as a gay man, was closeted in respect to social conventions, which demanded a "don't ask, don't tell" façade, yet his life as a creative artist and philosopher allowed him to present his views on sexual difference, by writing on the importance of self-expression and value relativity.[73] He was aware of his privileged position as a person of letters, but he thought all artists could spread democratic values of reciprocity and parity. Value study should be personal and retain a sense of soul-searching, as well as being cultural. "To be democratic is as important as it is to be treated democratically; democracy is a two-way process and accomplishment."[74]

Self-expression and forming self-identity can be thought of as an artistic process, specifically in terms of relativistic value-making. Filmmaking is a process medium, which is particularly adaptable to presenting a multivalence of emotions in relation to characters, by projecting feelings and emotions to the viewer, for them to reimagine self-reflectively. In Locke's time, film was a cutting-edge medium, and artists recognized an opportunity to experiment and influence society in terms of transvaluing attitudes. Unfortunately, the medium's plasticity was used to create the worse kind of propaganda, such as the 1918 blockbuster silent film *The Birth of a Nation*, which erroneously dramatized the Civil War. While it received some critical reviews, it was a nation-wide success. It was the first film ever shown at the White House, and Woodrow Wilson invited a select audience for the screening.[75] Promoted as historically accurate and educational, its narrative and depictions are brutally racist. This film depicted African Americans, by employing White actors made up in black-face, as people with lesser intelligence, overly sexualized, and dangerous to a unified nationalistic culture. Blacks were prohibited, by authorities around the country, from viewing the film, because of the possibility of social unrest.

However, the film created a justified reaction by Black entrepreneurs, who responded by opening Black cinemas, thereby inspiring an interest in filmmaking by social activists and artists. Stefanie Laufs has written a hermeneutic study of the birth of the Black film industry, as rooted in the Black community's reaction to Griffith's film. She includes Locke's and Dubois's revisionist ideas on Black identity as vital to Black activism. She quotes Locke: "the Negro today wishes to be known for what he is [since] he resents being spoken of as a [...] minor, [...] and to be regarded [as] the sick man of American Democracy."[76] As Locke applauded and uplifted Black culture and its advances through film, he talked about his hopes for film to be advanced as a democratic, rather than an "aristocratic" media.[77]

Although Locke did not write extensively on film, he was active in developing progressive, educational, and democratic uses of film, specifically in the late 1940s and the early 1950s as a board member of the Film Council of America.[78] The mission of the Council was to help "people interested in films to get in touch with one another and to cooperate in using films to improve the quality of living in the United States." He highlighted a number of films representative of the "frontiers of culture" at a fraternity meeting at Howard University.[79] One of those films, *The Quiet One*, 1948, is comparable in tone, character studies, and cultural impact to the contemporary *tour de force* all Black production, Moonlight. Both films are profound investigations into the challenges for American Black boys and men in respect to personal and social identity.

The Quiet One is a pioneering semi-documentary film, dramatizing a true story through a compelling, poetic voiceover narrative and painterly cinematography.[80] We follow Donald, who was a young, Black impoverished boy from Haarlem, as he develops severe emotional problems, thereby becoming more and more antisocial. The troubled boy's loneliness and petty criminality are augmented by his illiteracy, but mostly his unhappy life can be traced to his uncaring and unloving home environment. He was constantly criticized and neglected, resulting in him becoming speechless. His ability to understand any sense of himself as a unique personality is stunted. After being arrested for petty theft, he boards at a school for wayward boys, beginning a new chapter of his life. The psychiatrist of the Wiltwyck School for emotionally disturbed boys narrates the action. Yet, the drama had initially unfolded through Donald's perspective in emotionally charged scenes of him alone, playing hooky in the City, feeling alienated in the apartment of his grandmother. However, while at the Wiltwyck, Donald connects with the aesthetic feeling of nature as the school is located outside of the city in upstate New York. Throughout the film,

Donald gradually develops his self-identity, becoming more and more engaged with the people at the school. He forms values of friendship, creativity, and love, once in his new environment, as friends, teachers, and advisers become part of his life.

At first his lack of communication skills is symptomatic of a deficiency of values in the city's and his family's aesthetic sense of community. In the city Donald was invisible, wandering aimlessly throughout the day, while no one questioned his truancy. Such an experience can be felt metaphorically as demonstrative of "the color line," as a society looks past certain people as if a cloak of invisibility covers them. Donald rarely speaks upon first arrival at Wiltwyck, in part due to his lack of understanding of how his feelings and attitudes involve those of other people, yet he eventually begins to relate and laugh with his fellow schoolmates. Valuing companionship becomes personal when he begins to trust Clarence, the school's counsellor. After learning his mother had moved out of their apartment in the City, his feelings of abandonment and loneliness are positively transposed to more lasting friendships with people he can trust. Through this experience, he develops his sense of valuing friendships and his personal sense of self-identity. During one episode, Donald, confused and still somewhat without a sense of his own value as an individual, lies down alongside a riverbed, feeling the passing tidal currents. He refashions a clay sea shell, which he had made in crafts class for his mother, to become a vessel, planting small flowers within the groove, in some fresh wet dirt. As he admires his creation, then realizing his feelings of being valued by Clarence, and the others at the school, his growing self-appreciation and love for others awaken a sense of valuing his reciprocal feelings of love. He transvalues his unrequited love, so as to embrace trust and a sense of self-worth. He then gives the small clay planter to Clarence.

Progress has been made according to Locke's value ethics in terms of education. Writing about his era, he found that children were being educated to "minimize the hold over the irrationalism of prejudice, fear and suspicion of difference, lack of confidence and cooperative attitudes and the like."[81] We can realize today that as more people become more educated about their differences and relative natures and are able to trust their feelings and desires as forms of the practical and functioning values of our communities, we can continue to forge a more progressive, creative, and value-oriented world.

Personal identity, in respect to culture, begins with a sense of trust in one's personal feelings, as a matter of realizing and expressing one's connectedness with others. Locke mentions *The Quiet One* when speaking about fraternity, as a transcultural value, instead of an ethnic or a racial precondition. He does not recommend a cultural remedy exclusive to one group, but moral openness so we can trust in each other's loyalty, intelligence, and forthrightness. We can trust by allowing others to be themselves without shame. Racism is an embodied loss of personal and cultural identity, because people do not reach out honestly, so they have no heartfelt understanding of themselves in connection with others.

Locke understood value conflicts as a social schizophrenia, while attributing to Freud a breakthrough in the history of morality, uncovering that what we know as evil and good is not a matter of supernatural forces or biological determinism but a matter of early childhood training and moral education.[82] The scientific morality born of Freud's psychoanalysis, Locke hoped, would be implemented as a pragmatic mode of problem solving, in terms of transvaluation.[83] Locke proposes there are shared values that can transfigure devils, which is a phenomenon resulting from "parental and pedagogic ignorance and the social irrationalities of self-contradicting values in social usage and tradition."[84,85]

Locke alerts us to the self-deprecating aspects of such a phenomenon. He particularizes some of the most glaring self-contradicting social values:

> Contemporary society, much as it may dislike the diagnosis of sickness and schizoid tendencies, cannot escape it when it so patently, for example simultaneously professes war and the Christian doctrine of peace, when it tolerates a selfish secular ethics of business competition and exploitation and professes social security Christian charity and ethical altruism, nationalism and international racism and the brotherhood of man.[86]

The Quiet One spotlighted Haarlem as a place where, at that time, community values of caring and sharing were overshadowed by shaming and criminalization. I find that same theme presented again almost seventy years later in the monumental film *Moonlight*. *Moonlight* is the first all-Black film production to win top accolades by the established film industry.[87] But the film can be seen as making noninstitutional, philosophical achievements, presenting value-making as a matter of aesthetic processes. This film is similar to *The Quiet One* as the biographical story is focused on the characterization of a young black boy, who becomes aware of his personal and cultural values, through opening his own self-awareness. Charon, the main character, becomes attuned to his individuality and gay sexuality when realizing his love for a lost friend, who then reenters his life after ten years. Befriended and then shamed by that friend as a child, Charon comes to realize his gay sexuality and love for that very same friend, when sharing one another's feelings of vulnerability and need to fit into society.

Moonlight also presents a theme of an individual's embodied relationship with primal processes of nature. Feeling of one's connectedness with nature is a source of awareness, and consciousness, as the Atlantic Ocean, is the setting of the character's highly charged physical and emotional transformations. Charon, in several crucial scenes, is bathed in the reflective glow of such fluid consciousness.

The scenes on the seashore bring forward symbols of African American transgenerational histories, and a sense of identity, transcendent of time and place. In one such scene, Charon, nicknamed Black, is taught to swim, by his older friend and mentor, Juan, a Miami drug dealer. Juan was originally from Cuba, which could be nod to the plight of immigrants finding their place among the diverse cultures of the United States. Juan, despite his hypocrisy of being a drug dealer in the Black community, shares with Charon a moral understanding of the practical and spiritual needs of people to value one another as unique individuals. While learning to float, Charon is held by Juan, made lighter by the water's surface tension and its calm rippling. Charon becomes weightless, when baptized by Juan's words: "I got you, you are in the middle of the world." Once on shore, Juan shares a story of his childhood memories of running on the beach in Cuba:

> This old lady she stopped me, she said, "Running around catching the moonlight, the moonlight shines on you blue. I am going to call you Blue."

Such an awareness of the aesthetic feelings and consciousness of being Black, as reflective of his seminal human nature, is alike to transvaluing biological processes in respect to human consciousness. Juan goes on to teach Charon a moral lesson:

> At some point you have to decide for yourself who you are going to be, you can't let no one else make that decision for you.

In each of the three chapters of the film, Charon grows psychologically and physically, eventually coming to understand the value-laden impact he has on others.

When Charon realizes he is gay, his identity manifests by connecting with personal and community values. He begins to embody values in respect to his uniqueness, while experiencing such values through his most heartfelt relationships as part of varying environments, alike the color of one's spirit in the moonlight. Embracing the mutable, transformative nature of his sexuality,

Charon's character takes on a mythical consciousness as part of a shared, moral nature of all things. Moreover, Charon's sexuality becomes grounded in his revaluation of himself. Sexuality in the film is presented not as a static identity but as a human ability to transform while reaching out so as to revalue oneself and others. Yet, Charon's life is riddled with the societal maladies of shame, as he lives a labelled existence, named by our current society's lack of valuing our feelings, as we withhold opportunity, community recognition, and respect from people who are prejudiced against because of their physical color, sexual orientation, or economic status, judging them with a thin morality of praise and blame.

A personal dynamic of sexuality and valuation is sometimes forgotten contemporarily, as the LBGTQ community can be seen merely as a political platform. But the arts are often there to remind us of the moral importance of our personal feelings and attitudes. *Moonlight* reflects us, as feeling and desiring human beings, while we are baptized by our transvaluations. Art and science offer us values that are transformative and able to be expressed and traded to create communities sheltering and celebrating our shared humanity. Our identities, including our sexual identities, are colorful reflections of those universal values, only when they are shared. To stop trading and transforming those values is to stop being consciously human.

Leonard Harris devotes time to thinking about Locke's self-identity as a gay man, in relation to aesthetics, values, and social praxis. Recognizing Locke's curatorial control over the Harlem Renaissance as a statement of his gay identity, Harris thinks the philosopher brought to the forefront of morality and ethics, "universal aesthetic norms," of the value of diverse relationships.[88] Harris explains Locke's understanding of being singled out as different, in relation to his personal struggle for a public gay identity. Harris recognizes Locke's tireless fight for social justice for "minorities," as an artistic aesthetic, in that as part of progressive cultures, we all learn to share our feelings more expressively and then able to utilize those attitudes as values that cross gender and racial barriers.[89]

Harris points out Locke's philosophy of valuation and allows for personal uniqueness, including one's personal sexual attractions and preferences, dissolving notions that someone's identity is an inherited ontological position, or a set place of social status. An example is the LGBTQ pride movement, acting as cultural catalysts for liberation, in terms of their personal expressiveness.[90] Harris ends his essay with a revelatory statement in relation to the importance of lessons learned from such transvaluation:

Locke's philosophy is a living philosophy. Locke's approach allows us to see that group-transcendent norms are already embedded in particular communities; that trans-valuation is a normal feature of persons; that value fields are fields of desire, want, exaltation, and tension. Group-transcendent norms are already embedded in homosexual communities; specific norms are already the lines around which ontological unity is possible—never absolute, never completely stable, never static—yet a source of universality and empowerment, unsilenced.[91]

Locke's value theory designates a new universality as a more progressive world rises up to global challenges of culture wars and wars against scientific progress in areas such as same-sex conception.

To sum up, Locke thought of culture as moral transformation, best developed by personal realization and expression, and cultural democratization. Savvy of social problems while celebrating experiences of difference, he sought to cultivate a more fair and caring American culture. Since his time, our progressive cultures have flourished worldwide, but we have not yet been able to eradicate racial and sexual prejudices. As urgently as in the past, people now realize we cannot live in any kind of ethical world without continuing to work on solving deeply entrenched problems stemming from our racist and sexist attitudes. Such prejudices have burrowed into our educational, business, and scientific practices and so become entrenched in our personal identities. We still ask whether it is really possible that people can replace their sense of authoritative ethics with more democratic values, which are transferrable, never static, and transformative. To answer that question, we need to continue to reconsider Locke's value theory, which offers hope in respect to personal and cultural transformation, as intertwined with the endeavors of the arts and sciences.

9

Conclusion: Problem Solving with Cultural Aesthetics

We trend toward a philosophy of life when reading, thinking, and applying Classical American philosophy, as such wisdom is connected with the flourishing of all creatures in respect to our proactive meliorism. These philosophers were interested in the evolution of our individual creativity, as our making and doing are contingent upon our relationships. However, we should not turn away from logical analysis and abstract ideas, in that critical thinking is not distanced from our imaginings or practical matters. Our common sense is not tenable without our beliefs that we are bettering our human condition. We are most successful when we infuse how we learn and how we change our communities and environments by our reflections on our actions and our critical analysis in terms of our purposes and values. In this conclusion we will circle back to Chapter 1, expanding further Peirce's views on creativity, ethics, and love, highlighting how qualities of art and value-making help us navigate our progress-oriented aesthetic processes. We will then discuss how each of the book's interlocutors found social problem solving as an integral aspect of creative aesthetic processes.

The dictionary definition of "poeisis" is somewhat helpful, as the word could resurface in common parlay: "the activity in which a person brings something into being that did not exists before." Although I do not explain the complexities of distinguishing this denotation of poiesis from the ancient Greek distinctions between poiesis, praxis, or techne, I begin our discussion with Dewey's understanding in terms of art and aesthetics, surmising that poiesis is a foundation of pragmatic aesthetics. As Dewey finds, "Not only is art itself an operation of doing and making—a poiesis expressed in the very word poetry—but esthetic perception demands, as we have seen, an organized body of activities, including the motor elements necessary for full perception."[1] I find that all of our interlocutors uphold an active, evolutionary unfolding of our experiences as the crux of human creativity, and art communicates such an unfolding for all to understand.

For Peirce, poiesis is our creative making and doing as transformative for communities, and our creativity is integrated with the evolutionary nature of all of existence. David O'Hara in his brief essay "Peirce, Plato and Miracles" explains that for Peirce creativity is a matter of us acting on the possibilities of life so as to become more moral.[2] Peirce comes to understand Plato's moral idealism as a cosmological matter, so that reality is a continuously evolving potential for beauty and goodness. True changes in our existence occur because of morality. Social progress, scientific discovery, and artistic production are aesthetic processes stemming from and feeding into the creative and moral potential of all of existence. Our moral nature produces miraculous change moving us toward what is progressive for all. For Peirce this creative process is manifested with "movement beyond time of birth and decay," meaning what we make enshrining values of beauty and goodness potentially has eternal implications. Community is integral to the continuity of creativity, as it takes generations for the processes of miraculous change to unfold and to be recognized.

Peirce also explains how avoiding prejudice and bias, by living morally and practicing ethical science, is part of this creative process, as we discover new relationships of change. O'Hara expounds on Peirce' idea that creativity is connected to culture, particularly science, pointing to reality as not explained dogmatically or in terms of positivism, but as part of this miraculously ethical and continuous mode of existence.

> The resulting view of history is fallibilistic, realistic and evolutionary, in which miracles are not violations of laws of nature but are to be expected as evolutionary variations that form part of the ongoing self-revelation of the cosmos. Miracles, like all events in history must not be viewed prejudicially by adherents or distractors, but must be taken into careful account in the grand induction of history and science.[3]

As well, cosmic love is a sensuous process of manifestation and transformation, and David O'Hara quotes Dylan Thomas to make this point about the importance of aesthetics and beauty: "I hardly need add that this is all the more reasonable if Agape turns out to be the force that through the green fuse drives the flower."[4]

Aesthetics, for Peirce, involves community-building processes, in terms of value-making, by our making and interpreting general and fully experiential representations. Beginning with an individual's contemplation of an object, which remains good as long as the object remains acceptable to the person experiencing the object, the aesthetic process is partly reflective. Beauty and ugliness are not states of purity for Peirce, in that our feelings of like and dislike are embodied with many qualities of an object. The wholeness of our perceptions of the objects of our experience is, however, necessarily good.[5] So if a worm in our chocolate nauseates us, then we have drawn our attention away from the goodness of the worm feeding itself.

How we develop moral practices is a matter of ever-more fully comprehending phenomena, so representations assist us by allowing us to experience matters in a general, community-oriented manner. Peirce thought we could solve the problems of humanity by embodying our community values for a more moral world with the moral meanings of our semiotic technologies, such as language and art.

> If the meaning of a symbol consists in *how* it might cause us to act, it is plain that this "how" cannot refer to the description of mechanical motions that it might cause, but must intend to refer to a description of the action as having this or that *aim*.[6]

Art can envision our moral aims for the future, as well as prepare us for taking up necessary practices. Peirce explains:

> In order to understand pragmatism, therefore, well enough to subject it to intelligent criticism, it is incumbent upon us to inquire what an ultimate aim, capable of being pursued in an indefinitely prolonged course of action, can be.[7]

O'Hara finds that Peirce reveals a belief that we are all one community of creative visionaries. For such a community, philosophy is not merely thinking in retrospect or advance about our moral decisions but a science of learning and problem solving undertaken for the sake of unfolding what is not yet known in respect to everyone. Disinterestedness does not mean our ideas are not constitutive of our moral decisions, as our arts and ideas are not causal nor utilitarian, but creative ideas are community-oriented modes of inquiry. O'Hara writes:

> Furthermore, his turn to Plato, like his constant returns to Duns Scotus and Aristotle, is the lived evidence of his commitment to a real community of inquiry in which ideas are real, and in which, through the loving attendance of disinterested inquirers, the ideas themselves may be seen to grow.[8]

We depend on art and philosophy as a source of ideas to gauge and guide our social progress. In the first chapter, we discussed connections of imaginative ideas with the practices of making representations by drawing and dancing, and the problem-solving significance of such symbols. Let us look more closely at Peirce's aesthetic processes as it suggests a problem-solving method. Peirce claims that our engagements with representations of our values guide our thinking. Using symbols, which we create, we interpret our experiences in relation to what we already know and have felt. Pushing past our feelings of doubt because of our common values, we are then able to solve complex problems in respect to new circumstances. He distinguishes belief from doubt, as the latter disrupts our method. Cessation of doubt ushers us into the realm of belief, occurring as we act (and think) on our beliefs without complete empirical assurance of the outcome of our actions.[9] Belief, therefore, is an aesthetic and matter, as it is based on our feelings, opinions, and our values. Peirce writes, "Hence, the sole object of inquiry is the settlement of opinion."[10] Opinion is personally intuitive to us becoming more believable through our cultural engagements. Opinion is contingent on our ongoing interactions with our symbols and changing environments. Now to hold a misguided belief by tenacity only, such as white people believing they are more intelligent or civilized than other people, is untenable, realistically and socially. In respect to clinging to beliefs without taking on board the understanding of other others, Peirce explains:

> But this method of fixing belief, which may be called the method of tenacity, will be unable to hold its ground, in practice. The social impulse is against it. The man who adopts it will find that other men think differently from him, and it will be apt to occur to him, in some saner moment, that their opinions are quite as good as his own, and this will shake his confidence in his belief. This conception, that another man's thought or sentiment may be equivalent to one's own, is a distinctly new step, and a highly important one. It arises from an impulse too strong in man to be suppressed, without danger of destroying the human species. Unless we make ourselves hermits, we shall necessarily influence each other's opinions, so that the problem becomes how to fix belief, not in the individual merely, but in the community.[11]

Fixing our beliefs is a matter of communicating our values throughout our communities. We can think in terms of the success or failure of our values, such as sustaining human life, family, trust, freedom, in terms of how we create representations of our values. Peirce, thereby, sets the tone of pragmatic aesthetics as problem solving in accord with our value-making and how we share our creative ideas among others in our communities.

A contemporary example of creative value-making is the supposed difference of saluting the flag of the United States and taking a knee to protest the murder of people of color by police. Both are symbols that orient us toward a major aim of democracy, the free flow of constructive ideas so all may live well and prosper. The meaning of the national flag should evolve to reveal racial justice in the face of brutal violence against people of color. The controversy disputing the reverence and/or legitimacy of either of these two symbols/actions is a distraction from our communities' aims of parity, liberty, and justice.

As noted, for Peirce, transforming moral communities and our global ethical society is a matter of representing and developing ultimate aims; ultimate aims are such as the example offered in Chapter 1 in respect to world peace. When we create an idea embodied with our aesthetic feelings (a notion of an object's wholeness), an "ultimate end of action" indicates our moral intentions. For Peirce, "the only moral evil is not to have an ultimate aim." He explains:

> Now, the approval of a voluntary act is a *moral* approval. Ethics is the study of what ends of action we are deliberately prepared to adopt. That is right action, which is in conformity to ends, which are prepared deliberately to adopt. That is all there *can* be in the notion of righteousness, as it seems to me. The righteous man is the man who controls his passions, and makes them conform to such ends as he is prepared deliberately to adopt as *ultimate*.[12]

We act on aesthetic ideas artistically by constructing symbols, with creative and purposeful actions, as a matter of intelligent ethical action. Therefore, each person develops creative aptitudes in respect to aesthetic qualities, allowing us to embody our aims in relation to the relativity of our personalities and circumstances. Peirce continues:

> In order that the aim should be immutable under all circumstances, without which it will not be an ultimate aim, it is requisite that it should accord with a free development of the agent's own aesthetic quality.[13]

Peirce informs us that the agent's aesthetic qualities are bound with our changing circumstances and our community's aims, as the "ultimate action of experience upon him is part of one's aesthetic total."[14] To discern which actions are most ethical, we consider the possibilities of our common experiences, while we venture to act on faith, in respect to our values, in that providential circumstances and engaged individuals ensure us of innovation.

Risking our community security for a moral idea involves individuals developing their aesthetic sense of unity, as we are continually relating to diverse points of view. We do this by realizing the moral progress at stake (our collective ultimate aims), so meliorism is not merely a philosophical concept but an aesthetic practice. So, showing up for a women's rights rally feels good, as we emotionally engage with our fellow activists, but our presence cannot be separated from the ultimate end of transforming the values of people who think in terms of their superiority over others. Peirce's aesthetics can be understood as a moral field of play by which we gauge a community's cultural effectiveness. We must realize our ultimate aims are not universally ordained moral judgments but are constitutive of our problem-solving symbols, values, and practices, all of which involves us with a myriad of relationships, circumstances, and opportunities. However, our ultimate aims are based on our voluntary aesthetic decisions, and because we are guided by our values, these aims logically recommend themselves to us, as ethical people, as reasonable in themselves (aside from any ulterior considerations).[15]

At this point, we can discern how aesthetics, ethics, and logical analysis are entwined. Peirce explains:

> It must be an admirable ideal, having the only kind of goodness that such an ideal *can* have, namely esthetic goodness. From this point of view the morally good appears as a particular species of the esthetically good.[16]

Peirce recognizes the matter of semiotic reasoning as normative to our communities, so our aesthetic ideals, progressive actions, and ethical decisions can be made by all people. If we are not prepared to appreciate the aesthetic qualities of an idea that is good for others and to act on ultimate ends for the community, we are unethical. However, in respect to such moral generality, we often do not embrace our moral decision immediately nor intuitively but by critical thinking or what Peirce explains as diagrammatic reasoning in terms of symbols. We involve ourselves with representations, thinking about them creatively, so as to be able to adjust to changing circumstances, thereby enabling us to involve ourselves more fully with wide-ranging ethical actions.

To conclude, practical methods of pragmatic aesthetics according to Peirce can include acculturating humanistic attitudes, by encouraging people to be creative in respect to the moral progress of their communities. We should keep our communal actions directed toward ultimate aims, while being alert to new possibilities in respect to ethical changes.

Josiah Royce thought of our creative interpreting of arts, histories, sciences, and symbols as the de facto method for solving the problems of man. We employ our aesthetic processes by applying our wills to committing to our community-oriented purposes. Interpreting cultural artifacts allows us to question outmoded reasoning in light of our contemporarily relevant purposes, while our novel reinterpretations help us redirect our actions through renewed loyalty to our community.

Royce's aesthetics, which we discussed in Chapter 2, highlights the importance of employing the arts and sciences for social problem solving, specifically in respect to how solutions can be spread among diverse communities. Furthermore, as someone not shy of thinking about metaphysics, Royce ties his practical aesthetics to our individual commitments to our community and how we represent universal, yet pluralistic values. He works with universal values in terms of his philosophy of loyalty to loyalty. Loyalty to loyalty requires us to use the dedication we feel to our communities, thereby assisting us when interpreting and acting in response to social challenges, while realizing that each person feels such loyalty.

Alike to Peirce, Royce calls our attention to how our societal problems become embodied with our cultural arts. Royce refers to long-standing unsolved community problems as lost causes, such as war and environmental stresses, because of human oppression and greed. Yet, he identifies lost causes as opportunities for artists and experimental scientists to create new and ever-more diverse interpretations of our cultural artifacts. As we vary our perspectives, we open up our understanding of complex problems. Through culturally embodied interpretive processes, we unlock answers, as we take on board ever-wider consensus. I offer an example of when we have problems with our intimate love relationships, which are often symbolized by marriage commitments. However, we know personal relationships can take evil turns in respect to domestic abuse and violence. However, such personal, seemingly intimate problems are effectively solved by programs organized within one's community, such as offering greater food and financial security, mental health care, and social programs offering us opportunities for meaningful purpose in respect to community commitments. Community welfare programs are culture building and artefactual, similar to the other value-generating institutions, such as the institution of marriage.

In Chapters 3 and 4 we inquired into how we integrate our beliefs, and faith in making our lives better, with our aesthetics of everyday activity. William James emphasized individual's optimistic, future-oriented attitudes as key to developing solutions to personal and social problems. He highlights problem solving as our ability to create novel possibilities out of seemingly depressing situations, by forging deeper and sometimes new emotional relationships by contemplation, critical thinking, and personal/community relationships. In difference to Peirce, James stresses a pluralistic phenomenology, which he sees as contrasting to Peirce's monism. Philosophy, supposedly the study of the meaning of life, falls short, according to James, in that it often leaves out the color, sights, sounds, joys, failures, strivings, hopes, and dreams of our experiences. Belief in a better future has to do with our healthy thoughts and actions, without disregarding our somber moods, which alert us to the power of recovery from our struggles and failures. Doubt is a lack of faith and prevents action, which is contrary to our healthy morality, but it is not without merit as we begin to realize how we feel about our situations.

Questioning, for James, is followed by feelings of relief once a solution is found.[17] Phyllis Rooney, as an aspect of her comparison of feminist philosophy with pragmatism, finds problem-solving aesthetic processes as part of James's pragmatic philosophy. Rooney describes James's problem-solving process:

> In his essay "The Sentiment of Rationality," he notes that "the transition from a state of puzzle and perplexity to rational comprehension is full of lively relief and pleasure" and that a distinguishing mark for the philosopher in attaining a "rational conception" is a strong feeling of ease, peace, and rest.[18]

She points to this sentiment of rationality as a peaceful approach to societal problems, which feminists act with when striving for a more caring, fair, and peaceful world.

Directly to the point of our current conversation, James makes clear that an aesthetic aspect of problem-solving processes is radically empirical, meaning critical thinking is imbued in man's faith in a better future. Pleasant and stable feelings of moral goodness are born out of our moral imaginings and our relationships with others and our environments. James is adverse to a disinterested attitude, separating thought and action from creativity, relationships, and practical results. James writes:

> This is why so few human beings truly care for Philosophy. The particular determinations which she ignores are the real matter other aesthetic and practical needs, quite as potent and authoritative as hers. What does the moral enthusiast care for philosophical ethics? Why does the AEsthetik of every German philosopher appear to the artist like the abomination of desolation? What these men need is a particular counsel, and no barren, universal truism.[19]

Aesthetics is often referred to as an attempt to explain matters according to social codes, without situational context and the complexities of people's interpersonal relationships. However, James finds aesthetics as more than our explanations of existing circumstances, in that as we employ our beliefs, including our feelings embedded in our memories and attitudes in which we undertake our daily tasks. As well we often take actions far outside of the norm in respect to situations not yet completely understood.[20] Because we sometimes act on faith, our false starts and mistakes are understandable and forgivable; however, our inactivity in the face of moral challenges lessens our well-being.

James's understanding offers insights into our personal and cultural motivations to pursue progressive activism in respect to social change of systemic moral problems. His words clarify the meaning of meliorism:

> Faith means belief, in something concerning which doubt is still theoretically possible and as the test of belief is willingness to act, one may say that faith is the readiness to act in a cause the prosperous issue of which is not certified to us in advance. It is in fact the same moral quality, which we call courage in practical affairs, and there will be a very widespread tendency in men of vigorous nature to enjoy a certain amount of uncertainty in their philosophical creed, just as risk lends a zest to worldly activity.[21]

John Dewey connects inquiry and problem solving with aesthetics as a matter of how we test our preferences, traditions, norms, then communicating about better social practices to bring about social change when we experiment with art, employing a natural, creative method of inquiry available to everyone.[22] Dewey draws a clear picture of pragmatic aesthetics as a democratic way of life in his brief explication, "Creative Democracy: The Task Before Us."[23] As Hilary Putnam explains:

> The claim, then is this: Democracy is not just a form of social life among other workable forms of social life: it is the precondition for the full application of intelligence to the solution of social problems.[24]

Dewey clarifies democracy as creative, as our social habits are imbued with our moral attitudes and values. Our attitudes are guided by our common sense in relation to a "free play of facts and ideas." Aesthetic practices are cultural habits, reconfirming our shared values in terms of participating with each others so as to solve our problems, such as free assembly, voting to initiate social programs, and speaking out against social injustice. While we are engaged with solving the problems of our communities, we uphold a common faith in human nature.[25]

Let's look closely at this creative, aesthetic process in terms of how democratic habits evolve our values. Our democratic self-reliance, for Dewey, is not a matter of disinterested idealism but tied with our expression of freedoms to one another, as our personal human nature is independent and contrary to "coercion and imposition from others."[26] Dewey claims our primary ethical responsibilities are to act as citizens, striving to create the social conditions for all people to live freely. Our democratic habits build values of human freedom and social cooperation, such as valuing living in a world without slavery and affording equal opportunities.

How is art important, in respect to value-making processes, so as to inspire our civic participation through democratic habits? Dewey's understanding of aesthetics hinges on our moral imaginations, as we can find possibilities for a more just world in our common experiences. Art carries us beyond relating facts, to moral imagination by way of experimental acts and productions. According to Dewey, artists are directly involved with resolving natural creative tensions when making art. Values are embedded in our interactions with our environments, and the arts offer us examples of meaningful resolutions of conflicts. It can be challenging for diverse cultures to motivate progressive values for all, but the arts serve as vehicles for pluralism, and culture is progressively advanced through the arts. Art presents the artistic process to audiences by communicative mediums, for example when we read a painting, listen to the blues, or find meanings of films and theatre performances relevant to our lives.

Dewey clarifies that academic moral theory has been separated from discussions of art, politics, and science because of entrenched "divisions in economic and political institutions."[27] Many people justify and cling to social norms in terms of theoretical prescriptions, because of fears of being upset by views of people from different cultures, as class and economic privilege create a false aesthetic. An example would be people exercising racist segregation and imprisonment in order to control who prospers in a community, while justifying their behavior with a doctrine of moral superiority. Dewey's naturalistic aesthetic is a contrasting understanding of art and culture. In the United States today, there exists a white supremacy movement, attempting to do just that, without any pretense of their racist motivations. Yet, the pulling down of racist statues is visionary and creative, offering us new values of equality and fair community. The activist's experiences consummate a social tension, setting the stage for the challenge of putting better moral social habits in place.

Jane Addams's philosophy is perhaps the most pertinent to solving contemporary social problems, as her aesthetics is focused by her example of bettering the lives of people who are socially, economically, and politically marginalized. As we discussed in Chapter 6, Addams explains how violence, oppression, and poverty are interrelated culturally. We looked closely at how Addams suggests the practice of propagating cultural memory, as an artistic mode of intelligence, so as to cross barriers of class and socioeconomic disparity. Addams offers us a warning against adopting aesthetic attitudes of privilege. Alike to Dewey, she emphasizes the importance of democratic culture as a ground for social justice. To refresh our understanding, let us revisit her aesthetic theories.

> The man who disassociates his ambition, however disinterested, from the cooperation of his fellows, always takes this risk of ultimate failure. He does not take advantage of the great conserver and guarantee of his own permanent success which associated efforts afford. Genuine experiments toward higher social conditions must have a more democratic faith and practice than those, which underlie private venture. Public parks and improvements, intended for the common use, are after all only safe in the hands of the public itself; and associated effort toward social progress, although much more awkward and stumbling than that same effort managed by a capable individual, does yet enlist deeper forces and evoke higher social capacities.[28]

In respect to advising us against economically controlled aesthetics, we can recollect our discussions in Chapter 6 on Addams's thoughts of adjusting the scientific community's values, from bellicose and greedy to values promoting human flourishing.

Addams recommends aesthetic practices to solve social problems in respect to three main values: relationality/realizing intersectionality, participatory/activism, and socializing care/sympathetic understanding and fellowship.[29] Relationality includes contextualizing social problems in terms of our personal and collective histories as well as our contemporary circumstances. As citizens of our communities, we need to follow threads of personal experience to expose our most heartfelt values. Addams thinks good citizens seek out opinions from others who do not share their views. For example if we have problems finding time to care for our children while working to provide financially for our family, we should speak out publically and advocate for social child care programs, on the grounds that valuing and caring for our family's well-being is embedded with our community's future. However, we should realize these programs will not be used by everyone, so costs to sustain such programs need to be justified by our shared values rooted in care for the communities' well-being.

I find a second aesthetic practice as participatory/activism. Addams makes clear that people establishing laws and putting forward social norms should retain proximity to their community. Again we can think in terms of voicing our concerns, as a step toward cooperative and collective action for social change. The voices of the most vulnerable against social injustice are especially vital to the welfare of our communities, in that they embody and can express our most critical and urgent problems.

A third practice Addams puts forward is socializing care, as fellowship and sympathetic understanding is at the heart of culture. Communities must take up civic housekeeping, meaning we should organize our social institutions with the care we run our homes. Tidiness, economy, health care, and general well-being are hallmarks of community responsibility.

Many practical methods of social justice have been associated with Addams's aesthetics. Ethics of care in the medical field ties the heroism of medical practitioners with moral progress by increasing our understanding of the social reasons for illness and the benefits for preventive medicine. Additionally Addams's social work, such as her founding and running of Hull House, was synergistic with her political activism. Her methods of enriching a community through educating people about each other through the arts have been inspirational for strengthening our communities. As well, her views about caring for our public lives in the same way we care for our private/family lives is central to the contemporary fields of occupational therapy and social occupational therapy.[30] A renaissance in those fields puts forward social practices of citizenship and standing up for one's equal rights (certainly in respect to gender injustices), as part of a therapeutic method. Practicing democratic building therapies is beneficial to people struggling to cope with personal/behavioral/psychological problems amid oppressive economic and societal conditions.

Alaine Locke offers us the most compelling explanation of the arts as a mode of valuation, in terms of correcting racial injustice by culture and art.[31] He spotlights self-cultivation and education as effective aesthetic practices. Community culture is founded on personal culture, which can be cultivated by mentorship, self-expression, art appreciation, conversation, even good manners. Redefining aesthetics in terms of individual and cultural identity, Locke explains:

> For culture without personal culture is sterile—it is that insincere and hypocritical profession of the love of the beautiful which so often discredits culture in the eyes of the many.[32]

Being artistic and cultured in the arts "[b]rings his mind under the quickening influence of cultural ideas and values."[33] Locke agrees with other pragmatists, such as Dewey, when realizing how practicing and appreciating the arts enable us to become more socially powerful. Locke writes, "Whoever would achieve this must recognize that life itself is an art, perhaps the finest of the fine arts because it is the composite blend of them all."[34]

Our sense of personal and cultural identity enables us to participate fully in our democratic political culture. Referring to racial prejudice and bias against Black people in the United States, Locke describes our motivations for aesthetic activism and cultural reform:

> Moreover, personal representativeness and group achievement are in this respect identical. Ultimately a people is judged by its capacity to contribute to culture. It is to be hoped that as we progressively acquire in this energetic democracy the common means of modern civilization, we shall justify ourselves more and more, individually and collectively, by the use of them to produce cultural goods and representative types of culture.[35]

He continues:

> It is, therefore, under these circumstances something more than your personal duty to be cultured it is one of your most direct responsibilities to your fellows, one of your most effective opportunities for group service.[36]

Participation in the arts and culture should not be left only to the artists and audiences but also scientists, as creative ethical citizens. Locke recommends we employ our intellectual skills to analyze our values, comparing values from different communities in respect to our personal feelings and emotions. He recommends a social science of value analysis, claiming that with such research we "temper our loyalties with intelligence and tolerance."[37]

We can take an example from two contrasting music genres, when discussing Locke's relativity of the values. Rap music is a value-making popular art form and part of Hip Hop culture. Positive values often represented by rap songs, such as freedom, independence, success, happiness, caring for friends and family, can also be heard in Country Western songs.[38] Although these two musical genres have traditionally represented clashing racial cultures and political approaches, Black and White, Liberal and Conservative, Country Rap songs merge their styles and iconography, expressing the acceptance of both cultures for each other's values. Common values of tolerance and reciprocity of kindness and respect grow out of such hybrid art forms. While we should continue to critique the capitalistic self-oriented trappings of the American middle class, and whether popular culture ignores people deprived of education or opportunity for economic success, we can find some moral progress in this music in terms of changing racial prejudices.

Valuing our common purposes is at the heart of Classical American philosophy, and contrary to some people's understanding, pragmatic theory supports imaginative and relative thinking in this field, especially when conflated with aesthetic processes. Contemporarily, societal problems are felt globally while political fellowships and policy making seem to move along trails forged by competitive innovation, economic success, and corporate technological progress, untouched by many people's suffering and unrealized dreams. Yet, we have focused on problem-solving theories that lie outside of those well-worn and unsuccessful paths: Peirce's theory of understanding our world as a matter of probability and creative thinking rather than certainty, Royce's realization that morality and science is interpretive and historically bound, James's thinking on the value of what is unseen and the relevant truth of our beliefs, Dewey's emphasis on our moral imaginations and our abilities to experience fully our connection with nature, Addams's lasting philosophy marking the vital importance of our human resources to care for one another, and Locke's emphasize on embracing one's unique identity in contrast to depending on value-neutral science and racial prejudice and profiling.

Currently we find ourselves in a world culture brought to its knees by a global pandemic, which has been called an "invisible enemy." Researchers have traced the causes of the virus to bad community habits such as our worldwide disregard for wildlife and nature. The pandemic is a wicked problem, in that it is rooted in a complexity of social injustices. While over hundreds of thousands of people were losing their lives in the United States, disparities in health care and financial security were exposed. George Floyd was murdered in Minneapolis, Minnesota, by police officers, on a public street as fellow citizens recorded and transmitted the murder via social media. His memory sparked worldwide protests against racial injustice. Yet, hope is apparent in the rapid responses by scientific and medical communities around the world to the pandemic, alongside direct actions of protesters against racial and gender injustices.

Basic tenets of the philosophies we have discussed can guide us to further analysis and community actions. At least three philosophical tenets can offer us hope for the future: (1) our acceptance that human nature is integrated with Mother Nature, (2) understanding morality as depending on our individual creativity in relation to our community's moral progress, and (3) artistic representations and scientific research as visionary modes of inspiring action and propagating moral futures. Our problem-solving methods, modeled by these tenets, are perpetually in the making and remaking, in that we should continually question, knowing we could be wrong about our assumptions, plans, and actions.

So pragmatic aesthetics do help us find our way out of wicked problems, such as global climate change, pandemics, nuclear waste, poverty, gender prejudice, and racism. Realizing these problems as unessentially to our human condition, we recognize the importance of complexity and change. Our creativity hinges on our common belief that we can make our world better, as we bring forth new ideas and social conditions.

Notes

Chapter 1

1. John Dewey, *Reconstruction in Philosophy* (The Project Gutenberg EBook, Release date June 26, 2012: EBook #40089), 213.
2. Richard Shusterman, "Pragmatist Aesthetics: Roots and Radicalism," *The Critical Pragmatism of Alain Locke*, ed. Leonard Harris (Oxford: Rowman & Littlefield Publishers, Inc., 1999), 97–110.
3. Charles Sanders Peirce, on p. 293 of "How to Make Our Ideas Clear," *Popular Science Monthly*, v. 12, 286–302. Reprinted widely, including *Collected Papers of Charles Sanders Peirce* (CP), v. 5, paragraphs 388–410. Peirce writes a pragmatic maxim: "Consider what effects that might have practical bearing we conceive the object of our conception to have. Then our conception of these objects is the whole of our conception of the object."
4. Josiah Royce, *Josiah Royce's Late Writing: A Collection of Unpublished and Scattered Works*, "The Social Character of Scientific Inquiry," ed. and intro. Frank Oppenheim, (Bristol, UK: Thoemmes Press, 2001), Vol. I, 24. (*Josiah Royce's Late Writings: A Collection of Unpublished and Scattered Work*, Vol. I, 20–38).
5. John Dewey, *Art as Experience*, (New York: Penguin Group, 1934), 157–8.
6. Charles Sanders Peirce, "Trichotomic," *The Essential Peirce*, ed. Nathan House and Christian Kloesel (Bloomington and Indianapolis, IN: Indiana University Press, 1992), Vol. I, 282.
7. Richard Shusterman, "Pragmatist Aesthetics: Roots and Radicalism," *The Critical Pragmatism of Alain Locke*, ed. Leonard Harris (Oxford: Rowman & Littlefield Publishers, Inc., 1999), 97–110.
8. Charles Sanders Peirce, "Some Consequences of Four Incapacities," *Essential Peirce*, ed. Nathan Houser and Christian Kloesel (Bloomington and Indianapolis, IN: Indiana University Press, 1992), Vol. I, 53.
9. Josiah Royce, *The Problem of Christianity; Lectures Delivered at the Lowell Institute in Boston and at Manchester College*, (Oxford and Chicago, IL: Regnery Co, 1968), Vol. II, 430.
10. William James, Original lecture given at *Bryn Mawr* in 1892 and published in 1900 (New York: Henry Holt and Company), http://philosophy.lander.edu/intro/articles/jameslife-a.pdf, accessed February 20, 2020.

11 John Dewey, *The Essential Dewey, Volume 1*, ed. Larry A. Hickman and Thomas M. Alexander (Bloomington and Indianapolis, IN: Indiana University Press, 1998), 408–9.
12 Jane Addams, *Newer Ideals of Peace* (Chautauqua, NY: The Chantagua Press, 1907), 100.
13 Alain Locke, *The Works of Alain Locke*, ed. Charles Molesworth (New York: Oxford University Press, 2012), 494.

Chapter 2

1 Thinking of Peirce as a pragmatic aesthetician can be debated and the theoretical bonds that tie such a group together are dependent on interpretations of their writings. However, two sources place Sanders as a precursor to John Dewey's more tightly articulated aesthetics: First, Richard Shusterman's essay "Somaesthetics and C.S. Peirce" (Penn State University Press, *The Journal of Speculative Philosophy*, 23(1) (2009): 8–27) and secondly a review of the tenets of pragmatic aesthetics. The caveat to citing this essay is that Shusterman does not point directly to Peirce's connections to fluid expressions and gestures. For an outline of pragmatic aesthetics, in relation to nature and interpretation, see Richard Shusterman, *Pragmatist Aesthetics: Living Beauty, Rethinking Art* (Lanham, Boulder, New York and Oxford: Rowman & Littlefield Publishers, Inc., 2000).
2 See Charles Sanders Peirce, *Peirce on Signs: Writings on Semiotics*, ed. James Hoopes (Chapel Hill, NC and London: University of North Caroline Press, 1991). When writing this chapter I found particularly helpful Michael Leja, "Peirce, Visuality and Art," *Representations*, 72 (2000): 97–122. Dinda L. Gorlee, "A Sketch of Peirce's Firstness and its Significance to Art," *Sign, Systems Studies*, 37(1/2), University of Tartu, University of Tartu Press: 2009.
3 See Charles Sanders Peirce, "What Is a Sign," *The Essential Peirce*, Nathan Houser and Christian Kloesel (Bloomington and Indianapolis, IN: Indiana University Press, 1992), Vol. II, 4–10.
4 See Charles Sanders Peirce, "Excerpts from Letters to Lady Welby (1906–08) and Excepts from Letters to William James (1909)," *The Essential Peirce*, ed. Nathan Houser and Christian Kloesel (Bloomington and Indianapolis, IN: Indiana University Press, 1992), Vol. II, 477–91.
5 Charles Sanders Peirce, "Trichotomic," and "Evolutionary Love," *The Essential Peirce*, ed.Nathan Houser and Christian Kloesel (Bloomington and Indianapolis, IN: Indiana University Press, 1992), Vol. II, 280–4, 352–71.
6 Peirce, "Trichotomic," 283.

7   Ibid.
8   Nathan Houser and Christian Kloesel, eds., "Intro to 'Evolutionary Love,'" *The Essential Peirce* (Bloomington and Indianapolis, IN: Indiana University Press, 1992), Vol. II, 352.
9   It is interesting to note, Peirce uses an example from geometry, drawing of physically applicable lines, to show that "tychasm and anancasm are degenerate forms of agapasm." "Evolutionary Love," 362.
10 Ibid, 364.
11 See "Trichotomic," 282.
12 Peirce states, "The one intelligible theory of the universe is that of objective idealism, that matter is effete mind, inveterate habits becoming physical laws." Charles Sanders Peirce, "The Architecture of Theories," *The Essential Peirce*, ed. Nathan Houser and Christian Kloesel (Bloomington and Indianapolis, IN: Indiana University Press, 1992), Vol. I, 293. See also, more on his explanation of how feelings become thoughtful habits and virtues. Ibid, 297.
13 For a thorough explanation of synechism, see: Charles Sanders Peirce, "The Law of Mind," *Essential Peirce: Vol. I*, ed. Nathan Houser and Christian Kloesel (Bloomington and Indianapolis, IN: Indiana University Press, 1992), 312–33.
14 See Charles Sanders Peirce, "Evolutionary Love," *Essential Peirce: Vol. I*, ed. Nathan Houser and Christian Kloesel (Bloomington and Indianapolis, IN: Indiana University Press, 1992), 361.
15 He wrote about his interests in the normative sciences, "esthetics," ethics, and logic. He used the word "esthetics," for what I term "aesthetics" as a main focus of this study. "For normative science in general being the science of the laws of conformity of things to ends, esthetics considers those things whose ends are to embody qualities of feeling, ethics those things whose ends lie in action, and logic those things whose end is to represent something." Charles Sanders Peirce, "The Three Normative Sciences," *The Essential Peirce*, ed. Nathan Houser and Christian Kloesel (Bloomington and Indianapolis, IN: Indiana University Press, 1992), Vol. II, 200.
16 F.C. Northrop applies his aesthetics and value theory to American Modern dance, painting, and drawing. He states the processes and meanings of art express values indeterminately: "Thus world-embracing common denominator invariants are achieved but not at the expense of differences." See, F.C. Northrop, "Toward a General Theory of the Arts," *The Journal of Value Inquiry*, I(2) (1967): 113.
17 Peirce wrote in a letter to James, about phenomenology: "It is a branch of philosophy I am most deeply interested in and which I have worked upon almost as much as I have upon logic." I bring these references into the discussion to refer to how Peirce's profound interests of phenomenology did include radical (or open) interpretations of human experience. This aspect of his thinking on consciousness is born out in another quote from Peirce's letters to James, which according to scholars carries the caveat "phenomenology has nothing to do with psychology,"

possibly proving my point that for Peirce, it has everything to do with aesthetics and ethics, and with an open-ended/experiential manner of radical empiricism. Peirce wrote that "the conception of the real is derived by a melioration of the constraint-side of double-sided consciousness. Therefore to say that it is the world of thought that is real is, when properly understood, to assert emphatically that reality of the public world of the indefinite future as against our past opinions of what it was to be." See C.S. Peirce, *Letter to W. James, Oct. 3, 1904. James Papers, Houghton Library, Harvard University*, MS 58. Accessed October 2019.

18 Peirce writes, "The tendency to regard continuity, in the sense in which I shall define it, as an idea of prime importance in philosophy may conveniently be termed *synechism.*" He goes on to write,

> What the law is: Logical analysis to mental phenomena shows that there is but one law of mind, namely that ideas tend to spread continuously and to affect certain others which stand to them in a peculiar relation of affectability. In this spreading they lose intensity, and especially the power of affecting others, but gain generality and become welded with other ideas.
> Peirce, "The Law of Mind," *Essential Peirce*, Vol. I, 313.

19 Peirce explains, "Thus, the very origin of the conception of reality shows that this conception essentially involves the notion of a community, without definite limits, and capable of an indefinite increase of knowledge." Peirce, "Some Consequences of Four Incapacities," *Essential Peirce*, Vol. I, 53.

20 Synechism being productive engaging existence as we reach out to others through thinking while acting, ever more intuitively, thereby encountering new ethical perspectives and territories. Peirce writes in "Evolutionary Love":

> Growth by exercise takes place also in the mind. Indeed, that is what it is to learn. But the most perfect illustration is the development of a philosophical idea by being put into practice. The conception which appeared, at first, as unitary, splits up into special cases; and into each of these new thought must enter to make a practicable idea. This new thought, however, follows pretty closely the model of the parent conception; and thus a homogeneous development takes place.
> *Essential Peirce*, Vol. I, 361.

21 Erick Hawkins, *The Body Is a Clear Place and Other Statements on Dance*, forward by Alan Kriegsman (Pennington, NJ: Princeton Book Co., 1992), 37.

22 See in this anthology, Louis Kavouras, "Early Floating in the Here and Now: The Radically Empirical Immediate Dance Poetry of Erick Hawkins and Lucia Dlugoszewski." 2017.

23 Northrop writes, "Dlugoszewski and Hawkins are widely read in the theory and philosophy of art, both Western and Zen Buddhist. It is to be noted in this connection that radical empiricism is always nominalist, any symbol denoting a differentiated sequence of perishing particulars each one of which is unique. Consequently, radically empirical art in its first function, be it contemporary Western, Southeast or Chinese Oriental, or Zen Japanese Buddhist, is, when consistently expressed, always an existentialist art and philosophy. Such radical empiricism shows in the title of Hawkins' and Dlugoszewhki's dance and music, "Here and Now with Watchers" and "Dazzle on a Knife's Edge."" F.S.C. Northrop, "Toward a General Theory of the Arts," *The Journal of Value Inquiry*, I(z. 1) (1967): 111.

24 Radical Empiricism in terms of William James and Charles S. Peirce.

25 Northrop was surely acquainted with Peirce's influence on James's philosophy, as it is common knowledge. It is such influence in relation to radical empiricism that is pertinent to our current discussion, not a comparison of James's pragmatism and Peirce's pragmaticism. As a reference of such influence see, E.I. Taylor, ed. and R.H. Wozniak, ed. and intro., *Pure Experience, the Response to William James* (Bristol: Thoemmes Press, December 1997), ix–xxxii.

26 From my understanding, John J. McDermott would agree, as he explains in a footnote of his introduction to James's *Essays in Radical Empiricism*, "In a critical reading of this Intro, Max Fisch contends that a striking similarity exists between the relationship of radical empiricism and pragmatism in the thought of James and the relation of synechism and pragmatism in the thought of C.S. Peirce." William James, *Essays in Radical Empiricism*, Introduction by John J. McDermott (Cambridge, MA: Harvard University Press, 1976), ft. 19, 27.

27 I do not detail the many versions of Peirce's triad of conscious existence or semiotics or his definitions of signs and symbols. But generally, it is important to note that interpretations of signs are ongoing. Peirce writes:

> Symbols grow. They come into being by development out of other signs, particularly from likenesses or from mixed signs partaking of the nature of likenesses or from mixed signs partaking of the nature of likenesses and symbols. We think only in signs. These mental signs are of mixed nature; the symbol-parts of them are called concepts. If a man makes a new symbol, it is by thoughts involving concepts. So it is only out of symbols that a new symbol can grow. *Omene symbolum de symulo*. A symbol, once in being, spreads among the peoples. In use and in experience, its meaning grows.
>
> C.S. Peirce, "What Is a Sign?" *Essential Peirce*, Vol. 2, 10.

28 Peirce quotes Henry James to offer a realization of agapism and creativity:

> Henry James, the Swedenborgian, says: "It is no doubt very tolerable finite or creaturely love to love one's own in another, to love another for his conformity

to one's self: but nothing can be in more flagrant contrast with the creative Love, all whose tenderness *ex vi termini* must be reserved only for what intrinsically is most bitterly hostile and negative to itself." This is from *Substance and Shadow: an Essay on the Physics of Creation*. It is a pity he had not filled his pages with things like this, as he was able easily to do, instead of scolding at his reader and at people generally, until the physics of creation was well nigh forgot.
Peirce, "Evolutionary Love," *Essential Peirce*, Vol. I, 353.

29 I will be referring often to Peirce's essay "Trichotomic," in which he makes a connection between Delsarte Method of elocution and his phenomenological concepts of synthetic "esthetic understanding," and growth. See "Trichotomic," *The Essential Peirce*, Vol. II, 280–4.
30 See Jaime Nubiola and Sara Barrena, "Charles Peirce's First Visit to Europe, 1870–71: Scientific Cooperation and Artistic Creativity," *European Journal of Pragmatism and American Philosophy*, I.1 (Associaziche Pragma, 2009), ISSN: 2036–4091. http://lnx.journalofpragmatism.eu/?page_id=10, accessed March 3, 2017.
31 See Tullio Viola, "Bistable Images and the Serpentine Line: A Chapter in the Prehistory of the Duck-Rabbit," *Das Bildnerische Denken: Charles S. Peirce*, ed. Franz Engel, Moritz Queisner, Tullio Vila, Series Actus et Imagio 5 (Berlin, Germany: DeGruyter, November 2012), 123. Viola references Peirce's thinking on phenomenology, bringing forward a visual reference: "This must be a science that does not draw any distinction of good and bad in any sense whatever, but just contemplates phenomena as they are, simply opens its eyes and describes what it sees" (*Essential Peirce*, Vol. 2, 143). Ibid, 119.
32 Viola, 118. We might note here that another of Perice's students, John Dewey, would also understand embodied artistic processes as curiosity or interest, as he explains in "The Reflex Arc Concept in Psychology" (1896), transferring that idea to artistic experience in *Art as Experience* (1934). See John Dewey, "The Reflex Arc Concept in Psychology," *The Essential Dewey, Vol. 2: Ethics, Logic and Psychology*, ed. Larry A. Hickman and Thomas M. Alexander (Bloomington, IN: Indiana University Press, 1998), 3–10. Also John Dewey, *Art as Experience* (London, UK: Penguin Books, 1934), throughout and 165–6.
33 Viola, 117.
34 Ibid.
35 Aesthetic meanings can be immediate; then they can be added to take on objective meanings. C.S. Peirce, "Some Consequences of Four Incapacities," *Essential Peirce*, Vol. I, 43.
36 Peirce correlates drawing pictures with communicating by gesture, as he explains that drawings are useless in meaning unless they convey an experience of growing out of a time, place, and situation. He gives an example in his essay "What Is a Sign" of a serpentine line, which in the context of a second drawing becomes "ovals

flattened together." Ibid. He also confers that drawing itself is a process done by the artist as a mode of reflecting on whether that artist's "proposes will be beautiful and satisfactory." Peirce, "What Is a Sign?" *The Essential Peirce*, Vol. II, 6–7.

37 Peirce, "The Doctrine of Chances," *Essential Peirce*, Vol. II, 141. For an explanation of what Peirce's serpentine line drawings offer inspirationally and technically to the practice of drawing and for good images of some of Peirce's drawing from the Houghton Harvard Library archive, see: Seymour Simmons, "C.S. Peirce and the Teaching of Drawing," *Peirce on Perception and Reasoning from Icons to Logic*, ed. Kathleen A. Hull and Richard Kenneth Atkins, (New York: Routledge, 2017), 119–32.

38 See: Nancy Lee Chaifa Ruyter, "American Delsartism: Precursor of an American Dance Art," *Educational Theatre Journal*, 25(4) (December 1973): 420–35.

39 See C.S. Peirce, "Trichotomic," *The Essential Peirce*, Vol. I, 280–4. Peirce wrote his essay "Trichotomic" to emphasize the similarity between his semiotics and Steele MacKaye's elaboration on Delsarte's semiotics.

40 Iris Smith Fischer, "Theatre at the Birth of Semiotics: Charles Sanders Peirce, François Delsarte, and Steele MacKaye," *Transactions of the Charles S. Peirce Society*, 49(3) (Summer 2013): 385.

41 Fischer, "Theatre at the Birth of Semiotics," 371.

42 See ibid, 391.

43 Ruyter, 429.

44 Ibid.

45 Ruyter writes:

> Stebbins stressed the importance of correct breathing in the right functioning of the body, and taught breathing techniques. [26] She developed the concept of human motion patterning itself on what she considered the basic motion in nature –the spiral curve, or spiral wave-motion (what we might call a spiral successional movement). In the service of these concepts, as well as of those she had inherited from Delsarte and Mackaye, Stebbins collected and created a multitude of exercises. What is most impressive is that, if the nineteenth-century aesthetic is stripped away, much of her theory and many of her exercises conform to present-day approaches to dance and actor training.
>
> Ruyter, 428.

46 As Viola says about drawing, "The training of the eye aims at bringing to the fore that factual dimension of what we perceive, which we always tacitly relay on in order to abductively build up the world we inhabit… recovery of the innocence of the eye brings to our attention said about drawing." Viola, 119.

47 Ruyter, 429.

48 Peirce writes:

> Pantomime many itself be divided, on the same principle, into three varieties; artistic pantomime which merely exhibits the mane?, his general disposition and what there is uppermost in him at the moment, and is to be contemplated without analysis; dynamical pantomime, as where one points with finger or shakes or holds up the finger to impress what one is saying, or when one shakes the fist, or knocks the interlocutor down; and sign-language, mostly (owing to the peculiar nature of pantomime) of an imitative kind but yet involving analysis and being really rather language than pantomime proper.
>
> Peirce, "Trichotomic," 282.

49 See Peirce, "Trichotomic," 282. Peirce writes:

> Expression is a kind of representation or signification. A sign is a third mediating between the mind addressed and the object represented. If the thirdness is undegenerate, the relation of the sign to the thing signified is one which only subsists by virtue of the relation of the sign to the mind addressed; that is to say, the sign is related to its object by virtue of a mental association. Conventional modes of expression, and other modes dependent on the force of association, enter largely into every art.
>
> 281

50 For Peirce, MacKaye's technique of dramatic expression/movement is a semiotics of synechism.

> Mr. Mackaye's division of the principles of being has considerable resemblance with this. What he calls the vital or passional principle, which sustains life, seems to be nearly what I call the simple consciousness of Feeling; what he calls the affectional or impulsive principle is my dual consciousness plus Desire and minus Sense; what he calls Reflection is probably Reason with the esthetic understanding.
>
> Peirce, "Trichotomic," 283-4.

51 Ibid, 282.
52 Peirce, "Evolutionary Love," 353.
53 Ibid.
54 For an explanation of the history of Peirce's philosophy in relation to discrimination, prejudice, and racial bias, see Lana Trout, *The Politics of Survival Peirce, Affectivity, and Social Criticism* (New York: Fordham University Press, 2010).
55 Peirce, "Evolutionary Love," 354.
56 Peirce writes:

> If it could be shown directly that there is such an entity as the "spirit of an age" or of a people, and that mere individual intelligence will not account

for all the phenomena, this would be proof enough at once of agapastcism and of synechism. I must acknowledge that I am unable to produce a cogent demonstration of this, but I am, I believe, able to abduct such arguments as will serve to confirm those which have been drawn from other facts. I believe that all the greatest achievements of mind have been beyond the powers of unaided individuals; and I find, apart from the support this opinion derives from synechistic considerations, and from the purposive character of many great movements, direct reason for so thinking in the sublimity of the ideas and in their occurring simultaneously and independently to a number of individuals of no extraordinary general powers.

Peirce, "Evolutionary Love," 368.

57   Ibid.
58   Peirce says, "The scientific man is not in the least wedded to his conclusions. He risks nothing upon them. He stands ready to abandon one or all as soon as experience opposes them" (Peirce, "Philosophy and the Conduct of Life," 33). Note, Peirce reads Plato as coming to his senses on the truth in relation to the continuity of life, rather than the Heraclitean Cratylus's notion that "Continuity implies Transitoriness" and that what is truly continuous is what is eternal, namely, Space and Time. But as said, Plato comes to understand that the potentiality of ideas is continuous in a very real sense. Peirce explains, "The dialogue of the *Sophistes,* latterly shown to belong to Plato's last period, when he had, as Aristotle tells us, abandoned Ideas and put Numbers in place of them,—this dialogue, I say, gives reasons for abandoning the Theory of Ideas which imply that Plato himself had come to see, if not that the Textual Essences are continuous, at least, that there is an order of affinity among them, such as there is among Number. Thus, at last, the Platonic Ideas became Mathematical Essences, not possessed of Actual Existence but only of a Potential Being quite as *Real,* and his mature philosophy became welded into mathematics." Peirce, "Philosophy and the Conduct of Life," 35.
59   Ibid.
60   Ibid, 34.
61   Ibid, 39.
62   Ibid.
63   Princess Edmond De Polignac commissioned Satie. De Polignac was part of a group of lesbian intellectuals who memorized and presented to audiences Plato's dialogues. For a comprehensive and concise history of the Satie commission and the milieu's interests in Socrates's and Plato's philosophies, and their involvement with elocution, see the undergraduate Honors Theses of Andrea Decker Morena. The thesis has been published online by the Utah State University. Morena's thesis is very well documented, including many scholarly references. She includes

biological information and memories from and about both Satie and De Polignac, among others, such as: Alan Gillmor, *Erik Satie* (Boston: Twayne, 1988). and Peito Dossena, "À la recherché du vrai Socrate," *Journal of the Royal Musical Association* (Web: Taylor & Francis, Ltd.) 133(1) (2008): 1–31. See Andrea Decker Morena, *The Cult of Socrates: The Philosopher and His Companions in Satie's Socrates* (Logan, UT: Utah State University, 2013). http://digitalcommons.usu.edu/cgi/viewcontent.cgi?article=1141&context=honors, accessed September 5, 2017.

64 In this first act, the dancers dressed in three different colors, maybe symbolic of three classes of citizens of the *polis*, or three basic elements of air, earth, and water.

65 Peirce wrote about "the essential character of a line" in relation to the continued existence of the soul, which Peirce understands as having its telos in existence. In his manuscript on the Phaedo he writes, "To apply this argument to actual existence, and maintain that no real line could be terminated because no ideal line is terminated without infringement of its essential character would be if I rightly apprehend it, the precise parallel to the Phaedian argument for the immortality of the soul." Peirce, Charles S. Peirce Papers, Logic IV. 115. Houghton Library Harvard University, 1787–1951 (MS Am 1632).

66 Peirce, "Philosophy and the Conduct of Life," 41.

67 Peirce, *The Essential Peirce*, Vol. 2, 3.

68 Allastair Macaulay, "How a Mark Morris Dance Reimages Love," *The New York Times*, August 8, 2018, https://www.nytimes.com/2018/08/08/arts/dance/mark-morris-love-song-waltzes-breakdown.html, accessed August 8, 2018.

69 Peirce, "Evolutionary Love," 354.

Chapter 3

1 See Tommy J. Curry, *Another White Man's Burden: Josiah Royce's Quest for a Philosophy of White Racial Empire*, Suny Series in American Philosophy and Cultural Thought (Albany, NY: State University of New York Press, 2018).

2 Josiah Royce, *Race Questions Provincialism and Other American Problems* (New York: The Macmillan Company, 1908).

3 For a summary of his thinking on interpretation, see Joshua Royce, *The Problem of Christianity; Lectures Delivered at the Lowell Institute in Boston and at Manchester College* (Oxford and Chicago, IL: Regnery Co, 1968), Vol. II, 158–9.

4 Frank M. Oppenheim S.J., "Graced Communities: A Problem in Loving," *Theological Studies*, 44 (4): 605, 604–24, https://doi.org/10.1177/004056398304400404. Oppenheim goes on to explain: "Unlike perception and conception, interpretive knowing has for its object 'minds and signs of minds.' Consisting in a cognitive process rather than a single act, interpretation

is distinctive because, operating in a field of signs, its basic logical structure is not dyadic (subject-object), as perception and conception, but triadic (threefold): from sign-sender through sign interpreter to sign-receiver."

5   Royce, *The Problem of Christianity*, Vol. II, 147. "The triadic structure of interpretations is strictly analogous, both to the psychological and to the metaphysical structure of the world of time." Royce borrows from Bergson an understanding of time as an interpretation or artifact of the cosmos. But Royce disagrees with Bergson's aesthetics as grounded in perceptual formulations of our intuitions. See Royce, *The Problem of Christianity*, Vol. II, 139.
6   Oppenheim, "Graced Communities," 604–5.
7   Robert S. Corrington, *The Community of Interpreters: On the Hermeneutics of Nature and the Bible in the American Philosophical Tradition* (Savanah, GA: Mercer University Press, 1987), 3.
8   Corrington, *The Community of Interpreters*, 15.
9   Royce, *Problem of Christianity*, Vol. II, 163.
10 Ibid, Vol. II, 111–12.

> A community, as we have seen, depends for its very constitution upon the way in which each of its members interprets himself and his life. For the rest, nobody's self is either a mere datum or an abstract conception. A self is a life whose unity and connectedness depend upon some sort of interpretation of plans, of memories, of hopes, and of deeds. If, then, there are communities, there are many selves who, despite their variety, so interpret their lives that all these lives, taken together, get the type of unity which our last lecture characterized. Were there, then, no interpretations in the world, there would be neither selves nor communities.

11 Ibid, Vol. II, 151. "For where either God or man is in question, interpretation is demanded. And interpretation,—even the simplest, even the most halting and trivial interpretation of our daily life,—seeks what we hath not seen, and ear hath not heard, and what it hath not entered into the heart of man to conceive,—namely, the successful interpretation of somebody to somebody."
12 Ibid.

> Interpretation says: It is nigh thee—even in thine heart; but shows us, through manifesting the very nature of the object to be sought, what general conditions must be met if anyone is to interpret a genuine Sign to an understanding mind. And withal, interpretation seeks a city out of sight, the homeland where, perchance, we learn to understand one another.

13 Royce, *The Problem of Christianity*, Vol. II, 138. See Peirce, "A Neglected Argument for the Reality of God." When using musement to speculate metaphysically, Peirce realizes that logic will not suffice and that one might

begin their investigations by looking at what is not known in its entirety. "Some of the best will be motived by a desire to comprehend universe-wide aggregates of unformulated by partly experienced phenomena." He goes on to describe details about disclosing truths amid past uncomprehensive and not completely satisfactory understandings of profound questions, such as how one goes about proving God's existence. "I would suggest that the Muser be not too impatient to analyze these, lest some significant ingredient be lost in the process; but that he begin by pondering them from every point of view, until he seems to read some truth beneath the phenomena."

14   Corrington, 15. "Royce came to realize that knowledge must evolve across time and must take more forms than monism allows. This pluralism was reinforced by the temporal analysis of sign interpretation. For Royce the individual is actually a microcosmic community and is constituted by sign series. So Royce redefines the Finite Self."

15   Royce, *The Problem of Christianity*, Vol. 1, 306–7.

16   Ibid, Vol. I, 310.

> Therefore, if indeed you suppose or observe that, in our human world, such creative deeds occur, you see that they indeed do not remove, they do not annul, either treason or its tragedy. But they do show us a genuinely reconciling, a genuinely atoning, fact in the world and in the community of the traitor. Those who do such deeds solve, I have just said, not the impossible problem of undoing the past, but the genuine problem of finding, even in the worst of tragedies, the means of an otherwise impossible triumph. They meet the deepest and bitterest of estrangements by showing a way of reconciliation, and a way that only this very estrangement has made possible.

17   See Josiah Royce, "Shop Talk," *The Relation of the Literary Artist to Philosophy,*" *Josiah Royce's Late Writings, a Collection of Unpublished and Scattered Works*, Vol. 2, ed. and intro. Frank M. Oppenheim (Cincinnati, OH: S.J., Xavier University, Bristol, UK: Thoemmes Press, 2001), 194. Royce writes, "Yet there is a deep relationship between the philosopher who formulates his ideals of life, and the artist, who portrays what he sees. For both artist and philosopher are concerned, not with the merely literal report of the details of what happens in life. Both artists and philosopher are interested in the interpretation of the sense of life."

18   See John Clendenning, *The Life and Thought of Josiah Royce*, (Nashville, Tn.: Vanderbilt University Press, 1999) and more specifically for the aspect of this discussion which brings in T.S. Eliot, Piers Gray, "T.S. Eliot and Josiah Royce," *Stalin on Linguistics and other Essays*, ed. Colin MacCabe and Victoria Rothschild, (Houndmills, Basingstoke, Hampshire and New York: Palgrave, 2002), 81–109.

19 Josiah Royce, *The Basic Writings of Josiah Royce, Culture, Philosophy and Religion*, ed. and intro. John J. McDermott, (New York: Fordham University Press, 2005), 394.
20 Ibid, 395.
21 Ibid, 395.
22 Ibid, 394.

> Abstract however from the time form of music and what is left of any musical form whatever? If the gods listen to music at all they must appreciate it sequences. Wherein consists, however, a true musical appreciation? Whoever aimlessly half listens to the musical accomplishments of a dance or a public festival, may indeed be so absorbed in the passing instant's sound that he gets no sense of the whole.

23 Royce, *The Basic Writings of Josiah Royce, Culture*, 395. Royce explains:

> Well, such a view, as I take it, comes nearer to getting the sense of what real life is than does any view which considers it world merely as timeless. If, then, I try to conceive how God views things, I can only suppose, not that the absolute view ignores time, but that the absolute view sees at a glance all time past, present, future, just as the true appreciator of the music knows the entirety of the sequence as a sort of higher or inclusive present—a present in which the earlier stages do not merely vanish into the later stages, and yet on the other hand, are not all devoid of time relations to the later states. For this inclusive view, as I suppose, sees the totality of the significant deeds and will attitudes as a single life process—temporal because it is both significant and volitional, and present not in the vanishing, but in the inclusive and eternal sense present not as a timeless whole, but as an infinite sequence, "one undenied soul of many a soul," one life in infinite variety of expression.

24 Josiah Royce, "Shelley and the Revolution," *Fugitive Essays* (Cambridge: Harvard University Press, 1920), 66–95. Royce wrote the essay in 1880.
25 Royce, "Shelley and the Revolution," 82.

> Shelley, the practical reformer, is the inspirer of such conceptions as the *Prometheus,* or as the *Revolt of Islam.* Shelley, the poet of great experiences sparkles in a multitude of rare gems of lyric poetry. Shelley, not only as lyric poet, but also as seer and mystic produces such marvels as the *Triumph of life,* the *Epipsychidion,* or the *Adonis,* and adorns the *Prometheus* itself. In all these three directions of activity Shelley is the child of the Revolution in so far forth as his aims, his problems, and his beliefs are framed by the revolutionary spirit.

26 Ibid, 78. Royce writes:

> Hence, along with the fact of ceaseless activity in human thought and life goes the no less far reaching fact of ceaseless economy of energy, of perennial laziness,

in human thought and life. The world of though for men is at each moment what men choose to end it, but let men alone, and they will choose to find or construct is at each moment just like the world of the previous moment. Without stimulus, without definite ends in view, men will indeed go rebuilding their ideas every instant, but the rebuilding will not be a reformation, in the ordinary sense, but a building after old models. That is what we mean by conservatism.

27 Josiah Royce, "The Temporal and the Eternal," *The Basic Writings of Josiah Royce*, Vol. I, ed. John McDermott and Ignas K. Skrupskelis (Chicago, IL: University of Chicago Press, 1969), 611.

28 Ibid, 619.

29 As said, my project is not to redeem Eliot (nor Royce for that matter) from such criticisms, nor do I ponder whether the Eliot's cultural contributions remain valid. I am no apologist for Eliot, or others who had incorporated anti-Semitic prejudice into their art.

30 See Anthony Julius, *T.S. Eliot, Anti-Semitism and Literary Form* (Cambridge, UK: Cambridge University Press, 1995).

31 Thomas Pfau, "Personhood, Community, and Love: Can Theology and Literature Regain what Philosophy has Lost?" at Religion & Ethics, ABC Broadcasting Corporation –Australia (23 September 2018), https://www.academia.edu/37457045/_Personhood_Community_and_Love, Accessed December 10, 2019, 3:45 EST.

32 Julius, *T.S. Eliot, Anti-Semitism and Literary Form*, 13.

33 Piers Gray, "T.S. Eliot and Josiah Royce," *Stalin on Linguistics and Other Essays*, ed. C. MacCabe (New York: Palgrave, 2001), 84. Introducing Royce's hermeneutics by a connection with American Idealism, specifically the St. Louis school (I assume he refers to Hegel's influence), and Eliot's like-mindedness, Gray writes:

> Throughout his career, Royce understood the first two of the *Journal's* triad of considerations as aspects of a single problem. The displacement of traditional religious sentiment was creating a moral vacuum in which the individual could survive only by becoming a center unto himself. A society composed of a plurality of disparate national and cultural groups was, as a result, held together by the determinations of specific economic functions and a superstructure of repressive laws. Such an America was, for Royce, a "realm of the self-estranged spirit" because consciousness of conduct, self-consciousness, could arise only through the conflict of individual will within a social structure. Eliot's poems themselves are imbedded with the doubt of those times, certainly at the very least beginning with *The Love Song of J. Alfred Prufrock* till and including *The Wasteland*.

34 Gray, 73. Gray refers to an early paper by Eliot, in which the poet asserts that ritual does not change with interpretive meanings. Gray finds a cultural limitation that Royce does not share: "The passage is significant in asserting the necessity of

interpretative acts; no less important is its recognition of the *limits* of those acts." Gray is referring here to Eliot's introduction to his mother's poem *Savonarola*. See Gray, footnote, 6, 107, Charlotte Eliot, *Savonarola: A Dramatic Poem* (London: 1936), viii.

35 To gain understanding of Royce's move to an absolute pragmatism, see Mary Briody Mahowald, *An Idealistic Pragmatism: The Development of the Pragmatic Element in the Philosophy of Josiah Royce* (The Hague: Martinus Nijhoff, 1972), 123. Mahowald explains Royce's absolute pragmatism by contrasting, as Royce does, Bergson's emphasis on perception and intuition, with James's emphasis on the inadequate mere synthesis of conception and perception in relation to the cash value of experience. In explaining a difference of Royce to James in relation to interpretation, Mahowald brings forward the image of a journey, referred to by both philosophers. She finds that Royce confirms truth as absolute by one's will of purpose, whereas James is left with a relativism concerning how good an action works out, not being able to confirm the good intentions and plans that might change as also true.

36 Royce, *The Basic Writings of Josiah Royce, Culture*, 396. Royce continues:

> Our own will is the will of the world, conscious in us, and demanding our individual variety as its own mode of expression. We conspire with the world even when most we seem to rebel. We are one with it even when most we think of ourselves as separate. Art, ethics, reason, science, service all bear witness both to our unity with its purposes, and to its need that all unity of purpose should be expressed through an endless variety of individual activities.

37 Leone Montagnini, *Harmonies of Disorder: Norbert Wiener: A Mathematician-Philosopher of Our Time* (Cham, Switzerland: Springer Publishing, 2017), 33. In regard to the seminar, Montagnini has researched Royce's influence on Wiener, "revealing a definite interest for interdisciplinarity and investigations into the nature of the various scientific methods used in science."

38 Joseph Maddley, *The Making of T.S. Eliot: A Study of Literary Influences* (Jefferson, NC and London: McFarland & Company, 1979), 56.

39 Norbert Wiener, *Ex prodigy: My Childhood and Youth* (Cambridge, MA and London, UK: MIT Press, 1953), 171.

40 Wiener, *Ex-prodigy,* 165–6. Wiener writes: "I had two different sorts of contact with Josiah Royce. One was in his course on mathematical logic. Although I did not regard his contributions to mathematical logic as of major character, he introduced me to the subject. Royce was a many-sided man, coming at a critical period in the intellectual world when the old religious springs of philosophical thought were drying up and new scientific impulses were bursting into life. His mathematical logic bore the signs that almost always indicates a brilliant man who has come too late into a field to obtain a perfect mastery of it."

> This position of facing both the past and the future was also clear in Royce's seminar on scientific method, which I attended for two years, and which gave

me some of the most valuable training I have ever had. Royce welcomed into this little group every sort of intellectual who was carrying out a reasonable program of work and who was articulate concerning the methods by which he had come to his own ideas and concerning the philosophical significance thereof.

41 Norbert Wiener, *The Human Use of Human Beings: Cybernetics and Society* (Boston, Massachusetts: Da Capo Press and Boston, Massachusetts: Houghton Mifflin Harcourt, reprinted by arrangement with Houghton Mifflin Co., 1954), 122. "In anything like a normal situation, it is both far more difficult and far more important to us to ensure that we have such an adequate knowledge than to ensure that some possible enemy does not have it. The whole arrangement of a military research laboratory is along lines hostel to our own optimum use and development of information."

42 Montagnini, *Harmonies of Disorder*, 33. Also Wiener and Royce share an understanding about the scientific method, as probabilistic. On the basis of similar arguments of those used by neo-idealists,

> Wiener concluded that in no significant sense can we assert the existence of self-sufficient knowledge, because there is nothing that is devoid of essential relationships with others, and our consciousness forever modifies the observed object. From this observation he comes to the most radical conclusion. "But if no knowledge is self-sufficient, none is absolutely certain" (14d, 566). To deny certainty is not to say, in his opinion, denying the possibility of knowledge.

43 Ibid, 20.

> Royces' magnum opus, *The world and the individual*(1900–1901), represents a supreme effort to settle the idea of the absolute as unity and multiplicity, obtaining a marriage between absolutism and pragmatism, the so-called "absolute pragmatism" (Cf. Mahowald 1972). Ideas are conceived by Royce, not so much as cognitive entities, but rather as volitional entities, and the meaning of an idea is seen to reside in its intentional character. In a pragmatist way he believes that ideas are true if they work, but in turn they only work because they are in harmony with the purposes of the absolute. Generally speaking, individuals, with their individual plans, but also any element of nature like a stick or a stone, although unaware, constitute a network of teleological relationships, sometimes on purpose, within a divine cosmic plan.

44 Wiener, *The Human Use of Human Beings*, 50.
45 Ibid.

> Most of us in the United States prefer to live in a moderately loose social community, in which the blocks to communication, among individuals and classes are not too great. I will not say that this ideal of communication is

attained in the United States, until white supremacy ceases to belong to the creed of a large part of the country it will be an ideal from which we fall short. Yes even this modified formless democracy is too anarchic for many of those who make efficiency their first idea. These worshipers of efficiency would like to have each man move in a social orbit meted out to him from his childhood, and perform a function to which he is bound as the serf was bound to the clod.

46 Ibid, 50–1. He goes on to explain:

> These worshipers of efficiency would like to have each man move in a social orbit metered out to him from his childhood, and perform a function to which he is bound as the serf was bound to the clod. Within the American social picture it is shameful to have these yearnings, and this denial of opportunities implied by an uncertain future. Accordingly, many of those who are most attached to this orderly state of permanently allotted functions would be confounded if they were forced to admit this publicly. They are only in a position to display their clear preferences through their actions. Yet these actions stand out distinctly enough. The businessman who separates himself from his employees by a shield of yes-men, or the head of a big laboratory who assigns each subordinate a particular problem, and begrudges him the privilege of thinking for himself so that he can move beyond his immediate problems and perceive its general relevance, show that the democracy to which they pay their respects is not really the order in which they would prefer to live. The regularity ordered state of pre-assigned functions toward which they gravitate is suggestive of the Leibnitzain automate and does not suggest the irreversible movement into a contingent future which is the true condition of human life.

47 Ibid, 92. "But as efficient as communications' mechanisms become, they are still, as they have always been, subject to the overwhelming tendency for entropy to increase, for information to leak in transit, unless certain external agents are introduced to control it." 92.

48 Ibid, 94,

> The desire to apply Cybernetics of semantics, as a discipline to control the loss of meaning from language, has already resulted in certain problems. It seems necessary to make some sort of distinction between information taken brutally and bluntly, and that sort of information on which we as human beings can act effectively or, *mutatis mutandis,* on which the machine can act effectively. In my opinion, the central distinction and difficulty here arises from the fact that it is not the quantity of information sent that is important for action, but rather the quantity of information which can penetrate into a communication and storage apparatus sufficiently to serve as the trigger for action.

49 Ibid, 34. By singularity Wiener meant a machine creating an ongoing process around itself, to fight off entropy. "The machine, like to living organism, is, as I have said, a device which locally and temporarily seems to resist the general tendency for the increase of entropy. By its ability to make decisions it can produce around it a local zone of organization in a world whose general tendency is to run down."

50 Mark Graves, "Shared Moral and Spiritual Development Among Human Persons and Artificially Intelligent Agents," *Theology and Science*, 15(3) (2017): 333–51. Published, Mark Graves (2017) Theology and Science, 15:3, 333–51, DOI: 10.1080/14746700.2017.1335066, Theology and Science, Vol. 15, 2017—Issue 3.

51 Wiener, *The Human Use of Human Being*, 185.

52 Royce, *Josiah Royce's Late Writing: A Collection of Unpublished and Scattered Works*, "The Social Character of Scientific Inquiry," ed. and intro. Frank Oppenheim (Bristol, UK: Thoemmes Press, 2001), Vol. I. 24 (*Josiah Royce's Late Writings: A Collection of Unpublished and Scattered Work*, Vol. I, 20–38).

53 Ibid, 23.

54 Ibid. He goes on to write:

> To sum up our results: whatever the methods which are characteristic of the natural science, they depend upon and express a very clear and conscious recognition on the part of the scientific inquirer in the range of inductive science that the truth which he seeks when he deals with nature is truth that belongs to the community. And thus the methods of inductive science and the practical attitude of the loyalist have an intimate and close connection which we need to understand somewhat better than we usually do.

55 Ibid, 23–4. Royce writes:

> What I am interested now in emphasizing is that in so far as this takes place, philosophical thought without ceasing to be independent thinking and to use individual inventions and the freedom of individuals, will become increasingly loyal in method, will be more and more an effort to express, as the natural scientific method expresses, the purposes, the insights, the discoveries of the community.

56 See ibid, 25.

57 Ibid, 28.

58 Royce, *Problem of Christianity*, Vol. II, 96.

59 Josiah Royce, *The World and the Individual* (New York, London: The Macmillan Company, 1900), 103. Royce writes:

> Our interest in discriminating is expressed in the joyous "I see" of discoverer. But this is the joy of living, of creating, as well as finding, as world. For in merely acknowledging facts one may indeed be said to find (in the sense I here have in mind) something that, as once conceives, another might have found

as well. But one is conscious of creating, only in so far as one believes that the expression of one's purpose is an unique and individual fact, that has nowhere else in the world of Being its likeness. In consequence, the whole truth is that one discriminates, indeed at every step and in doing so acknowledges what one does not regard as one's present creation. But this very act of discrimination is, in the life of one who sees a present, an individual, and in so far a creative expression of purpose. And the world in permitting this expression reveals its true essence better than the mere description of the serially arranged data reveals the final truth of things. Whoever observes merely the series of linked and discriminated facts, has therefore but to reflect in order further to observe that one's discrimination and linking of acts is itself also a fact, yet not a fact in the series discriminated, but rather one stage in a life of self-expression. Thinking also is living. Science is justified as a type of action. And this is why we never can be content with discovering that the world is describable, but must note that all description is valuable as a process occurring in a life. That is why, moreover, we must always hold that the very facts themselves which we can at present interpret only in terms of description, are the incidents of an orderly life of divine Self Expression.

60   Norbert Wiener, *Invention: The Care and Feeding of Ideas* (Cambridge, MA and London, UK: The MIT Press, 1993), 87.
61   Mark Graves, *Mind, Brain and the Elusive Soul: Human Systems of Cognitive Science and Religion*, (Hampshire, UK and Burlington, VT: Ashgate, 2008), 127. To clarify, Graves writes, "As discussed in Chapter 3, one can study most human activity as occurring on subatomic, physical, biological, psychological, and cultural levels where the boundaries occur in atomic, biochemical, neurological, and linguistic systems, respectively." He continues, "The selection of abstractions resulting in third-order emergence and the incompatible types of causality and function for each level preclude a single unified view of the human person."
62   Ibid, 128. An example given is the integrated collaboration of mind and nature, as Graves explains the importance of a transcendent sixth field of human activity, as well as a third-order understanding rather than merely through a dualistic position of material or idealistic. Graves explains, "Perhaps nature not only has physical quality, a 'life-like' quality, and a 'mind-life' quality, but it also as a 'community-like' quality, and perhaps a 'transcendent-like' or 'spirit-like' quality. Again, one should not project human systems onto nature but recognize the selection influences that occur on human systems by third-order emergence in nature."
63   Ibid, 129.
64   Ibid, 132. Graves finds a concrete example in dialogues between Christians, Buddhists, Muslims: "A clear example of a transcendent relationship example occurs in dialogue between Christians and Buddhists (or Muslims) when each practitioner recognizes in the other's key 'classic' founder an insight for

understanding the practitioner's own religion. In sustained dialogue respectful of plurality, one finds a new, cross-cultural (cross-religion) relationship that strengthens the coherence, integrity, and autonomy of each system."
65   Ibid, 134.
66   Ibid, 136. "Cultural-level systems can become transformed by their participation in transcendent level processes from the interaction of cultural systems that support attributes which break symmetries in constraints, develop emergent boundary conditions that apply to the whole system, and create information meaningful only at the transcendent level."
67   Ibid, 132. Another important aspect is the topic of universals as "classics," referring to art. Graves explains, "A more nuanced account than universalizing cultural systems occurs in the work of the contemporary Christian theologian David Tracy, who defines "classics" as texts, events, images, persons, rituals, or symbols that reveal permanent possibilities of meaning or truth. Classics within any religious tradition so disclose a compelling aspect of truth about human lives that one cannot deny them a kind of normative status. The classic refers to a norm that crosses cultures (or historical periods within a tradition) and thus indicates possibilities for cross-cultural constructions that may result in transcendent level systems" (Ftn. 7). David Tracy, *The Analogical Imagination: Christian Theology and the Culture of Pluralism* (New York: Crossroad, 1981), 8.
68   Graves, *Mind, Brain and Elusive Soul*, 136.
69   Ibid, 136. "Royce articulates a philosophy of loyalty that supports the second-order emergence of cross-cultural relationships and initiates the formation of transcendent-level systems. His community of interpretation results in the emergence of spirit, that I claim results in third-order emergence and the emergence of the transcendent level."
70   Ibid, 137.
71   Royce, *The Problem of Christianity*, Vol. II, 50.
72   Ibid, Vol. I, 350. He reiterates this call as continually creating a unity of people, as an individual yet community endeavor.Nevertheless, the principle of principles in all Christian morals remains this:—"Since you cannot *find* the universal and beloved community,—*create* it." And this again, applied to the concrete art of living[,] means: Do whatever you can to take a step towards it, or to assist anybody,—your brother, your friend you neighbor, your country,—mankind,—to take steps toward the organization of that coming community.
73   Ibid, Vol. I, 359.
74   At the same time people realize more and more how affective cultural signs are, in all their varied modes and techniques, when making political, cultural statements, such as Green Peace activism through on the water protests, women's bare-breasted protests, whole food movements by restaurants and food truck vendors, pet shelters advocating for pet rights as well as wild animal rights, sports figures participating

in social justice protests on their playing fields, and countless other examples. Such creative and symbolic protests are not abstracted from the more formal worlds of art and science when seen in respect to spiritual understandings, as well as open questioning of authoritative practices, of unity by loyalty to the values of communities.

75 Royce, *Problem of Christianity*, Vol. II, 430.
76 Petr Bogatyrev, "Folk Song from a Functional Point of View," *Semiotics of Art*, ed. Ladislav Matejka and Irwin R. Titunik (Cambridge, MA and London, UK: MIT Press, 1976), 21.
77 Ibid.
78 Bogatyrev, 29.
79 Ibid.
80 Political functions are not the only modes by which folk song and literature were integrated as Bogatyrev mentions pure aesthetic inspiration, and "Among the symbolists the dominant function of folk song was aesthetic or mystic" (Bogatyrev, 29).
81 Royce, *Problems of Christianity*, Vol. I, 158.
82 See Ben Sisario, "Accusations About Bob Dylan's Nobel Prize Lecture Rekindle an Old Debate." *New York Times*, June 14, 2017, https://www.nytimes.com/2017/06/14/arts/music/bob-dylan-nobel-lecture-sparknotes.html, accessed, April 18, 2018, 11:50 am.
83 "A Hard Rain's Gonna Fall" was For more information on Dylan's lyrics, there are many scholar sources. I particularly found helpful an archival site online: http://bob-dylan.org.uk/archives/1550.
84 Tony Attwood, "A Hard Rain's Gonna Fall." http://bob-dylan.org.uk/archives/1550. Posted on September 4, 2015. Accessed, April, 2018, 11:20 am.

> *This piece has been updated several times. The latest update was 23 September 2017. Throughout 2016/17 it was the most read article on this site.* By Tony Attwood. "And that is not just in the form of the lyrics, but also the music, for Hard Rain uses a most unusual technique, varying the number of lines in the middle section. In verse one we have a nine line verse (five in the middle, starting with the misty mountains). Verse two is 11 lines, (seven in the middle, starting with the new born babe). Verse three (just to make sure we were not getting the hang of these changes) is the same again—11 lines. The fourth verse (it's a ten line verse with six in the middle "I met a yound child beside a dead pony"), and we finish with the all encompassing 16 line verse (12 in the middle) "I'm a-goin' back out 'fore the rain starts a-fallin.'" The extension of the last verse is singularly powerful. Of course as listeners, we haven't counted the number of lines in each verse but somehow we know this is going on and on—not just by the feel but by the change from "where" to the four subsequent lines before

the two chorus lines.It is also the power and determination of the singer to go out and change the world that accorded with the times—at least for some of us".
85 Peter Burke, *Popular Culture in Early Modern Europe*, (New York: New York University Press, 1978). See specifically for explanation of schism, chapters 1 and 2.
86 Burke, 22.
87 Burke, 242. Here is referring to Spanish reformers in 1762:

> In the next generation, a group of Spanish reformers put forward arguments—secular arguments—against bull-fights, against street ballads, and against the mystery plays of Calderón. Calderón's plays had already been attacked for "mixing and confusing the sacred and the profane," but in 1762 the nobleman Nicolas Fernández de Moratín criticized them on more aesthetic grounds, in the manner of Gottsched and Sonnenfels, for breaking the rules laid down by reason and good taste, in other words the unities of time, place and action. The plays were condemned as irregular, capricious, extravagant.

88 Royce, *Problem of Christianity*, Vol. I, 70.
89 Ibid, Vol. II, 269.

Chapter 4

1 See, Kenneth W. Stikkers essay, "Dialogue Between Pragmatism and Constructivism in Historical Perspective," *John Dewey Between Pragmatism and Constructivism*, ed. Larry A. Hickman et al. (New York: Fordham University Press, 2009), 67–83. See also: Max Scheler, *Cognition and Work: A Study Concerning the Value and Limits of the Pragmatic Motivation in the Cognition of the World*, English translation unpublished manuscript, Zachary Davis, St Johns University, Queens, New York City. Davis has noted to me in a personal correspondence: "There on the influence James had on Scheler. It is not clear what exactly Scheler read of James other than James' *Pragmatism*." Scheler does mention James's *Varieties of Religious Experience*, but only as a criticism. Zachary Davis 12/06/12, 9:01 pm Commented. For Scheler's thoughts on James's notions on ethics and morality in *Varieties*, see Max Scheler, "On the Rehabilitation of Virtue." trans. Eugene Kelly, *American Catholic Philosophical Quarterly*, 79(1) (2005): 21–37.Note: Throughout this chapter I am indebted to Professor Stikkers and Professor Davis for their comments and keen insight. This does not mean that those two agree on Scheler's understanding and support of pragmaticism. As well, I do not assume that either agrees with my reading here. However, I do rely on their scholarship and advice. I attempt to endnote their contributions accordingly.
2 Kenneth W. Stikkers's reading in the Preface to *Problems of a Sociology of Knowledge*, trans. Manfred S. Frings (London: Routledge and Kegan Paul, 1980).

As well as other essays: i.e. Larry A. Hickman's essay "The Homo Faber Debate in Dewey and Max Scheler," *Pragmatism as Post-Postmodernism: Lessons from John Dewey*, (New York: Fordham University Press, 2007), 231–40.

3. See Randall Auxier's general overview of process aesthetics in an essay critiquing Suzanne Langer. He quotes Langer, to explicate a central tenet of a "process aesthetic"; "since it is only when we are aware of the structure or form of a thing that it becomes available for comparison, the process of symbolization is dependent initially on the logical analysis of a single entity." *Process Studies*, 26 (January 1998), 86-106. Cf. Langer, *The Practice of Philosophy*, 115.

4. Richard Shusterman, "The Pragmatist Aesthetics of William James." *British Journal of Aesthetics*, 51(4) (2011): 356. "A key theme of pragmatist aesthetics is the continuity and combination of the aesthetic with the practical, a theme expressed in the integration of art and life, the recognition that bodily appetites and desires can also be aesthetic and the appreciation of the functionality of art and aesthetic experience."

5. Professor Davis has pointed out that in Scheler's "Metaphysics and Art," that art is *bilden* (construction) and a "manifestation of a sense image in some medium like painting or sculpture." Sent Zachary Davis, December 6, 2012 9:08 pm commented.

6. Max Scheler, "Metaphysics and Art," *Max Scheler (1874–1928) Centennial Essays*, ed. Manfred S. Frings, (The Hague: Martinus Nijhof, 1974), 112.

7. Shusterman, The Pragmatist Aesthetics of William James, 348.

8. Ibid.

9. See John Daniel Wild, *The Radical Empiricism of William James* (Westport, CT: Greenwood Press, 1969, 1980), 395. I refer to John Wild's explanation of *pure experience* with reference to a phenomenological approach to James's thought. Wild clarifies: In opposition to traditional rationalism, as well as traditional empiricism, James maintained from the beginning that relational patterns are directly felt and perceived. Immediate experience cannot be dismissed as a set of isolated data. It involves relational structures of the most basic kind, including selective attention, consciousness, continuous transition, and the search for truth. These patterns have always been a central concern of philosophy, because it is only through them that our discrete experiences are gathered together into a meaningful world. In the past, however, they have been identified with the sense-giving activity of a separated mind. According to James this supposition is unnecessary, for these patterns are already known by direct acquaintance independent of language and conceptual thought and may become articulate and communicable by a certain kind of conceptual analysis.

10. In respect to James's and community, see John J. McDermott, "The Promethean Self and Community in the Philosophy of William James." *The Rice University Studies*, 66(4) (1980): 87–102. Although James is known for his "individualism" of perception, the relational aspects of his psychology bring forth the common

element between his views and Scheler's, that the individual's choices are not choices at all unless they are functional in society among the pluralism of relationship.

11 Such influence is complex, but the thrust of Henry James Sr.'s influence on William James's philosophy lies in the area of virtues and metaphysics. Accordingly, this is the relevance of this matter in regard to this comparison of William James and Scheler. For how the influence relates generally, see Gérard Deledalle, "William James and His Father: A Study in Characterology," *The Philosophy of William James*, ed. Walter Robert Corti, (Hamburg: Felix Meiner, 1976). For explanations of the Swedenborgian influences on specific Jamesian concepts such as *pure experience* and *fringe*, see Armi Värila, *The Swedenborgian Background of William James* (Helsinki: Suomalainen Tiedeakatemia, 1977).

12 See David A. Cleveland, *A History of American Tonalism 1880–1920* (New York: Hudson Hills, 2010).

13 I refer those interested in this, to date, undeveloped connection to Dennis Crockett, *German Post-Expressionism* (Pennsylvania, PA: Pennsylvania State University Press, 1999).

14 For a brief exploration into John Dewey's pragmatic aesthetics, which were influenced by James, and European art movements of the first half of the twentieth century, see Krystyna Wilkoszewska, "Dewey's Philosophy of Art as a Challenge for European Aesthetics," *Pragmatism and Values, the Central European Pragmatist Forum*, ed. John Ryder and Emil Visnovsky (Amsterdam and New York: Rodipi, 2004). Please note that Wilkoszewska can be debated on several accounts; mainly in regard to ignoring Dewey's association with progressive art trends and Dewey's important passages on aesthetics in *Nature and Experience*.

15 Corocoran Gallery of Art, Washington DC, 1891, 48 ½ × 72 1/8 in (122.2 × 183.2 cm), Museum Purchase, Gallery Fund 91.10.

16 Orville, Hiestand, *See America First*, Kessinger Publishers, before 1929. 77. Now part of the Guttenberg Project; http://www.gutenberg.org/etext/3547.

17 Most notably Dix and Scheler shared an interest in Nietzsche's philosophy. Dix modeled busts of Nietzsche from bronze. See "Nietzsche and the Future of Art." *Hyperion: On the Future of Aesthetics*, a web publication of *The Nietzsche Circle*: www.nietzschecircle.com, December 2007. Copyright © 2003 Friedrich Ulfers and Mark Daniel Cohen. http://www.nietzschecircle.com/hyperion0728.html September 9, 2012 5:24 pm Central Europe Time.

18 Scheler, *Cognition and Work*, 293. Scheler makes clear his critique:

> Pragmatism bears a close affinity to the advancement of Kantian philosophy, an advancement Fichte had completed. For pragmatism, the world is only the material for a free activity of the ego, and, under pragmatism, the task of theoretical cognition loses its independence from the practical, moral consciousness. Also for pragmatism and its modern successors such as Chr.

V. Sigwart, W. Windelbrand, H. Rickert, H. Münsterberg, the concept of being is reduced to the concept of value, the concept of "object" is reduced to the experienced ought of the recognition of a content through the judgment that should be a type of "assessment." We will describe in the future the above mentioned theses as pragmatism in the broader sense to which we contrast, as pragmatism *in the stricter sense*, the pragmatism of James, Schiller and Dewey.

19 Stikkers, *Problems of a Sociology of Knowledge*, 76. Also, I must note Davis's comments that clarifies Scheler does not necessarily embrace pragmaticism but "applauds the pragmatists treatment of mastery of knowledge, i.e., the type of knowledge gained through action and work that tends to some practical or useful end." Zachary Davis December 6, 2012 9:08 pm, commented.
20 Scheler, "Metaphysics and Art."
21 Shusterman, 350.
22 See William James, *Meaning of Truth* (New York: Longmans, Green and Co., 1911), 210.
23 Ibid. As mentioned, James thinks of these intuitions as harmonies between "objects of thought." Scheler thinks of intuitive feelings or emotions as a priori; however, both understand that the agent is pulled toward immediate experience by an aesthetic valence that is preferred and that is consequentially acted on.
24 Once again Davis points out what Scheler means by vital soul, as "what is 'comprehended' by a living being and phantasy as an act executed by the human being a living being, not a spiritual being." Zachary Davis December 6, 2012 9:08 pm, commented.
25 See William James, "A World of Pure Experience (1904)," first published in *Journal of Philosophy, Psychology, and Scientific Methods*, 1, 533–43, 561–70 and McDermott, "The Promethean Self and Community in the Philosophy of William James" as cited in note 9 of this chapter.
26 Stikkers, *Problems of a Sociology of Knowledge*, 77.
27 See William James, "The Dilemma of Determinism," *The Will to Believe and Other Essays in Popular Philosophy*, ed. Frederick Burkhardt et al., *The Works of William James*, Vol. 6 (1897; Cambridge: Harvard University Press, 1979), 115.
28 Scheler, "Metaphysics and Art," 106.
29 Ibid.
30 Ibid.
31 See ibid, 116–19. For a precise explanation of creative, aesthetics productive imagination that includes valuation of life, Scheler provides a full description of his thinking:

> On the contrary, there is *productive* imagination in every living being of higher, more complex structures—driven forward through the automotoric

functions of drives in the vital soul. Only gradually does this imagination become subjected to correction, critique, or selection, during the maturation of sense perception and noetic acts of the mind. It is not extinguished, however, in the mature and optimal state of a human being. Rather, it more and more enters into the service of the mind which, in the function of reasonable willing, restrains and regulates drive-impulses and directs phantasy to the mind's own goals: through spiritual, aesthetic value-feeling phantasy enters into the service of aesthetic goals.

32 1935, oil on masonite, 40-17-03/57, Private Collection, Location: Vaduz, Liechtenstein.
33 Ibid.
34 Scheler, "Metaphysics and Art," 113.
35 Ibid, 106.
36 Ibid, 114.
37 William James, *Principles of Psychology* (New York: Henry Holt 7 Co., 1890), Vol. 11, 329.
38 James, *Principles of Psychology*, Vol. 11, 333.
39 Shusterman, 355.
40 Ibid.
41 Scheler, "Metaphysics and Art," 118.
42 James, *The Principles of Psychology*, 345–6.
43 Ibid.
44 Thomas M. Alexander, "Pragmatic Imagination." *Transactions of the Charles S. Peirce Society*, 26(3) (Summer 1990): 333.
45 See Alexander, "Pragmatic Imagination," 335. Alexander connects James with community as do other scholars such as McDermott. He does this on an aesthetic basis, and he then traces this pragmatic aesthetic to an influence on Dewey's aesthetics of experience and the formulation of what he calls the "moral imagination." For a full understanding of his term "moral imagination," see Thomas M. Alexander, "John Dewey and the Moral Imagination: Beyond Putnam and Rorty Toward a Postmodern Ethics." *Transaction of the Charles S. Pierce Society*, 29(3) (1993): 391. "A moral imagination requires experience, a body of developing habits, education, an ability to understand the way other people think and live, and the ideal of discovering through cooperative action solutions to conflicts."
46 Alexander, "Pragmatic Imagination," 340.
47 Ibid, 390.
48 Ibid, 341.
49 Scheler, "Metaphysics and Art," 108.
50 Ibid, 109.

51 Otto Dix, *Lustmord (Sex Murder)*, 1922, oil on canvas, 165 × 135 cm (65 × 53 1/8 in.). Missing. The quote was gathered by the art historian Olaf Peters. It makes clear the revaluation of values converging with phantasm that is depicted in opposition to the ideal.
52 Maria Tatar, *Lustmord: Sexual Murder in Weimar Germany* (New Jersey: Princeton University Press, 1995), 19.
53 Dietrich Schubert, "Painting, a Medium of Cool Execution," *Otto Dix*, ed. Olaf Peters (Munich, New York: Prestel, and New York:Neue Galerie and Montreal: The Montreal Museum of Fine Arts, 2010), 92–108, 102.
54 For a full account of the *life-community* and its virtues, see Max Scheler, *Philosophical Perspectives* (Boston, MA: Beacon Press, 1958), 89.

Chapter 5

1 "Serhiy Kvit: The ideology of the EuroMaidan Revolution," *KyivPost*, Public Media, http://www.kyivpost.com, March 24, 2014, 5:41.
2 Marcin Mamon, "The Cross and the Sword: The Making of a Christian Taliban in Ukraine," *THE//Intercept*, online magazine, https://firstlook.org/theintercept/2015/03/18/ukraine-part-3/, 11:30 am CST, March 18, 2015.
3 Throughout this chapter I rely heavily on textual analysis of John Dewey, *Art as Experience* (New York: Penguin Group, 1934) and William James, *Varieties of Religious Experience* (New York: Penguin Group, 1902).
4 See Randy L. Friedman, "Deweyan Pragmatism," William James Studies, Vol. 1, https://williamjamesstudies.org/1.1/friedman.html#_ftn1. Friedman investigates Dewey's religious philosophy and makes a point that his brand of pragmatism differs from James's in respect to religious belief. For Friedman the main difference is that Dewey thinks of religious experience as born out through reconstruction of society. I find that James also alludes to melioristic aspects of religion. Friedman writes:

> This first step allows Dewey to level the playing field. Through a turn to experience, dogma is replaced by religious beliefs that are now working hypotheses whose meaning is no longer assumed or accepted by virtue of their status as religious beliefs. Perhaps this move on Dewey's part is what he finds lacking in James' description (and endorsement) of certain religious experiences in *Varieties*—that is, these experiences reflect but do not reflectively reconstruct religious beliefs.

5 See Hannah Arendt, *Lectures on Kant's Political Philosophy* (Chicago, IL: The University of Chicago Press, 1992).

6   I concur that public discussions and thinking about collective goals as a matter of concepts and decisions, which are methods for peace at the center of Arendt's political philosophy, are also successful tools for nonviolent social change. However, religions do structure (through tradition) what is important to this discussion, namely *religiousness*. Therefore, Arendt's views on religion are relevant in that they bear out the fact that although she does not negate the "mood" of revolutionaries altogether, she stresses that human matters must be imbued with a secular attitude. Arendt is, however, pragmatic when she writes:

> Politically, the outstanding characteristic of the Christian era had been that this ancient view of world and man—of mortal men moving in an everlasting or potentially everlasting world—was reversed: men in possession of an everlasting life moved in an ever-changing world whose ultimate fate was death; and the outstanding characteristic of the modern age was that it turned once more to antiquity to find a precedent for its own new preoccupation with the future of the man-made world on earth. Obviously, the secularity of the world and the worldliness of men in any given age can best be measured by the extent to which preoccupation with the future of the world takes precedence in men's minds over preoccupation with their own ultimate destiny in a hereafter.

See Hannah Arendt, *On Revolution* (London, UK: Penguin Books Ltd., 1990), 230. Online edition, https://archive.org/stream/OnRevolution/ArendtOnrevolution_djvu.txt, accessed May 10, 2015, 11:30 a.m.

7   See Ronald Beiner, "Hannah Arendt on Judging," *Lectures on Kant's Political Philosophy* (1982), 124. In Beiner's interpretive essay to Arendt's lessons on Kant's aesthetics and politics, he describes the crucial anomaly, in that disinterestedness cannot lead to a sense of culture as a group of political and creative people hoping for a more free and inclusive state of affairs, without making moral judgments the same as political judgments. He does point out though that Arendt was taken by Kant's moment of beauty "purposiveness without purpose," which allows creativity without attaching morality to politics. However, this cannot allow Arendt to move past her conclusions that political and aesthetic movements depend on the judgment of spectators. This is the opposite of what I argue as the essence of artistic, religious, and political engagement. Beiner writes: "It is worth noting that the two actualities by which Kant here distinguishes political judgments namely universality and disinterestedness are the very same two outstanding marks of judgment ascribed by Kant to aesthetic taste. This famous passage shows unmistakably that political judgment, like aesthetic judgment is reserved to the spectator."

8   See John Dewey, "Natural Development and Social Efficiency as Aims," *The Essential Dewey*, ed. Larry A. Hickman and Thomas M. Alexander (Bloomington

and Indianapolis, IN: Indiana University Press, 1998), Vol. 1, 264. In fact Dewey's definition of culture is based not only on education but also on inclusiveness and the broadening of people's views. Dewey writes:

> But social efficiency as an educational purpose should mean cultivation of power to join freely and fully in shared or common activities. This is impossible without culture, while it brings a reward in culture, because one cannot share in intercourse with others without learning—without getting a broader point of view and perceiving things of which one would otherwise be ignorant. And there is perhaps no better definition of culture than that it is the capacity for constantly expanding the range and accuracy of one's perception of meanings.

9 John Dewey, "Religion Versus the Religious: From a Common Faith," *The Essential Dewey*, ed. Larry Hickman, Thomas Alexander (Bloomington and Indianapolis, Indiana: Indiana University Press, 1998), Vol. 1, 401. I have also relied on the following text for my use of the term *religiousness*. Thomas M. Alexander, *John Dewey's Theory of Art, Experience and Nature the Horizons of Feeling* (Albany, NY: State University of New York, 1987).

10 Dewey, *Art as Experience*, 362. Dewey sums up the connection of both personal and practical relationships between people and imaginative and broad-reaching ideas communicated through art and morality. Dewey writes:Imagination is the chief instrument of the good. It is more or less a commonplace to say that a person's ideas and treatment of his fellows are dependent upon his power to put himself imaginatively in their place. But the primacy of the imagination extends far beyond the scope of direct personal relationships. Except where "ideal" is used in conventional deference or as a name for a sentimental reverie, the ideal factors in every moral outlook and human loyalty are imaginative. The historic alliance of religion and art has its roots in this common quality. Hence it is that art is more moral than moralities.

11 See Thomas M. Alexander's introduction to *A Common Faith*. Alexander quotes Dewey: "The religious attitude," Dewey says, would be "a sense of the possibilities of existence" and "devotion to the cause of these possibilities" (Late Works 4:242). What Dewey proposes, in other words, is the replacement of what might be called a "spirituality of the actual" with a "spirituality of the possible." Dewey, "Introduction," *A Common Faith: Second Edition*, Dewey, *A Common Faith*, introduction by Thomas M. Alexander (New Haven: Yale University Press, 2013). Dewey also directly connects art with revolution: "Moreover, resistance and conflict have always been factors in generating art; and they are, as we have seen, a necessary part of artistic form." *Art as Experience*, 353.

12 James, *The Varieties of Religious Experience*, 454.

13 Ibid.

14 Ibid, 455.

15 See James' lines on his pragmatic way of thinking about the existence of God, and his critique of transcendentalism. "But all facts are particular facts, and the whole interest of the question of God's existence seems to me to lie in the consequences for particulars which that existence may be expected to entail." *The Varieties of Religious Experience*, 522.
16 James writes, "In many persons, happiness is congenital and irreclaimable. 'Cosmic emotion' inevitably takes in them the form of enthusiasm and freedom. I speak not only of those who are animally happy. I mean those who, when unhappiness is offered or proposed to them, positively refuse to feel it, as if it were something mean and wrong." *The Varieties of Religious Experience*, 79–80.
17 Dewey writes,

> Man excels in complexity and minuteness of differentiations. This very fact constitutes the necessity for many more comprehensive and exact relationships among the constituents of his being. Important as are the distinctions and relations thus made possible, the story does not end here. There are more opportunities for resistance and tension, more drafts upon experimentation and invention, and therefore more novelty in action, greater range and depth of insight and increase of poignancy in feeling. As an organism increases in complexity, the rhythms of struggle and consummation in its relation to its environment are varied and prolonged, and they come to include within themselves an endless variety of sub-rhythms. The designs of living are widened and enriched. Fulfillment is more massive and more subtly shaded.
>
> *Art as Experience*, 23.

18 Dewey, *Art as Experience*, New York City: Penguin Group, 1934, 202.
19 John Dewey, *The Essential Dewey, Volume 1*, ed. Larry A. Hickman and Thomas M. Alexander (Bloomington and Indianapolis, IN: Indiana University Press, 1998), 408–9.
20 James, *Varieties*, 48.
21 Ibid, 518.
22 See ibid, 516. James writes, "Yet the unseen region in question is not merely ideal, for we are turned into a new man, and consequences in the way of conduct follow in the natural world upon our regenerative change."
23 John Dewey, *The Essential Dewey*, Vol. 1, ed. Larry A. Hickman and Thomas A. Alexander, (Bloomington and Indianapolis, Indiana: Indiana University Press, 1998), 410.
24 Dewey, *Art as Experience*, 340.
25 Dewey explains an important connection between values, meaning, history, and art.

> For while the roots of every experience are found in the interaction of a live creature with its environment, that experience becomes conscious, a matter of perception, only when meanings enter it that are derived from prior experiences. Imagination is the only gateway through which these meanings enter it that are derived from prior experiences. Imagination is the only gateway through which these meanings can find their way into a present interaction: or rather, as we have just seen, the conscious adjustment of the new and the old *is* imagination. Interaction of a living being with an environment is found in vegetative and animal life. But the experience enacted is human and conscious only as that which is given here and now is extended by meanings and values drawn from what is absent in fact and present only imaginatively.
>
> He goes on to say,
>
> There is always a gap between the here and now of direct interaction and the past interactions whose funded result constitutes the meaning with which we grasp and understand what is now occurring. Because of this gap, all conscious perception involves a risk; it is a venture into the unknown, for as it assimilates the present to the past it also brings about some reconstruction of that past.
>
> *Art as Experience*, 283–4.

26 See Hannah Arendt, *Lectures on Kant's Political Philosophy*, (Chicago, IL: The University of Chicago Press, 1992).

27 Ibid.

28 Arendt denied that judging and being creative was completely rational, yet she contradicted herself as is noted by Ronald Beiner in his interpretative essay in *Lectures on Kant's Political Philosophy*. Beiner writes, "We have already mentioned that in 'What is Freedom?' Arendt aligns judgment with intellect or cognition, in stark contrast to her eventual denial that judgment is an intellectual faculty or is indeed cognitive at all." He goes on to write, "So we see that it was only gradually that Arendt came to regard judging as a separate mental activity, distinct from both intellect and will; and, by the time she had settled this question in her own mind, she had come to reformulate the very relation between judgment and politics—between 'the life of the mind' and 'the world of appearances.'" 139.

29 See Hannah Arendt, *The Human Condition* (Chicago, IL: The University of Chicago, Press, 1958), 27–9.

30 "Disinterestedness" is required for Kant's universal subjectivity. It means being free from desire. See Emmanuel Kant, 1790, *Critique of Judgement*, trans. Meredith (Oxford: Oxford University Press, 1928), 42–50.

31 Arendt, *Kant Lectures*, 27.

32 Kant, 307.

33 Arendt does admit that Kant never thought in terms of cultural plurality, but this is not the problem pragmatically. The problem with Arendt and Kant is that creativity and aesthetic imagination is conceptually unavailable to everyone. Arendt interprets Kant in a political context when she agrees with his aesthetics of the spectator:

> Only what touches, affects, one in representation, when one is uninvolved, like the spectator who was uninvolved in the actual doings of the French Revolution—can be judged or ugly, or something in between. One then speaks of judgment and no longer of taste because, though it still affects one like a matter of taste, one now has, by means of representation, established the proper distance, the remoteness or un-involvedness or disinterestedness, that is requisite for approbation and disapprobation, for evaluating something at its proper worth. By removing the object, on has established the conditions for impartiality..
>
> (67)

34 Original lecture given at *Bryn Mawr* in 1892 and published in 1900 (New York: Henry Holt and Company), http://philosophy.lander.edu/intro/articles/jameslife-a.pdf, accessed February 20, 2020, 11:30 AM.

35 Ibid.

36 Dewey, *Art as Experience*, 347. Dewey writes about the discrete and continuous nature of cultures: "Each culture has its own individuality and has a pattern that binds its parts together. Nevertheless, when the art of another culture enters into attitudes that determine our experience genuine continuity is affected. Our own experience does not thereby lose its individuality, but it takes unto itself and weds elements that expand its significance." Dewey, *Art as Experience*, 349.

37 Dewey, *The Essential Dewey*, Vol. 1, p. 410. Dewey writes, "Any activity pursued in behalf of an ideal end against obstacles and in spite of threats of personal loss because of conviction of its general and enduring value is religious in quality. Many a person, inquirere, artist, philanthropist, citizen, men and women in the humblest wals of life, have achieved, without presumption and without display, such unification of themselves and of their relations to the conditions of existence."

38 *Art as Experience*, 340.

39 See Antoine Arjakovsky, *The Role of the Churches in the Ukrainian Revolution*, ABC Religion and Ethics, Updated March 7, 2014 (First Posted March 6, 2014) http://www.abc.net.au/religion/articles/2014/03/06/3958163.htm, accessed January 2, 2015, 1:30 pm.

40 The pro-Russian separatists also held icons and priests supported both sides of the conflict. For a full description of the Ukrainian clash of religions, cultures, politics from the pro-European perspective, see http://maidantranslations.com/2014/04/13/

inside-sloviansk-april-13-2014/, accessed April 20, 2015, 12:30 pm. An example of the influence of religious icons on contemporary sociopolitical affairs is the art exhibition: "Iconart: Visions of a World Unseen, Contemporary Sacred Art from Ukraine": The Ukrainian Institute of America is pleased to announce a group exhibition of eighteen artists from Ukraine, "Iconart: Visions of a World Unseen." Organized in cooperation with Iconart Gallery of Contemporary Sacred Art, located in Lviv, Ukraine, the exhibition draws from the work of Ukrainian artists associated with the gallery. Independently working in different media, the artists focus on spiritual and religious concerns within the contemporary cultural context in which they live. http://iconart.com.ua/ua/events/111, accessed February 11, 2015, 1:30 pm.

41 For a scholarly account of the religious factions at play in the Russian Revolution and how the common people both supported and split from those factions, see Vera Shevzov, *Russian Orthodoxy on the Eve of Revolution* (Oxford, New York: Oxford University Press, 2004).

42 Leonid Ouspensky and Vladimir Lossky, *The Meaning of Icons* (Crestwood, NY: St Vladimir's Seminary Press, 1983), 166.

43 Ibid.

44 Ibid.

45 Dewey, *Art as Experience*, 12. Dewey writes about the more general aspects of nature, in terms of all living creatures. He writes:

> The first great consideration is that life goes on in an environment; not merely *in* it but because of it, through interaction with it. No creature lives merely under its skin; its subcutaneous organs are means of connection with what lies beyond its bodily frame, and to which, in order to live, it must adjust itself, by accommodation and defence but also by conquest. At every moment, the living creature is exposed to dangers from its surroundings, and at every moment, it must draw upon something in its surrounding to satisfy its needs. The career and destiny of a living being are bound up with its interchanges with its environment, no externally but in the most intimate way.

46 Ibid, 352, "From one point of view the problem of recovering an organic place for art in civilization is like the problem of reorganizing our heritage from the past and the insights of present knowledge into a coherent and integrated imaginative union."

47 Ibid, 346.

48 William Dean, "Radical Empiricism and Religious Art," *The Journal of Religion* (Chicago : The University of Chicago Press), 61 (2) (April 1981): 168–87. Dean's thoughts on religious art and radical empiricism are relevant here. He thinks that to judge the interpersonal and creative value to religious/aesthetic experiences, one must look to its effects. Dean writes about religious art as a matter of its effects in

the world, and this helps explain how spirituality is reality through art. Dean makes a point about the phenomenology of religious art, in that he thinks it brings to the surface what is deep within our consciousness, without losing the mystery and unknown qualities, and it shows us those qualities as feelings and values that are evidentially real. Dean explains:

> Finally, however, from the perspective of radical empiricism, religious art is most important for what it shows empirically about the world rather than for what it accomplishes subjectively for the beholder. Religious art is important not primarily because it engenders a uniquely two-faceted experience in the self, but because it defines that in the world which can engender that experience and because it can do so without clarity.

49 See Lydia S. Tonoyan and Daniel P. Payne, "The Visit of Patriarch Kirill to Ukraine in 2009 and Its Significance in Ukraine's Political and Religious Life," *Religion, State and Society*, 38(3) (2010): 253–64, http://dx.doi.org/10.1080/09637494.2010.499283 , accessed June 12, 2014, 11:30 am.
50 James, *Varieties*, 334.
51 *Saint Sergius and Saint Bacchus*, Original found at Saint Catherine's Monastery, Mount Sinai, Egypt, now housed at the Bohdan and Varvara Khanenko Museum of Arts, Kiev, Ukraine.
52 See John Boswell, *Same Sex Unions in Pre-Modern Europe* (New York: Vintage Books, Random House, 1994).
53 See Slavoi Žižek, "What Europe Should Learn from Ukraine," *Blog Da Boitempo*, March 31, 2014, http://blogdaboitempo.com.br/2014/03/31/zizek-what-europe-should-learn-from-ukraine/, accessed January 10, 2015, 11:30 pm. And "Why Both the Left and the Right Have Got It Wrong on Ukraine," *The Guardian*, http://www.theguardian.com/world/2014/jun/10/ukraine-slavoj-zizek-lenin, Tuesday June 10, 2014, 05.00 EDT.
54 See Žižek, "What Europe Should Learn from Ukraine," *Blog Da Boitempo*, March 31, 2014, http://blogdaboitempo.com.br/2014/03/31/zizek-what-europe-should-learn-from-ukraine/, accessed January 10, 2015, 11:30 pm. He writes in his ongoing blog:

> The Ukrainian Rightist nationalism is part of a renewed anti-immigrant populist vogue which presents itself as the defense of Europe. The danger of this new Right was clearly perceived a century ago by G.K. Chesterton who, in his *Orthodoxy*, deployed the fundamental deadlock of the critics of religion: "Men who begin to fight the Church for the sake of freedom and humanity end by flinging away freedom and humanity if only they may fight the Church." Does the same not hold for the advocates of religion themselves? How many fanatical defenders of religion started with ferociously attacking the contemporary

secular culture and ended up forsaking any meaningful religious experience? And does the same not hold also for the recent rise of the defenders of Europe against the immigrant threat? In their zeal to protect Christian legacy, the new zealots are ready to forsake the true heart of this legacy.

55 Dewey, *Art as Experience*, 343.
56 Jon Lee Anderson, "Revolutionary Relics." *New Yorker*, May 1, 2014, http://www.newyorker.com/culture/photo-booth/revolutionary-relics, accessed June 15, 2014, 11:30 am.
57 István Rév, *Retroactive Justice: Prehistory of Post-communism* (Stanford, CA: Stanford University Press, 2005), 98.
58 Žižek, "Why Both the Left and the Right Have Got It Wrong on Ukraine," *The Guardian*, http://www.theguardian.com/world/2014/jun/10/ukraine-slavoj-zizek-lenin, Tuesday June 10, 2014, 05.00 EDT.

Chapter 6

1 See Nathan Crick and David Tarvin, "A Pedagogy of Freedom: John Dewey and Experimental Rural Education." *Inter-American Journal of Philosophy*, 3(2) (Fall 2012): 68–83. However, I emphasize aesthetic factors playing an important part in the way individuals orient themselves to their communities and environments, while enriching their natural environments. Also particularly enlightening to this line of research is Deron Boyles, "John Dewey's Influence in Mexico: Rural Schooling, 'Community,' and the Vitality of Context." *Inter-American Journal of Philosophy*, 3(2) (Fall 2012): 98–113.
2 See John Ryder, *The Things in Heaven and Earth: An Essay in Pragmatic Naturalism* (New York: Fordham University Press and New York City Press, 2013). I will describe pragmatic naturalism, taking cues from John Ryder's essay.
3 See J. Christopher Eisele, "History of Education Society John Dewey and the Immigrants." *History of Education Quarterly*, 15(1) (Spring 1975): 67–85. Published by History of Education Society Online, http://www.jstor.org/stable/367821, accessed May 6, 2016, 00:18 UTC. For a thorough overview of Dewey's references on immigration, as well as an explanation of his views on intercultural relations rather than assimilation, see this essay.
4 John Dewey, *Art as Experience* (New York: Penguin Group, 1934), 350.
5 Dewey's introduction of an 1945 edition of Jane Addams's 1922 work, *Peace and Bread in Time of War*. See John Dewey, "Democratic versus Coercive International Organization: The Realism of Jane Addams" in introduction to Jane Addams, *Peace and Bread in Time of War* (New York: King's Crown Press, Rev. ed., 1945), xvii–xviii. Dewey wrote in respect to Addams book:

What fits the United States, she holds, for assuming this leadership is precisely the fact that democratic development in this country has in fact increasingly cut under and cut across barriers of race and class. If nothing is Miss Addams' book more-timely than in its sense of the positive values contributed by our immigrant populations. The pattern of American life, composed of multiple and diversified peoples, hostile in the countries from which they came but living in reasonable amity here, can and should be used to provide the pattern of international organization. One of the ironies of the present situation is that a war caused in large measure by deliberate Nazi provocation of racial and class animosity has had the effect in this country of stimulating the growth of racial fear and dislike, instead of leading to intelligent repudiation of Nazi doctrines of hate. The heart of the democratic movement, as Miss Addams saw and felt it, is "to replace coercion by the full consent of the governed, to educate and strengthen the free will of the people through the use of democratic institutions" in which "the cosmopolitan inhabitants of this great nation might at last become united in a vast common endeavor for social ends." Since the United States had demonstrated on a fairly large scale the practicability of this method, Miss Addams put her faith in extension of the democratic process to the still wider world of peoples.

6   See Dewey, *Art as Experience*, 363.

While perception of the union of the possible with the actual in a work of art is itself a great good, the good does not terminate with the immediate and particular occasion in which it is had. The union that is presented in perception persists in the remaking of impulsion and thought. The first intimations of wide and large redirections of desire and purpose are of necessity imaginative. Art is a mode of prediction not found in charts and statistics, and it insinuates possibilities of human relations not to be found in rule and precept, admonition and administration.

7   Gregory Fernando Pappas, "Dewey's Philosophical Approach to Racial Prejudice." *Social Theory and Practice*, 22(1) (Spring 1996): 47–65. Published by: Florida State University Department of Philosophy, https://www.jstor.org/stable/23559023.
8   Dewey, *Art as Experience*, 350.
9   Edgar Holger Cahill, "American Resources in the Arts," *Art for the Millions Essays from the 1930's by Artists and Administrators of the WPA Federal Art Project*, ed. Francis O'Connor (Greenwich, CT: New York Graphic Society Ltd., 1973), 34.
10 Cahill, "American Resources in the Arts," 34.
11 Dewey, *Art as Experience*, 359.
12 Ibid, 297. Dewey explains that the meaning of art is in accord with what is done with it, including and importantly culturally.

For, as we have already seen, the more a work of art embodies what belongs to experiences common to many individuals the more expressive it is. Indeed, failure to take account of the control exercised by objective subject-matter is the just ground for the criticism directed against the subjectivist, theories latterly under discussion. The problem for philosophic reflection concerns, them, not the presence or absence of such objective material but its nature and the way in which it operates in the developing movement of an aesthetic experience.

13 John Dewey, "The Moral Self," *The Essential Dewey: Ethics, Logic, Psychology*, ed. Larry Hickman and Thomas Alexander, Vol. II (Bloomington and Indianapolis, IN: Indiana University Press, 2009), 349.
14 Dewey, *Art as Experience*, 363.
15 Dewey, "The Moral Self," 349.
16 John Ryder, *The Things in Heaven and Earth: An Essay in Pragmatic Naturalism* (New York: Fordham University Press and New York City Press, 2013), 277.
17 See Silvia Navarette Bouzard, "Breaking Free: 'Outsider' Artists in the Iron Babylon," *México 1900–1950*, ed. Agustin Arteaga (New Haven, CT and London: Dallas Museum of Art, Yale University Press, 2017), 213–48.
18 See Dallas Museum of Art, Time and Place, "Meeting of Two Worlds (1920–1950)." https://collections.dma.org/essay/PmVOzRA3, accessed December 1, 2020. "Shortly after the Mexican Revolution and until right before World War II, Mexico became a meeting point for poets, painters, filmmakers, and photographers from the United States and Europe, transforming the country into a melting pot of visual languages and movements. Surrealism encountered magical realism and generated its own genre."
19 Raquel Tibol, *Frida Kahlo an Open Life*, trans. Elinor Randall (Albuquerque, NM: University of New Mexico Press, 1993), 6–7.
20 See Richard J. Bernstein, "Dewey's Encounter with Trotsky." *Inter-American Journal of Philosophy*, 3(2) (Fall 2012): 5–15, Texas A & M University, Online/Peer-Reviewed, ISSN 2157-1694. The report was entitled "Report of the Commission of Inquiry into the Charges Made Against Leon Trotsky." The commission was headed by Dewey and included Alfred Rosmer, Fernand Charbit, and André Breton.
21 John Dewey, "Mexico's Educational Renaissance." *New Republic*, 48 (September 22, 1926): 116–18. Dewey also wrote two other exposes, published in the New Republic, explaining his thoughts on his travels through Mexico; "Church and State in Mexico." *New Republic*, 48 (August 25, 1926): 9–10; "From a Mexican Notebook." *New Republic*, 48 (October 20, 1926): 239–41.
22 Tibol, *Frida Kahlo an Open Life*, 94. Tibol documents:

Frida owes much to the charming photographic portraits painted in Mexico in the second half of the past century, as well as to the *retablos* that thank God or the saints for a continuation of life in spite of the most horrendous misfortunes; and—more than to anything or anybody—she owes to popular Mexican art the manorial pride shown in fragile materials, in the monumental force developed in small dimensions, and in ironic disorder before the macabre. These contradictory factors are the best proof of her rebellion against adversity. Life and work as affirmation and reaffirmation of the living.

23 See Carolyn Kastner, "The Cosmopolitan Circles of Miquel Covaburrbias." *American Art*, 30(1) (Spring 2016): 11–15.
24 See Miguel Covarrubias, *Indian Art of Mexico and Central America* (New York: Alfred A. Knopf, 1958).
25 Frida Kahlo, Self Portrait Along the Border Line between Mexico and the United States, 1932, Oil on Metal, Private Owner. Frida Kahlo, original title Alla Cuelga Mi Vestido, known as My Dress Lies There, 1933, Oil on Masonite and Collage, FEMSA Monterrey, Mexico.
26 For a description of Kalho's teaching, see Tibol, *Frida Kahlo an Open Life*, 177–24.
27 Ibid, 182.
28 Bouzard, "Breaking Free Outsider Artists of the Mexican School," 220. Art historian Silvia Navarrete Bouzard has noted the revolutionary dynamics of María Izquierdo, whose iconography is similar to Kahlo's art. Explaining Izquierdo's paintings she writes, "Her still lifes, improvised memento mori, and images of traveling circuses adopted the sentimental and slightly ungainly style of nineteenth century popular art with ex-votos."
29 Frida Kahlo, Self-Portrait with a Thorn Necklace and Hummingbird, 1940, Oil on Canvas, Harry Ransom Humanities Research Center, Austin, Texas.
30 See Nancy Deffebach, *María Izquierdo & Frida Kahlo: Challenging Visions in Modern Mexican Art* (Austin, TX: University of Texas Press, 2015), 59.
31 Albert Durer, *Ecce Homo*, 1512, Oil on Canvas, Aite Pinakothek, Munich.
32 See *Frida Kahlo's Garden*, ed. Adriana Zavala, Mia D'Avanza, and Joanna L Groarke, The New York Botanical Garden (Munich, London, New York: Delmonico Books, Prestel, 2015).
33 Sarah M. Lowe, "Introduction," *The Diary of Frida Kahlo an Intimate Self-Portrait* (London: Bloomsbury, 1995), 26–7. Lowe writes:

> Kahlo's association with Surrealism as a movement, and with Breton as her supporter, is ambiguous, in large measure because of breton's compulsive need to arbitrate what exactly might be considered Surrealism—ironic in light of his movement's anarchic founding ideas. Kahlo was unmoved by Breton's charismatic self-importance, in part because of the predominantly intellectual and abstract cast of his notions. While Breton was inspired by what was alien to the rational world of the white European male—madness, women, the exotic—Kahlo's creative impulse came from her own concrete reality.
>
> Scholars give varied views of Kahlo's views on surrealism, but she personally did not identify with the movement. I found two somewhat different explanations helpful: for a view of Kahlo as an artist influenced by symbols

with a Freudian kind of automata style, see Lowe cited above. But for a different interpretation, more alike to a naturalistic aesthetic, which I have compared her approach to Dewey's, see Tibol, *Frida Kahlo an Open Life*, 126–7.

34 Kahlo, *The Diary of Frida Kahlo*, 255. Writing in her journal, November 4, 1952, Kahlo explains her mature views:

> Today I'm in better company than for 20 years) I am a self I am a Community. I know that the main origins are wrapped in ancient roots. I have read the History of my country and of nearly all nations. I know their class struggles and their economic conflicts. I understand quite clearly the dialectical materialism of Marx, Engels, Lenin, Stalin and Mao Tse. I love them as the pillars of the new Community world. Since Trotsky came to Mexico I have understood his error. I was never a Trotskyist. But in those days 1904—my only alliance was with Diego (personally) Political fervor. But one has to make allowances for the fact that I had been sick since I was six years old and for really very short periods of my life have I enjoyed truly good HEALTH and I was of no use to the Party. Now in 1953. After 22 surgical interventions I feel better and now and then I will be able to help my Community Party. Although I'm not a worker, but a craftswoman—And an unconditional ally of the Community revolutionary movement. For the first time in my life my painting is trying to help in the line set down by the Party. REVOLUTIONARY REALISM Before it was my earliest experience—I am only a cell in the complex revolutionary mechanism of the peoples for peace in the new nations, Soviets.

35 Kahlo, *The Diary of Frida Kahlo*, 256. Kahlo writes:

> Chinese—Czechoslovakians—Poles—united in blood to me. And to the Mexican Indian. Among those great multitudes of Asian people there will always be the faces of my own—Mexicans—with dark skin and beautiful form with limitless grace. The black people would also be freed, so beautiful and so brave. (Mexicans and negroes are subjugated for now by capitalist countries where all North America—U.S. and England.)

36 Dewey, *Art as Experience*, 346.

37 Dussel foresees a development of liberation ontology transforming pragmatist ethics, as the latter is relational with our awareness of our ethics with evolutionary love/naturalism. The drawback, he thinks, is that American philosophy has found white male Americans as the evolution of European cultures, disregarding others who have been oppressed. He mentions Dewey, but concentrates in Peirce and James when asking about the possible future of liberation philosophy and pragmatism. See Enrique Dussel, "The Pragmatism of Charles S. Peirce," *The Ethics of Liberation: In the Age of Globalization and Exclusion*, trans. and ed. Alejandro A. Vallega (Durham, NC and London: Duke University Press, 2013), 160–6.

38 Enrique Dussel, *The Underside of Modernity: Apel, Ricoeur, Rorty, Taylor, and the Philosophy of Liberation*, trans. and ed. Eduardo Mendieta (New Jersey: Humanities Press, 1996), Foreword Vii.

   The Philosophy of liberation that I practice regarding all types of oppression on the planet (of women, the discriminated races, the exploited classes, the marginalized poor, the impoverished countries in short, the immense majority of humanity) begins a dialogue with the hegemonic European-North American philosophical community... [with the] poverty of the greater part of humanity as a fundamental philosophical and ethical theme.

39 Enrique Dussel, "Being in the World Hispanically, A World on the Border of Many Worlds," trans. and intro. Alexander Stehn, *Comparative Literature*, 61(3), The Americas, Otherwise (Summer 2009): 273, 256–73.

40 See Nina Lakhani, "Mexico tortures migrants—and citizens—in effort to slow Central American surge," *The Guardian*, April 4, 2016, 07.10 EDT. Lakhani reporting from Ocosingo wrote that aid from the United States to stop the immigration flow from Central America has contributed to abuse of some indigenous people from Southern Mexico. She writes, "A growing number of indigenous Mexicans are being detained by agents looking for Central American migrants, amid a crackdown driven partly by aid from US." She tells the story of three teenage Mayans from the Chipas region, who were traveling to work on a farm in the North of Mexico. "They would have tripled their wages in comparison to their local wage 3.00 dollars a day. The brother and his sisters were taken off their bus because they were suspected of being Guatemalan trying to cross into the United States. The baffled youngsters—who speak Mayan Tzeltal but very little Spanish—were threatened and tortured with electric shocks to confess they were not Mexican. Their papers and the money they had saved for their trip was confiscated. Only through the efforts of human rights activists who visit the deportation centers on a regular basis, a lawyer was made aware of their situation and eventually they were freed and sent back to Chipas."

41 John Dewey, "Nationalizing Education." *Journal of Proceedings and Addresses of the National Education Association*, 183(25), (1916): 184–5.

42 Ibid.

43 J. Christopher Eisele, "John Dewey and the Immigrants." *History of Education Quarterly*, 15(1) (Spring 1975): 67–85 Published by: History of Education Society, http://www.jstor.org/stable/367821 accessed May 6, 2016, 00:18 UTC, According to Eisele, this is the only time Dewey comments on cultural pluralism.

   This letter is significant for two reasons. First, it is the only source in which Dewey comments directly on the theory of cultural pluralism, as Kallen or anyone else described it. Second, Dewey points out an aspect of Kallen's plan he finds objectionable, the possibility that it is segregationist in a way that could lessen the interaction of cultures and thereby negate the contribution of one culture to another.

44 See Dewey, *Art as Experience*, 267. As a concise definition of "doing and making" as poetic, Dewey writes, "Not only is art itself an operation of doing and making—a *poiesis* expressed in the very word poetry—but esthetic perception demands, as we have seen, an organized body of activities, including the motor elements necessary for full perception."
45 See Crick and Tarvin, "A Pedagogy of Freedom," 68–84.
46 Ibid, 69–70.

As the summer of 1926 drew to a close, John Dewey found himself on the road to Guadalajara with his daughter Evelyn and a Spanish translator. It was the end of his short stint as a guest lecturer at the National University in Mexico City where he had been invited to speak on "Contemporary Philosophical Thought" and "Advanced Educational Problems" to a group of approximately 500 largely U.S. teachers and students. Yet he was fascinated by the stories he heard from the Mexican teachers who came to his lectures. In the midst of the turmoil of the Mexican Revolution, as the new constitutional government struggled to build a nation, pockets of creative education were springing up in the newly founded rural schools. Consequently, although originally tasked primarily to lecture on "philosophy to a largely academic audience," by the end of his trip Dewey had requested a car and a translator in order to tour these schools and speak with the primarily indigenous population of teachers and students who taught and learned there.

47 Ibid, 70.
48 Ibid, 72.
49 Tibol, *Frida Kahlo an Open Life*, 181. "After Frida's death Rivera would write: "Frida shaped students who today figure among the most valued men and women artists of Mexico. She always encouraged them to preserve and develop their personalities in their work, and in the social and political clarification of their ideas.""
50 Francis V. O'Connor, "Introduction," *Art for the Millions*, ed. Francis V. O'Connor (Greenwich, CT: New York Graphic Society Ltd., 1973), 21. Dewey, *Art as Experience*, 350.
51 See Joel Artista, "IXCHEL'S DREAM." Brooklyn, NY, https://joelartista.com/.

Chapter 7

1. See Marilyn Fischer, "Trojan Women and Devil Baby Tales: Jane Addams on Domestic Violence," in *Feminist Interpretations of Jane Addams*, ed. Maurice Harrington (University Park, PA: The Pennsylvania State University Press, 2010), 81–107.
2. Jane Addams, "Helen Castle Mead," *Helen Castle Mead* (Chicago, IL: privately printed, 1929), 17–23: Found Mead Source Project, https://brocku.ca/MeadProject/Addams/HelenMeadTribute.html1/4/2020, 11: 17 am Central Standard Time.
3. Jane Addams, *Democracy and Social Ethics*, Ebook The Citizen's Library of Economics, Politics, and Sociology, 26, accessed January 20, 2020, CT 12:30 pm. https://iuristebi.files.wordpress.com/2011/07/democracy-and-social-ethics.pdf, Originally published Jane Addams, *Democracy and Social Ethics* (London: Macmillan Company, 1902).
4. See Charlene Haddock Seigfried, "Cultural Contradictions Jane Addams's Struggles with the Life of Art and the Art of Life," *Feminist Interpretations of Jane Addams*, ed. Maurice Hamington (University Park, PA: The Pennsylvania State University Press, 2010), 69. Seigfried writes,

   > Through accounts of Addams's early life demonstrating the discrepancies between events and feelings as recorded by Addams at the time in her journals and letters and the way they are recounted in her later published work, we can realize that in Twenty Years at Hull-House, she recast her earlier self to bring it in line with her later understanding, a process of memory with both conscious and unconscious aspects. Neither the literary achievement nor the philosophical acuity of the book can be fully recognized if it is believed that Addams's story of her early years is simply a fable, as Katherine Joslin claims. As an artist and thinker, she is recasting her life and the history of the Hull House settlement into a coherent expression of the insights and theories she has developed.

5. See George Herbert Mead, *Philosophy of the Present* (Amherst, NY: Prometheus Books, 2002). And Marilyn Fischer, *On Addams*, "Interpretation and Social Transformation: Reading Addams through Mead" (Australia and United Kingdom: Thomson Wadsworth, 2004).
6. Jane Addams, *Newer Ideals of Peace* (Chautauqua, NY: The Chantagua Press, 1907), 222–3.
7. Addams, *Newer Ideas of Peace*, 227. "Such a change having taken place, should we hold him royal in temper or worthy of the traditions of knight-errantry, if he were held back by commercial considerations, if he hesitated because the Krupp Company could sell no more guns and would be thrown out of business?"

8   Ibid, 222–3.
9   Jane Addams, *Democracy and Social Ethics* (London, UK: The Macmillan Company, 1902), 1.
10 Addams, *Democracy and Social Ethics*, 227.
11 Katherine Joslin, *Jane Addams: A Writer's Life* (Baltimore, MD: University of Illinois Press), 61.
12 For insight into a change in this view because of new translations by women, see Homer, *The Odyssey*, trans. Emily Wilson (New York and London, UK: W. W. Norton & Co., 2018). Homer, *The Iliad*, trans. Caroline Alexander (London, UK: Vintage Digital, 2016).
13 Addams, *Democracy and Social Ethics*, 65. "But all this happened before science had become evolutionary and scientific at all, before it had a principle of life from within."
14 Addams, *Newer Ideals of Peace*, 129–30.
15 Ibid, 26. Please note that Addams gives thanks to William James for also putting forward this idea of a moral equivalence for war on p. 24 of this same text.
16 Marilyn Fischer, *On Addams* (Australia, Canada, Mexico, Singapore, Spain, United Kingdom and United States: Wadsworth, 2004), 56.
17 Addams, *Newer Ideals of Peace*, 150.
18 Addams, *Democracy and Social Ethics*, 219.
19 James Addams, *The Long Road of Women's Memory* (Champaign, IL: University of Illinois Press, 2002).
20 Addams, *The Long Road*, 59.
21 Ibid, 59.

> He regretted that he was so accustomed to analysis that his mind would not let the general situation alone but wearily went over it again and again; and then he added that this war was tearing down the conception of government which had been so carefully developed during this generation in the minds of the very men who had worked hardest to fulfill that conception.

22 Ibid, 59.
23 Ibid, 60. The women continues saying, "They have known the daily stimulus of a wide and free range of contacts. They have become interpenetrated with the human consciousness of fellow scientists all over the world."
24 Ibid, 129.
25 Jane Addams, *The Excellent Becomes the Permanent* (New York: The Macmillan Company, 1932).
26 See Charlene Haddock Seigfried, "A Pragmatist Response to Death: Jane Addams on the Permanent and the Transient," *The Journal of Speculative Philosophy*, New Series, 21(2), Essays from the Meeting of the Society for the Advancement

of American Philosophy (2007): 133–41 (9 pages), Published By: Penn State University Press.
27 Seigried, "A Pragmatist Response to Death," 134.
28 Addams, *The Excellent Becomes Permanent*, 160–1.
29 Ibid, 161.
30 Addams, *The Long Road of Woman's Memory*, 67.
31 Ibid, 63.
32 See Addams, *Newer Ideals of Peace*, 18.
33 Ibid, 115.
34 Ibid, 100.
35 See Jane Duran, *Toward a Feminist Epistemology* (Savage, MD: Rowman & Littlefield Publishers, Inc., 1991), for a thoroughly comprehensive and uniquely insightful survey of the field of feminist and "naturalistic" epistemology.
36 Addams, *The Long Road of Woman's Memory*, 3. Childhood memories are brought to play in a present-day context, just as Addams reflects on images of her travel experiences, then relating those memories to the symbolic meanings embodied in ancient relics.
37 Ibid, 6. "It may suggest one more of obligations to Memory, that Protean Mother, who first differentiated primitive man from the brute; who makes possible our complicated modern life so daily dependent on the experiences of the past; and upon whom at the present moment is thrust the sole responsibility for guarding, for future generations, our common heritage of mutual good-will."
38 Joslin, *Jane Addams: A Writer's Life*, 200.
39 Addams, *The Long Road of Women's Memory*, 79.
40 Addams, *Newer Ideals of Peace*, 16. "An American philosopher has lately reminded us of the need to discover in the social realm the moral equivalent for war—something heroic that will speak to me as universally as war has done, and yet will be compatible with their spiritual nature as war has proved itself to be incompatible."
41 See Robert Ackerman, *The Myth and Ritual School: J.G. Frazer and the Cambridge Ritualists* (New York: Garland Pub, 1991) and K.J. Phillips, "Jane Harrison and Modernism," *Journal of Modern Literature*, 17(4) (Spring 1991): 465–76.
42 See Jane Ellen Harrison, *Ancient Art and Ritual* (The Project Gutenberg EBook: EBook #17087: Release Date: November 18, 2005).
43 Harrison, *Ancient Art and Ritual*, 136.
44 Ibid.
45 Ibid, 71–2.

> A very little consideration shows that he performs at first no abstraction at all; abstraction is foreign to his mental habit. He begins with a vague excited dance to relieve his emotion. That dance has, probably almost from the first,

a leader; the dancers choose an actual *person*, and he is the root and ground of *personification*. There is nothing mysterious about the process; the leader does not "embody" a previously conceived idea, rather he begets it. From his personality springs the personification. The abstract idea arises from the only thing it possibly can arise from, the concrete fact. Without *perception* there is no *con*ception. We noted in speaking of dances (p. 43) how the dance got generalized; how from many commemorations of actual hunts and battles there arose the hunt dance and the war dance. So, from many actual living personal May Queens and Deaths, from many actual men and women decked with leaves, or trees dressed up as men and women, arises *the* Tree Spirit, *the* Vegetation Spirit, *the* Death.

46 See Mary Jo Deegan, *Jane Addams: Social Reform and the Symbolic Interactionists* (New York: Routledge, 2017), Chapter 5.

47 George Herbert Mead, "The Imagination in Wundt's Treatment of Myth and Religion," *Psychological Bulletin* 3 (1906): 393–9. Mead writes,

> It would be difficult to convince one who approached without psychological presuppositions the history of primitive art and mythology, that the functions which the early products of a constructive imagination fulfilled in the social life of the group did not determine the psychological growth of the products themselves, that the function which the aesthetic image had in the social consciousness was not active until the product arose in response to the simple demand for a carrier of the feelings, that the selection which must have been responsible for their preservation had nothing to do with the inner activities by which they were produced; and yet this seems to me the logical result of Wundt's analysis. In a word, for him, the aesthetic image, whether existing simply in the mind or embodied in an outer form, has no function beyond that of responding to and heightening the affective experience. If such a statement seems an adequate psychological interpretation of the ideal artist and his creations it certainly breaks down when applied to primitive art.

48 Addams, "Helen Castle Mead," 17–23, https://brocku.ca/MeadProject/Addams/HelenMeadTribute.html1/4/2019, 11:17 am Central Standard Time.

49 Ibid.

50 George Herbert Mead, "The Social Nature of the Present," *The Philosophy of the Present*, ed. Arthur E. Murphy (LaSalle, IL: Open Court, 1932), 47. Mead writes, "A social character can belong only to the moment at which emergence takes place that is to a present."

51 Mead, *Philosophy of the Present*, 31. "If we had every possible document and every possible monument from the period of Julius Caesar we should unquestionably have a truer picture of the man and of what occurred in his life-time, but it would

be a truth which belongs to this present, and a later present would reconstruct it from the standpoint of its own emergent nature." Also, ibid, 88. "And this involves both the past and the future. In a sense his present takes in the whole undertaking, but it can accomplish this only by symbolic imagery, and since the undertaking is a whole that stretches beyond the immediate specious presents, these slip into each other without any edges."

52 Ibid, 52. "The social nature of the present arises out of its emergence. I am referring to the process of readjustment that emergence involves." Also, ibid, 47. "A social character can belong only to the moment at which emergence takes place, that is to a present… This function is a continual reconstruction as a chronicle to serve the purposes of present interpretation."

53 George Herbert Mead, *The Philosophy of the Act* (Chicago, IL: The University of Chicago Press, 1938), 54.

> But still more fundamentally, the building-up of a memory record involves, in the first place, a social world as definitely as the physical world, within which the events took place, and involves, in the second place, experience which was actually or potentially social in its nature to the extent that whatever happens or has happened to us has its character over against actual or possible audiences or observers whose selves are essential to the existence of ourselves, the mechanism of whose conversation is not only as immediate as our replies but, when imported into the inner forum, constitutes the mechanism of our own thought.

54 Mead, *Philosophy of the Present*, 33.

55 Ibid, 32. "The past and the future that appear in the present may be regarded as merely the thresholds of a minute bit of an unbounded extension whose metaphysical reality reduces the present to a negligible element that approaches the world in an instant." "The study of passage involves the discovery of events. These cannot be simply parts of passage. These events have always characters of uniqueness. Time can only arise through the ordering of passage by these unique events."

56 Ibid, 168.

> In the process of communication the individual is an other before he is a self. It is in addressing himself in the role of an other that his self arises in experience. The growth of the organized game out of simple play in the experience of the child, and of organized group activities in human society, placed the individual then in a variety of roles, in so far as these were parts of the social act, and the very organization of these in the whole act gave them a common character in indicating what he had to do. He is able then to become a generalized other

in addressing himself in the attitude of the group or the community. In this situation he has become a definite self over again the social whole to which he belongs.

57 Ibid, 175.
58 George Herbert Mead, "Fragments on the Process of Reflection," *The Philosophy of the Act*, ed. Charles W. Morris with John M. Brewster, Albert M. Dunham and David Miller, (Chicago, IL and London, UK: The University of Chicago Press, 1938), 81.
59 Mead, *The Philosophy of the Act*, 54.

> Memory images constitute but a minute part of the past that stretches out behind you. For most of it we depend upon records, which come back to one form or another of language, and we refresh our memory as really in inquiring of a companion what took place on a certain occasion as in questioning ourselves. His testimony may not be as trustworthy as our own because of difference of interest and possible prejudice, but on other occasions for the same reason his testimony may outrank our own in reliability. While the actual image of the event has an evidential character that is peculiar, not infrequently it may be shown by the testimony of others to have been the product of imagination or to have been shifted from its proper place in the record. But still more fundamentally, the building-up of a memory record involves, in the first place, a social world as definitely as the physical world, within which the events took place, and involves, in the second place, experience which was actually so potentially social in its nature to the extent that whatever happens or has happened to us has its character over against actual or possible audiences or overseers whose selves are essential to the existence of our own selves, the mechanism of whose conversation is not only as immediate as our replies, but, when imported into the inner forum, constitutes the mechanism of our own thought.
>
> 54.

60 Ibid, 498.

> A human community there must be, and there can be no human community unless it recognizes the values that are the goals of its strivings. As it is possible to find all the essential physiological processes of the most complex animal form in the life process of an amoeba, so we can discover in a primitive community all the functions that answer to the structures of highly elaborated institutions in complex societies, and these functions must persist even if the values which the institutions mediate find themselves in conflict.

61 Ibid, 503.

> As I think I have indicated, there are two approaches to the problem. One of them starts from present unquestioned values and, setting up standards fashioned on these values, proposes social regulations that tend to restrain the reproduction of certain strains of human stocks that by these standards are undesirable. The other approach is from the reinterpretation of the situations within which our values appear and which are responsible for the cast they have taken on.

62 Addams, *The Long Road of Woman's Memory*, 5. "The deduction was obvious that mutual reminiscences perform a valuable function in determining analogous conduct for large bodies of people who have no other basis for mindedness."
63 Ibid, 5.
64 Ibid, 5.
65 Mead, *Philosophy of the Present*, 33. "Furthermore the study of passage involves the discovery of events. These cannot be simple parts of passage. These events have always characters of uniqueness."
66 Fischer, "Interpretation and Social Transformation: Reading Addams Through Mead," 2008, 44. https://www.iupui.edu/~mpsg/Essays/Fischer_Midwest_revised.pdf, accessed January 30, 2020, EST 12:30 pm. "He believed that ethics cannot proceed by applying abstract rules to a given problem, but that the values pertaining to a given situation emerge out of that situation. What is most important is to identify all of the various interests involved and take them into account."
67 Addams, *The Long Road of Woman's Memory*, 9.
68 Ibid, 23.
69 Ibid, 23.
70 Ibid, 23.
71 Elena Ferrante, *My Brilliant Friend*, trans. Ann Goldstein (New York: Europa Editions, 2016), 33.
72 Addams, *Democracy and Social Ethics*, 71–2.
73 Ibid, 230–1.
74 Sarah Begley, "The Historical Truth behind Elena Ferrante's Neapolitan Novels." Sarah Begley, August 31, 2015. *Time*, History/Books, http://time.com/4010504/neapolitan-novels-hisotry, accessed January 30, 2020, EST 12:30 pm.
75 See Addams, *Democracy and Social Ethics*, 231.

> The alderman therefore bails out his constituents when they are arrested, or says a good word to the police justice when they appear before him for trial, uses his pull with the magistrate when they are likely to be fined for a civil misdemeanor, or sees what he can do to "fix up matters" with the state's attorney when the charge is really a serious one, and in doing this he follows the ethics held and practiced by his constituents. All this conveys the impression to the simple-minded that law is not enforced, if the lawbreaker has a powerful friend.

One may instance the alderman's action in standing by an Italian padrone of the ward when he was indicted for violating the civil service regulations.

76 Elena Ferrante, *Those Who Leave and Those Who Stay*, trans. Ann Goldstein (New York: Europa Editions, 2013), 280.
77 Roberto Saviano, *Gomorrah*, trans. Virginia Jewiss, (New York: Picador, 2007).
78 Deborah Acosta, "Step into a Refugee Camp." *New York Times*, website, December 30, 2016 | 10:48, https://www.nytimes.com/video/world/middleeast/.../who-are-the-syrian-refugees, accessed January 30, 2020, EST 12:30 pm.
79 See "Teenage Syrian Refugees 'Team Hope' win at Dubai Robotics Competition," Website NUAE, *The National*, October 27, 2019. https://www.thenational.ae/uae/teenage-syrian-refugees-team-hope-win-at-dubai-robotics-competition-1.929490.
80 Addams, *Newer Ideals of Peace*, 166.
81 George Herbert Mead, "Review of the Newer Ideals of Peace by Jane Addams." *American Journal of Sociology*, 13 (1907): 122–3.

Chapter 8

1 See Alain Locke, "Unity Through Diversity: A Bahá'í Principle," *The Bahá'í World: A Biennial International Record*, Vol. IV, April 1930–1932 (New York: Bahá'í Publishing Committee, 1933; Wilmette, IL: Bahá'í Publishing Trust, 1980), 372–74, reprinted in Alain Locke, The Bahá'í World: A Biennial International Record.
2 Alain Locke, *The Works of Alain Locke*, ed. Charles Molesworth (New York: Oxford University Press, 2012), 494.
3 Alain Locke, "Value and Imperative," *American Philosophy Today and Tomorrow*, ed. Horace M. Kallen, Sidney Hook (Freeport, NY: Books for Libraries Press, 1935, 1968), 313. Locke offers a mini-biography of his ideas he then calls a psychograph.
4 See Kenneth R. Manning, *Black Apollo, The Life of Ernest Everett Just* (New York and Oxford: Oxford University Press, 1983), 3–36. Kenneth R. Manning writes a description of the poverty and discrimination experienced by most Negros, when Locke was born, and most of his friends, in his biography of E.E. Just.
5 See Alain Locke, *The Concept of Value* (Washington, DC: Howard University, Alain Locke Papers, Coll. 164, Boxes 156, 157, 158, 1907–1910). See Finding Aid, by Staff, October 1, 2015—"Literary Heritage." 1907–1910. Studied at Hertford College, Oxford University, as the first Black Rhodes scholar wrote thesis, "Concept of Value."
6 See Leonard Harris and Charles Molesworth, *Alain L. Locke: The Biography of a Philosopher* (Chicago, IL and London, UK: The University of Chicago Press, 2008), 94.
7 See Harris and Molesworth, *Alain L. Locke: The Biography of a Philosopher,* 132.

8   Alain Locke, "The Ethics of Culture," *The Philosophy of Alain Locke: Harlem and Renaissance and Beyond* (Philadelphia, PA: Temple University Press, 1989), 177.
9   Harris and Molesworth, *Alain L. Locke: The Biography of a Philosopher*, 110.
10 Ibid, 133. Harris and Molesworth write, "This meant that all value judgments had a typical basis in feeling and yet had substantial structures that prevented them from being purely subjective. No one, Locke argued, is satisfied with the 'rigidly objective or the rigidly subjective interpretation of values.'"
11 Leonard Harris, "Introduction to 'Values and Imperatives,'" *The Philosophy of Alain Locke*, ed. Alaine Locke, (Philadelphia: Temple University Press, 1989), 31.
12 See Alain Locke, "Value and Culture," *The Works of Alain Locke*, ed. Charles Molesworth, (Oxford, England: Oxford University Press, 2012), 464. As well as see Harris and Molesworth, *Alain L. Locke: The Biography of a Philosopher*, 291. Harris and Molesworth explain while quoting Locke's "Value and Culture":

> Implicitly addressing Du Bois and others who were insisting that racism could be eliminated only through economic struggle based in class consciousness, Locke takes a meliorist view. In concluding his essay, he proposed a "non-Marxian principle of maximizing values." This was the idea of "loyalty to loyalty," the notion first advanced by Royce when Locke was still a student at Harvard. Locke summarizes Royce's argument: "In its larger outlines and implications it proclaimed a relativism of values and a principle of reciprocity." If "transposed to all the fundamental value orders," the notion of a loyalty to loyalty meant "reverence for reverence, toleration between moral systems, reciprocity in art, and had so good a metaphysician been able to conceive it, relativism in philosophy." Locke concludes by imagining a religion, a morality, an art, and a philosophy that would all be able to see that values were forms of feeling, but this did not mean values were phantasms or self-indulgences. Rather, they formed a set of truths that could be changed, tested by experience, and made into a way of corroborating ourselves and the allegiances that lie behind our common humanity.

13 Locke, "Value and Culture," 464.
14 See W. Malcolm Byrnes, "EE Just and Creativity in Science, the Importance of Diversity." *Journal of African American Studies* (New Brunsw), 19(3) (September 2015): 264–78. Doi:10:1007/s12111-015-9305-1.
15 Leonard Harris, "Outing Alain Locke: Empowering the Silenced," *Sexual Identities, Queer Politics*, ed. Mark Blasis (Princeton, NJ: Princeton University Press, 2001), 323.
16 Jeffrey C. Stewart, *The New Negro: The Life of Alain Locke*, (Oxford, NY: Oxford University Press, 2018), 452. Stewart makes a case for Locke's aesthetics in terms of diversity, rather than elitism, noting Locke's championing of Black gay artists. Also, Stewart points out that Locke's advocacy for "The Talented Tenth" was a means for

raising the economic standards of Blacks by way of educated leadership. Stewart concludes that although Locke was drawn to associate with social circles of rich, educated, and well-respected people, he thought that Black people could enjoy sophisticated lives while striving for full liberation from White privilege.

17 Locke, "Value and Culture," 457.
18 Locke, "Values and Imperatives," 40.

> For every value coupled by judgmental predication, thousands are linked by identities of feeling-mode; for every value transformed by change of logical pre-suppositions, scores are switched by a radical transformation of the feeling-attitude. We are forced to conclude that the feeling quality, irrespective of content, makes a value of a given kind, and that a transformation of the attitude effects a change of type in the value situation.

19 Locke, "Value and Culture," 457.
20 Locke, "Values and Imperatives," 44.
21 Locke, "Value and Culture," 460. "But by the theory that values are constituted by the primary modal quality of the actual feeling one does not have to go beyond that to explain the accurate appropriateness of the unusual predicates or the actuality of the attitude in the valuation. They are in direct functional relation and agreement." 44. "Here it is able to account for value conversions and value opposition in terms of the same factors, and thus apply a common principle of explanation to value mergings, transfers and conflicts. It is with this range of phenomena that the logical theories of value experience their greatest difficulties."
22 Feeling modes lay a nonrigid structure for an ethics, by which we can easily synthesize the content and context of our lives. We should keep in mind that new attitudes toward old values create new ground for cultures and progressive values, as well as expanding one's sense of who you are in relation to others.
23 Alain Locke, "A Functional View of Value Ultimates," *The Philosophy of Alain Locke*, ed. Leonard Harris (Philadelphia: Temple University Press, 1989), 91.
24 Locke, "A Functional View of Value Ultimates," 91.
25 Alain Locke, "Self Criticism the Third Dimension of Culture," *The Works of Alain Locke*, ed. Charles Molesworth, (Oxford, England: Oxford University Press, 2012), 485.
26 Richard Shusterman, "Pragmatist Aesthetics: Roots and Radicalism," *The Critical Pragmatism of Alain Locke*, ed. Leonard Harris (Oxford: Rowman & Littlefield Publishers, Inc., 1999), 97–110. Shusterman goes on to lay out twelve principles of pragmatic aesthetics, which Locke's philosophy helps to disclose.
27 See Alain Locke, "Frontiers of Culture," *The Philosophy of Alain Locke*, ed. Charles Molesworth, (Oxford, England: Oxford University Press, 2012), 231. Locke writes:

I, too, confess that at one time of my life I may have been guilty of thinking of culture as cake contrasted with bread. Now I know better. Real, essential culture is baked into our daily bread or else it isn't truly culture. In short, I am willing to stand firmly on the side of the democratic, rather than the aristocratic notion of culture and have so stood for many years, without having gotten full credit, however.

28 *Negro in Art: a Pictorial Record of the Negro Artist*, ed. and commentary Alain Locke (New York: Hacker Art Book, 1979), 291.
29 See Frank Mehring, "'The Unfinished Business of Democracy': Transcultural Confrontations in the Portraits of the German-American Artist Winold Reiss," *American Artists in Munich. Artistic Migration and Cultural Exchange Processes*, ed. Christian Fuhrmeister, Hubertus Kohle, and Veerle Thielemans (München: Deutscher Kunstverlag, 2009), 193–210. Reiss and Locke enjoyed a long-term friendship and collaborated on the journal/books mentioned as well as Locke's special edition of the *Survey Graphic: Harlem Mecca of the New Negro*, Vol. VI, No. 6 (New York: Metropolitan Life Insurance Company, March, 1925).
30 *The New Negro*, ed. Alain Locke (New York: Simon & Schuster, 1925).
31 Frank Mehring, "The Visual Harlem Renaissance: Or Winold Reiss in Mexico." *Amerikastudien/American Studies*, 55(4) African American Literary Studies: New Texts, New Approaches, New Challenges (2010): 633.
32 Mehring, "The Unfinished Business of Democracy," 201.
33 See: Richard J Bernstein, *The Pragmatic Roots of Cultural Pluralism*, The New School, July 23, 2014, https://www.resetdoc.org/story/the-pragmatic-roots-of-cultural-pluralism/. Also see Horace M. Kallen, "Democracy versus the Melting Pot I." *Nation*, 100(2590) (1915): 190–4. "Democracy versus the Melting Pot II: A Study of American Nationality." *Nation*, 100(2591) (1915): 217–20. Kellar includes cultural pluralism but does not stress the importance of individual difference, as Locke. Kallen was a long-time colleague of Locke's. Locke and Kallen knew each other throughout their lives, beginning with their Harvard undergraduate days.
34 Schomburg Center for Research in Black Culture, Manuscripts, Archives and Rare Books Division, New York Public Library. "The Brown Madonna," New York Public Library Digital Collections. http://digitalcollections.nypl.org/items/510d47df-958e-a3d9-e040-e00a18064a99, accessed February 14, 2020.
35 Alain Locke, "Who and What Is Negro?" *Philosophy of Alain Locke*, ed. Leonard Harris (Philadelphia: Temple University Press., 1989), 213.
36 Locke, "Who and What Is Negro?" 213.
37 Ibid, 213.
38 Sargent Johnson, *Mother and Child*, Frontispiece, Color Plate, *Negro in Art: A Pictorial Record of the Negro Artist*, ed. and commentary Alain Locke (New York: Hacker Art Book, 1979), 291.

39 See Jonathan Marks, *Is Science Racist?* (Cambridge, UK and Malden, MA: Polity Press, 2017).
40 Locke, "Who and What Is Negro?" 214.
41 Byrnes, "E.E. Just and Creativity in Science," 264–78. Published online June 24, 2015. doi: 10.1007/s12111-015-9305-1. Note that a shorter, modified version of this article was published under the title "The Forgotten Father of Epigenetics." *American Scientist*, 103 (March–April 2015): 106–9.
42 Byrne, "E.E. Just and Creativity in Science," 269.

> Consistent with Just's theory, a recent finding in cell and developmental biology may indicate that chromosomes have the ability to absorb factors from the cytoplasm during development. Pagliara et al. (2014) discovered that the nuclei of differentiation embryonic stem cells tend to acquire a property known as "auxeticity," that is, they expand when stretched, much the same way that a wad of balled-up paper expands when it is stretched. The physiological significance of this recent finding is unknown, but it could mean that the chromosomes of the cells can, in a selective sponge-like manner, absorb different sets of cytoplasmic factors as they change into various cell types (i.e., as they differentiate). If this is found to be true, then Just will have been more correct than one could have imagined.

43 See W. Malcolm Byrnes, "The Forgotten Father of Epigenetics." Website: American Scientist, https://www.americanscientist.org/article/the-forgotten-father-of-epigenetics, accessed January 2020 EST 12:45 am.
44 Byrnes, "The Forgotten Father of Epigenetics," website: American Scientist, https://www.americanscientist.org/article/the-forgotten-father-of-epigenetics. Byrnes explains Locke's thinking in this respect:

> A philosopher-turned-anthropologist, Locke argues that nations will prosper when they foster cultural exchange among the different racial or ethnic groups within and across their borders. He advocated for a kind of free trade between groups, emphasizing that the healthiest societal relationship is one in which each group is able to offer something of value to the other, and each group respects the other in autonomy.

45 Ernest Everett Just, *The Biology of the Cell Surface* (Philadelphia, PA: P. Blakiston's Son & Co., Inc., 1939), 367. Just writes, "Life is not only a struggle against the surroundings from which life came; it is also a co-operation with them. The Kropotkin theory of mutual aid and co-operation may be a better explanation of the cause of evolution than the prevailing popular conception of Darwin's idea of the struggle for existence."
46 Just, *The Biology of the Cell Surface*, 356. "Living substance cannot be considered abstracted either from time or from space. The organism cannot be separated from

its environment; they form together one inter-acting system. Two predominating characteristics exhibited by living organisms are: first, those changes which are time-ordered; and second, those which are environment-conditioned."

47 Ibid, 367.
48 Ibid, 356. "Living substance cannot be considered abstracted either from time or from space. The organism cannot be separated from its environment; they form together one inter-acting system. Two predominating characteristics exhibited by living organisms are: first, those changes which are time-ordered; and second, those which are environment-conditioned."
49 Maurizio Esposito, *Romantic Biology* (London: Pickering & Chatto, 2013).
50 Just, *Biology of the Cell*, 365.
51 John Dewey, "The Future of Philosophy," *The Later Works,* Vol. 17 1825–1953, Miscellaneous Works, ed. Jo Ann Boydston (Carbondale and Edwardsville: Southern University Press, 2008), 466.
52 Locke, " A Functional View of Value Ultimates," 83.Such a reduction of the position of all value functionalism to the ultra-relativism of the positivists is arbitrary and unwarranted. Granted that some relativist interpretations of value are subjective as to be completely atomistic and anarchistic, that is not the case with all. Particularly is this so with a type of analysis whose main objective is to give a consistent account of the relative permanencies of value-modes and their normative criteria and the readily observable phenomena of value change and value transposition in a way that they will not contradict one another.
53 John Dewey, *Art as Experience* (New York: Penguin Group, 1934), 352.
54 Locke, *The Philosophy of Alain Locke*, 89.
55 Ibid, 124.
56 See John Dewey, "The Logic of Judgments of Practice," *The Middle Work of John Dewey 1899–1924*, ed. Jo Ann Boydston (Carbondale, IL: Southern Illinois Press, 1915), Vol. 8, 47.
57 Locke, *The Philosophy of Alain Locke,* 125.
58 Ibid, 120. "In general, it may be concluded that since values inhere in all the "facts" that are recognized as such, they are themselves facts, and that the antithesis between values and facts cannot be made absolute. Values are not simply fortuitous and gratuitous and should be eliminated by strict science but are essential to cognitive process and compatible with any sort and degree of objectivity Facts too are always reactions—upon prior facts—and are generated by their evaluation: and, moreover, these prior facts may have been merely hypothetical, constructs recommended by their prospective value."
59 Leonard Harris, Intro to Locke's "A Functional View of Value Ultimates," 80.
60 Ibid.
61 Ibid.

62 Locke, "A Functional View of Value Ultimates," 82.
63 See Byrne, "E.E. Just and Creativity in Science."
64 Marks, *Is Science Racist?* 9. Marks explains that scientific racism has continued to take many forms since the 1800s. Referring to the racist writings and comments made by James Watson, the father of molecular genetics, and Nobel Laureate for the discover of DNA, Marks writes: Watson's comments about the relative innate intelligence of races [were] in fact quite normative for the biology and anthropology of the mid-1800's. Although other scientific fashions have come and gone since then—for example, creationism, the idea that species were zapped into existence, independently of one another; or phrenology, the idea that the fine features of the skull revealed the mental traits or personality quirks of its bearer: or eugenics, the idea that the state should take it upon itself to breed a better form of citizen, primarily through programs of mass sterilization—racism has never departed, even though it has taken several guises. Indeed, a testament to the power of racism in science is that it has only been minimally affected by the emergence of Darwinism.
65 "Moonlight," Barry Jenkins, Screenplay, Rarell Alvin McCraney, Story Writer (United State: A24 Copyright Holder; Plan B Entertainment, Pastel Productions, Production, 2016), A24 Rights Holder.
66 Alain Locke and Bernhard Joseph Stern, "Intro to Superiority Creeds and Race Thinking," *When Peoples Meet: A Study in Race and Culture Contacts*, Alain Locke and Bernhard Joseph Stern, (New York: Hinds, Hayden and Eldredge, 1946), 421–2. Locke lays out the consensus of social scientists to attest to the spuriousness of the term: "History, carefully traced, suggests social causes and historical explanation for practically everyone of the group traits commonly assigned by racialist doctrine to biological and hereditary factors."
67 Alain Locke, "Intro to 'Types of Social Change,'" *When People Meet: A Study of Race and Culture*, ed. Alain Locke and Bernhard Joseph Stern, (New York, New York: Hinds, Hayden and Eldredge, 1946), 234. Locke writes:

> Ironically enough, many a maharajah, looking down through centuries of caste tradition on subordinate layers of Hindu of superimposed political caste, with the minister resident or colonial "adviser" its obdurate symbol. This cannot be construed as mere political society, now finds himself the victim restriction and hierarchy as prevails between rulers of varying rank, for accompanying it is the arbitrary dictation of the governing group mores andetiquette as a symbol of cultural superiority superseding the traditional native etiquette.

68 Alain Locke, "Intro to 'Types of Social Cleavage,'" *When People Meet*, 240.
69 Locke, "Types of Social Cleavage," 236.

70 Locke and Stern, Intro to "Superiority Creeds and Race Thinking," 422–3. The complete quote is revealing:

> Racialism has become so inveterate a habit in popular thinking, however, that it carries on unabashed by scientific contradiction in many instances. Toynbee devotes passing but devastating attention to some of the more popular brands of race bias. So trivial or contrary to fact are most of these, that it is quite obvious that they not only originate on the level of uncritical thinking but remain there throughout their use and acceptance. They are entertained as unquestioned tribalisms, building up the norm of the group into a criterion for universal application. These are the equivalents in the sphere of physical qualities of the social contrast-concepts previously analyzed.

71 See Marks, *Is Science Racist?*, 15, Figure 1.1, "Frontispiece" of the 1868 first German edition of Ernst Haeckel's *The History of Creation* (Courtesy of the Max Planck Institute for the History of Science, Berlin).

72 Locke, "Frontiers of Culture," 236.

73 Harris, "Outing Alain Locke," 330 (complete essay for bibliography, 321–41).

74 Locke, "Frontiers of Culture," 236.

75 Stefanie Laufs, *Fighting a Movie with Lightening: "The Birth of a Nation" and the Black Community* (Hamburg: Anchor Academic Publishing, 2013), 39.

> It is also argued that Wilson, after seeing the movie said "It is like writing history with lightening. And my only regret is that it is all so terribly true," It is not clear if he ever made this statement. However, by using the real or fictitious approval of the president in newspapers as a means of publicity, Dixon and Griffith most probably assured a curiosity regarding the movie in the general public.
>
> 13.
>
> For more information also see: Melvyn Stokes, *D.W. Griffith's "The Birth of a Nation: A History of the Most Controversial Motion Picture of All Time"* (Oxford: Oxford University Press, 2007), 27, 55.

76 Laufs, *Fighting a Movie with Lightening*, 38–9. Laufs highlights the Harlem Renaissance, focused by Locke's "The New Negro." She combines Locke's and Dubois's views, while citing Booker T. Washington and other important Black social activists. She explains and quotes Locke: "A famous leader and spokesperson of the cultural New Negro movement, Alain Locke, stated that the time of 'mental passive resistance' had not advanced the black community in their fight for equal rights and freedom, but insisted direct actions that started in the northern USA were the key to acceptance and equality. In his thinking he was quite similar to WEB Dubois."

77 Harris, Brief Commentary, "Frontiers of Culture," 229.

78 See Glen Burch, "The FCS and the Film Council Movement." *Hollywood Quarterly*, University of California Press, 5(2) (Winter 1950): 138–43. In the 1950s Locke was on the board of the Film Council of America. Edgar Dale, who was also a member of the FCA advisory, explains that the organization was a nonprofit educational organization, whose members were devoted to "help people interested in films to get in touch with one another and to cooperate in using films to improve the quality of living in the United States."
79 See Locke, "Frontiers of Culture," 229–38. The other films mentioned are *Intruder in the Dust*, and *Home of the Brave*.
80 *The Quiet One*, 1948, U.S.A., 1 hour 5 min, documentary drama, distributed by Arthur Mayer and Joseph Borstyn, directed by Sidney Meyers, produced by Janice Loeb, written by Helen Levitt, Janice Loeb, Sidney Meyers, James Agee.
81 See Locke, "Frontiers of Culture," The Philosophy of Alain Locke, 229–38. The other films mentioned are, "Intruder in the Dust," and "Home of the Brave." See "The Quiet One," 1948, U.S.A., 1 hour 5 min, Documentary Drama, Distributed by Arthur Mayer and Joseph Borstyn, Directed by Sidney Meyers, Produced by Janice Loeb, Written by Helen Levitt, Janice Loeb, Sidney Meyers, James Agee, 503.
82 See Alain Locke, "Freud and Scientific Morality," *The Works of Alain Locke*, ed. Charles Molesworth, (Oxford, England: Oxford University Press, 2012), 502,

> Dynamic psychology has plunged into this cauldron of the times and found most promising clues. The diagnosis is disillusioning and hard to face, but under the scrutiny of social psycho-analysis society turns out to be the Great Sinner by reason of its own unresolved value irrationalities. We get the frank verdict of a sick society schizoid in terms of professing conflicting values, with no clear indication of priority and no radical effort to resolve the self-contradictions.

83 Locke, "Freud and Scientific Morality," 501–2. "This, in final analysis, is to make morals basically a socio-biological matter, where individual character and personality patterns are products primarily of the interaction between individuals and their social environments, especially their early social experiences. The evil in man ceases to have metaphysical and theological explanation and implications."
84 Ibid, 502.
85 Ibid, 501.

> The Works of Alain Locke, 501, In all of this, of course, one does not confuse part explanation with the whole many-sided situation that is not to be accounted for in terms of psycho-analytic factors solely. Nor should one confound original Freudianism with the many modifications of later dynamic psychology and psychoanalytic theory. The significant point is that human behavior once approached from this realistic and objective Freudian point of view can never

revert to the old view of an original or permanent human nature of an absolute, arbitrary and unchanging morality which was its associated corollary.

86 Ibid, 502.
87 *Moonlight*, 2016, U.S.A., Director: Barry Jenkins, Producers: Adele Romanski, Jeremy Kleiner, Dede Gardner, Writers: Barry Jenkins (screenplay), Tarell Alvin McCraney (story by), Stars: Mahershala Ali, Shariff Earp, Duan Sanderson.
88 Harris, "Outing Alain Locke," 330.
89 Ibid, 330. Harris writes, "Even if Locke was misguided in this effort to control how African-American folk culture should be reformed and presented as embodying, aesthetic norms, he was not misguided in trying to bring it out of the closet. Moving from the closet into normality—whether the closet was that hiding racial and culturally reality or, by association, the closet of hiding homosexuality—Locke struggled to elevate, transform, and create universality in a way that allowed for diverse sexuality and cultural diversity respected in everyday life."
90 Ibid, 336. "Representing the interest of a particularity was thus representing the interest of humanity; promoting the unique features of Negro culture as a contribution to universal civilization—*tout court*, for the homosexual community."
91 Ibid, 339.

Chapter 9

1 John Dewey, *Art as Experience* (London: Penguin Books, 1934), 287.
2 David O'Hara, "Peirce, Plato and Miracles on the Mature Peirce's Re-discovery of Plato and the Overcoming of Nominalistic Prejudice in History." Arisbe: The Peirce Gateway, posted October 22, 2007.
3 Ibid.
4 O'Hara, footnote 32: Dylan Thomas, "The Force that Through the Green Fuse Drives the Flower." From *The Poems of Dylan Thomas*, published by New Directions. Copyright © 1952, 1953 Dylan Thomas. Copyright © 1937, 1945, 1955, 1962, 1966, 1967 the Trustees for the Copyrights of Dylan Thomas. Copyright © 1938, 1939, 1943, 1946, 1971, 2003 New Directions Publishing Corp.
5 Charles Sanders Peirce, "The Normative Sciences," *The Essential Peirce* (Bloomington, IN: Indiana University Press, 1992), 201. "An object to be aesthetically good, must have a multitude of parts so related to one another as to impart a positive simple immediate quality to their totality, and whatever does this is, in so far, esthetically good, no matter what the particular quality of the total be."
6 Peirce, *The Essential Peirce,* Vol. 2, "The Three Normative Sciences," 202.

7   Ibid, 202.

> Whether or not this is really so, is a metaphysical question which it does not fall within the scope of normative science to answer. If it is not so, the aim is essentially unattainable. But just as in playing a hand of whist, when only three tricks remain to be played, the rule is to assume that the cards are so distributed that the odd trick can be made, so the rule of ethics will be to adhere to the only possible absolute aim, and to hope that it will prove attainable. Meantime, it is comforting to know that all experience is favorable to that assumption.

8   O'Hara, "Peirce, Plato and Miracles."
9   Peirce, "The Fixation of Belief," *The Essential Peirce Vol. II*, 111. "Thus both doubt and belief have positive effects upon us, though very different one. Belief does not make us act at once, but puts us into such a condition that we shall behave in a certain way, when the occasion arises. Doubt has not the least effect of this sort, but stimulates us to action. Until it is destroyed."
10 Peirce, "The Fixation of Belief," 114–15.
11 Ibid, 116.
12 The Essential Peirce, *The Three Normative Sciences*, 200.
13 Ibid.
14 Ibid, 203.
15 Peirce, "The Normative Sciences," 201.
16 Ibid.
17 William James, *The Sentiment of Rationality* (London and Bombay: Longmans; Green and Co., 1905), 69–70.
18 Phyllis Rooney, "Hypatia Feminist Pragmatist Revisionings of Reason, Knowledge, and Philosophy." May 1993 *Hypatia*, 8(2) (Spring 1993): 25.
19 James, *The Sentiment of Rationality*, 69–70.
20 Ibid, 109.
21 Ibid, 90.
22 John Dewey, "The Pragmatism of Peirce," *Journal of Philosophy, Psychology and Scientific Methods*, 13(26) (1916): 709–15, 712–13.
23 John Dewey, "Creative Democracy The Task Before Us," *The Philosopher of the Common Man*, ed. John Dewey (New York: Greenwood Press, 1968), 220–8.
24 Hilary Putnam and Ruth Anna Putnam, *A Reconsideration of Deweyan Democracy*, 63.S.Cal. L. Rev.1671 HeinOnline. https://heinonline.org/HOL/LandingPage?handle=hein.journals/scal63&div=46&id=&page=, accessed June 16, 2020.
25 Dewey, *Creative Democracy the Task Before Us*, 222.
26 Ibid.
27 Dewey, *Art as Experience*, 362.

28 Jane Addams, *Democracy and Social Ethics* (Urbana and Chicago, IL: University of Illinois Press, 2002), 153.
29 For an excellent analysis of applying Addams pragmatic methods to complex social problems, see Danielle Lake, "Jane Addams and Wicked Problems: Putting the Pragmatic Method to Use." *The Pluralist*, 9(3) (2014): 77–94.
30 See Rodolfo Morrison, "Pragmatist Epistemology and Jane Addams: Fundamental Concepts for the Social Paradigm of Occupational Therapy," *Occupational Therapy International*, 23(4) (December 2016): 295–304.
31 Alain Locke, *The Philosophy of Alain Locke Harlem Renaissance and Beyond*, ed. Leonard Harris (Philadelphia, PA: Temple University Press, 1989), 110.
32 Locke, "The Ethics of Culture," *The Philosophy of Alain Locke*, 179.
33 Ibid, 182.
34 Ibid, 181.
35 Ibid, 185.
36 Ibid.
37 Locke, "Pluralism and Intellectual Democracy," *The Philosophy of Alain Locke*, 60.
38 See Janet Mignon Kucia, "Values in Rap Music, The Impact of Rapy Music on Audience Value Structure." The University of Southern Mississippi, the Aquila Digital Community, Summer 8-1-2001, dissertation.

Selected Bibliography

Classical American Philosophy Poiesis in Public

Addams, Jane. *Democracy and Social Ethics*. London, UK: The Macmillan Company, 1902.

Addams, Jane. *Newer Ideals of Peace*. New York, NY: The Chantagua Press, 1907.

Addams, Jane. *The Excellent Becomes the Permanent*. New York, NY: The Macmillan Company, 1932.

Addams, Jane. *The Long Road of Women's Memory*. Champaign, IL: University of Illinois Press, 2002.

Arendt, Hannah. *The Human Condition*. Chicago, IL: The University of Chicago Press, 1958.

Burke, Peter. *Popular Culture in Early Modern Europe*. New York, NY: New York University Press, 1978.

Covarrubias, Miguel. *Indian Art of Mexico and Central America*. New York, NY: Alfred A. Knopf, 1958.

Deffebach, Nancy. *María Izquierdo & Frida Kahlo: Challenging Visions in Modern Mexican Art*. Austin, TX: University of Texas Press, 2015.

Dewey, John. *Art as Experience*. New York, NY: Penguin Group, 1934.

Dewey, John. *The Philosopher of the Common Man*. New York, NY: Greenwood Press, 1968.

Dewey, John. *The Essential Dewey, Vol. 1: Pragmatism, Education, and Democracy*. Editors Larry A. Hickman and Thomas M. Alexander. Bloomington, IN: Indiana University Press, 1998a.

Dewey, John. *The Essential Dewey, Vol. 2: Ethics, Logic and Psychology*. Editors Larry A. Hickman and Thomas M. Alexander. Bloomington, IN: Indiana University Press, 1998b.

Dewey, John. *A Common Faith*. Introduction by Thomas M. Alexander. New Haven, CT: Yale University Press, 2013.

Dussel, Enrique. *The Underside of Modernity: Apel, Ricoeur, Rorty, Taylor, and the Philosophy of Liberation*. Translated and edited by Eduardo Mendieta. Atlantic Highland, NJ: Humanities Press, 1996.

Ferrante, Elena, *Those Who Leave and Those Who Stay*. Translated by Ann Goldstein. New York, NY: Europa Editions, 2013.

Ferrante, Elena. *My Brilliant Friend*. Translated by Ann Goldstein, New York, NY; Europa Editions, 2016.

Graves, Mark. *Mind, Brain and the Elusive Soul: Human Systems of Cognitive Science and Religion*. Hampshire, England, and Burlington, VT: Ashgate, 2008.
Hawkins, Erick. *The Body Is a Clear Place and Other Statements on Dance*. Pennington, NJ: Princeton Book Co., 1992.
James, William. *Principles of Psychology*, Volumes 1 and 2. New York, NY: Henry Holt 7 Co., 1890.
James, William. *Varieties of Religious Experience*. New York, NY: Penguin Group, 1902.
James, William. *The Sentiment of Rationality*. London and Bombay: Longmans, Green and Co., 1905.
James, William. *Meaning of Truth*. New York: Longmans, Green and Co., 1911.
James, William. *Essays in Radical Empiricism*. Cambridge, MA: Harvard University Press, 1976.
Kahlo, Frida. *The Diary of Frida Kahlo an Intimate Self-Portrait*. London: Bloomsbury, 1995.
Locke, Alaine L. *When Peoples Meet, a Study in Race and Culture Contacts*. New York, NY: Hinds, Hayden and Eldredge, 1946.
Locke, Alaine L. *The Philosophy of Alain Locke: Harlem and Renaissance and Beyond*. Edited by Leonard Harris. Philadelphia, PA, USA: Temple University Press, 1989.
Locke, Alaine L. *The Works of Alain Locke*. Edited by Charles Molesworth. New York, NY: Oxford University Press, 2012.
Mead, George Herbert. *The Philosophy of the Present*. Edited by Arthur E. Murphy. LaSalle, IL: Open Court, 1932.
Mead, George Herbert. *The Philosophy of the Act*. Chicago, IL: University of Chicago Press, 1938.
Mead, George Herbert. *Philosophy of the Present*. Amherst, NY: Prometheus Books, 2002.
Peirce, Charles Sanders. *Peirce on Signs: Writings on Semiotics*. Editor James Hoopes. Chapel Hill, NC and London: University of North Caroline Press, 1991.
Peirce, Charles Sanders. *The Essential Peirce, Volume 1: Selected Philosophical Writings (1867–1893)*. Bloomington, IN, and Indianapolis, IN, Illinois: Indiana University Press, 1992.
Peirce, Charles Sanders. *The Essential Peirce, Volume 2: Selected Philosophical Writings (1893–1913)*. Bloomington, IN, and Indianapolis, IN, Illinois: Indiana University Press, 1998.
Royce, Josiah. *The World and the Individual*. New York, NY, and London, UK: The Macmillan Company, 1900.
Royce, Josiah. *The Problem of Christianity: The Christian Doctrine of Life. Volume 1*. New York, NY: Macmillan Company, 1913a.
Royce, Josiah. *The Problem of Christianity: The Real World and the Christian Ideas. Volume 2*. New York, NY: Macmillan Company, 1913b.
Royce, Josiah. *The Problem of Christianity; Lectures Delivered at the Lowell Institute in Boston and at Manchester College, Volumes 1 and 2*. Oxford, UK, and Chicago, IL: Regnery Co, 1968.

Royce, Josiah. *Royce's Late Writing: A Collection of Unpublished and Scattered Works*. Edited and Introduction by Frank Oppenheim. Bristol, UK: Thoemmes Press, 2001.

Royce, Josiah. *The Basic Writings of Josiah Royce, Volume 1, Culture, Philosophy, and Religion*. Editor John McDermott. New York, NY: Fordham University Press, 2005a.

Royce, Josiah. *The Basic Writings of Josiah Royce, Volume 2, Logic, Loyalty and Community*. Editor John McDermott. New York, NY: Fordham University Press, 2005b.

Ryder, John. *The Things in Heaven and Earth: An Essay in Pragmatic Naturalism*. New York, NY: Fordham University Press, 2013.

Scheler, Max. *Formalism in Ethics and Non-Formal Ethics of Values*. Evanston, IL: Northwestern University Press, 1973.

Scheler, Max. *Centennial Essays*. Edited Manfred S. Frings. The Hague: Martinus Nijhof, 1974.

Scheler, Max. *Cognition and Work*. Translated Zachary Davis. Evanston, IL: Northwestern Press, 2020.

Tibol, Raquel. *Frida Kahlo an Open Life*. Translated by Elinor Randall. Albuquerque, New Mexico: University of New Mexico Press, 1993.

Wiener, Norbert. *Ex Prodigy: My Childhood and Youth*. Cambridge, MA and London, England: MIT Press, 1953.

Wiener, Norbert. *The Human Use of Human Beings: Cybernetics and Society*. Boston, MA: Da Capo Press, reprinted by arrangement with Houghton Mifflin Co., 1954.

Wiener, Norbert. *Invention: The Care and Feeding of Ideas*. Cambridge, MA, and London: The MIT Press, 1993.

Secondary

Ackerman, Robert. *The Myth and Ritual School: J.G. Frazer and the Cambridge Ritualists*. New York: Garland Pub, 1991.

Alexander, Thomas M. "Pragmatic Imagination." *Transactions of the Charles S. Peirce Society*, Vol. 26, No. 3 (Summer, 1990), 325–48.

Blasis, Mark, Editor. *Sexual Identities, Queer Politics*. New Jersey: Princeton University Press, 2001.

Deegan, Mary Jo. *Jane Addams: Social Reform and the Symbolic Interactionists*. New York, NY: Routledge, 2017.

Duran, Jane. *Toward a Feminist Epistemology*. Savage, MD: Rowman & Littlefield Publishers, Inc., 1991.

Fischer, Iris Smith. "Theatre at the Birth of Semiotics: Charles Sanders Peirce, François Delsarte, and Steele MacKaye." *Transactions of the Charles S. Peirce Society*, Vol. 49, No. 3 (Summer 2013), 371–94.

Fischer, Marilyn. *On Addams*. Australia, Canada, Mexico, Singapore, Spain, United Kingdom, and United States: Wadsworth: 2004.

Harris, Leonard, Editor. *The Critical Pragmatism of Alain Locke*. Lantham, MD: Rowman & Littlefield, 1999.

Harris, Leonard and Charles Molesworth. *Alain L. Locke: The Biography of a Philosopher*. Chicago, IL, and London, UK: The University of Chicago Press, 2008.

Harrington, Maurice, Editor. *Feminist Interpretations of Jane Addams*. University Park, PA: The Pennsylvania State University Press, 2010.

Hickman, Larry A., Stefan Neubert and Kerten Reich, Editors. *John Dewey between Pragmatism and Constructivism*. New York: Fordham University Press, 2009.

Joslin, Katherine. *Jane Addams: A Writer's Life*. Urbana, IL: University of Illinois Press, 2004.

Julius, Anthony. *T.S. Eliot, Anti-Semitism and Literary Form*. Cambridge, UK: Cambridge University Press, 1995.

Kallen, Horace Meyer. *American Philosophy Today and Tomorrow*. Freeport, NY: Books for Libraries Press, 1968.

Manning, Kenneth R. *Black Apollo, the Life of Ernest Everett Just*. New York, NY, and Oxford, UK: Oxford University Press, 1983.

Mahowald, Mary Briody. *An Idealistic Pragmatism: The Development of the Pragmatic Element in the Philosophy of Josiah Royce*. The Hague: Martinus Nijhoff, 1972.

Montagnini, Leone. *Harmonies of Disorder: Norbert Wiener: A Mathematician-Philosopher of Our Time*. Cham, Switzerland: Springer Publishing, 2017.

Ruyter, Nancy Lee Chaifa. "American Delsartism: Precursor of an American Dance Art, Educational Theatre." *Journal*, Vol. 25, No. 4 (December 1973), 420–35.

Shusterman, Richard. *Pragmatist Aesthetics: Living Beauty, Rethinking Art*. Lanham, MD, Boulder, CO, New York, N.Y., and Oxford: Rowman & Littlefield Publishers, Inc., 2000.

Stewart, Jeffery C. *The New Negro: The Life of Alain Locke*. New York, NY: Oxford University Press, 2018.

Trout, Lana. *The Politics of Survival Peirce, Affectivity, and Social Criticism*. New York, NY: Fordham University Press, 2010.

Wild, John Daniel. *The Radical Empiricism of William James*. Westport, CT: Greenwood Press, 1969, 1980.

Index

Acosta, Deborah
   memories of refugees 135–6
   "Step into a Refugee Camp" 135
activism 5, 35, 50, 70, 113–15, 123, 129, 175, 178–9
   Black 160
   creative 115, 135
   feminist 134
   Green Peace 201 n.73
   social 99, 114, 145
Addams, Jane 2–8, 29, 125, 133–6, 176
   cosmic patriotism 122
   cosmopolitanism 123
   Democracy and Social Ethics 113, 115, 224 n.13, 229–30 n.75
   democratic culture 132–3, 177
   The Excellent Becomes the Permanent 121
   feminism *vs.* militarism 120, 122
   feminist values 113–16, 122
   heroism 117–18, 122, 125
   Hull House community 129–30, 134, 137, 178
   and James 224 n.15
   The Long Road of Woman's Memory 118, 124, 128, 225 n.36, 229 n.62
   memory 114, 128–9
      cultural 113, 116–26, 129, 131, 137
      militarism 114–15, 120–1
   Newer Ideals of Peace 115, 117, 123, 136, 223 n.7, 225 n.40
   Peace and Bread in Time of War 91, 216–17 n.5
   storytelling 118–21, 123, 126
   values of solving social problems 177–8
aesthetic experiences 1–3, 6, 12, 15–17, 59–60, 68–70, 73, 79
aesthetic reasoning 14, 21–6, 28
agapism theory 11, 13, 17, 22, 28, 186 n.28
Alexander, Thomas M. 58, 67–8
   A Common Faith 210 n.11
   on James 67
   "Pragmatic Imagination" 207 n.45
American Folk music 51
Americanism 61
American Modern Dance 14, 17, 19, 21–2, 184 n.16. *See also* Modern Dance
ananchasm (circumstantial and logical), evolution 13
Ancient Greeks 9, 17, 19, 21, 24, 104, 106, 167
Anderson, Jon Lee, "Revolutionary Relic" 86
Anglo-European culture 36
Anglo-Saxon culture 105
anthropology 65
   cultural 21, 98–9, 142, 151
   Eurocentric 90
   philosophical 57, 105, 151
anti-Semitism 36–7
aperion 19
Arendt, Hannah 72, 77–9, 209 nn.6–7, 212 n.28
   and Kant 213 n.33
Aristotle 25, 190 n.58
art(s) 3–5, 7, 11, 13, 32, 34, 38, 44, 53–4, 59, 74, 91, 155, 157, 164, 169, 176, 178
   aesthetic values of 65
   artistic making 16, 58, 63–4
   Byzantine 72, 82
   communicative 92–6
   education 89
   humanistic 101
   and imaginative value-making 60–2
   Mexican 5, 97
   as relativistic value-making 144–50
   religious attitudes and 72
   and ritual 125
   as sign-making process 13–17
   and soul 57, 62–70
artifacts 11, 31, 48
   Aztec/pre-Aztec 98

cultural 30, 71, 73, 76, 79, 91–2, 94, 114, 172–3
  imaginative and political 78–82
  Peirce on 23
Artificial Intelligence (AI) 30–1, 39, 41–2, 45–7, 49–50
Artista, Joel, *IX Chel* 110
Attwood, Tony, "A Hard Rain's Gonna Fall" 202 n.83
Auxier, Randall 204 n.3

baroque 25, 133, 148
Baumgarten, Alexander Gottlieb 54
Beiner, Ronald
  "Hannah Arendt on Judging" 209 n.7
  Lectures on Kant's Political Philosophy 212 n.28
Bethune, Mary McLeod 147
Black art 144
Black culture/people (African American) 5, 140, 149, 160, 179
  Locke's promotion of 139, 143–4, 147, 149, 152, 160, 231–2 n.16, 237 n.76
  paintings 148–50
  violence against 47, 151, 180
Black Lives Matter 47, 50
black market 133
Boas, Franz 141
Bogatyrev, Petr 51, 202 n.80
  "Folk Song from a Functional Point of View" 202 n.76
Bouzard, Silvia Navarrete 219 n.28
Breton, André 103, 219 n.33
Burke, Peter 54, 203 n.87
  Popular Culture in Early Modern Europe 53
Byrnes, W. Malcom 152, 156
  "E.E. Just and Creativity in Science" 234 nn.41–2
  "The Forgotten Father of Epigenetics" 234 n.44
Byzantine art 72, 82

Cahill, Edgar Holger 92–3
Camorra (international crime organizations) 134–5
Child, Francis James 52
Christianity 19, 50, 80–2
  and Kahlo 100

collective memory 4, 51, 114–16, 123, 127, 129–30, 137
collective thinking 6, 123, 126
communism/communist 81, 91, 96–7, 103
community 12–13, 46, 68, 70, 126–8, 132, 168, 192 n.10, 228 n.60
  and communication 32–3, 122
  community building 68, 79, 86, 168
  community of interpretation 55
  community-oriented education 89–90, 109, 111
  community-oriented values 94, 100, 133, 148, 162–3, 169
  and culture 70, 86, 111, 154, 178
  dancing 24–5
  indigenous 89, 98, 105, 107, 111
  of inquiry 169
  LBGTQ 164
  life-community 68, 70
  scientific 6, 44, 50, 119–20, 151, 177
  social responsibility 178
  welfare programs 173
consciousness 3, 21, 41, 43, 59
  self-consciousness 53, 77, 140, 195 n.33
  social 9, 27, 32, 36
  synthetic 12
  unity of 59–60
Corocoran Gallery of Art 205 n.15
Corrington, Robert S. 32–3, 193 n.14
cosmic love 168
cosmopolitan/cosmopolitanism 89–90, 92–6, 110, 123
  Dewey's aesthetics 103–7
  naturalism 96–103
  pedagogy 107–11
Covarrubias, Miguel 98
creativity 15–16, 21, 28, 39, 41, 46, 58
  collective 31
  creative thinking 2, 4, 6, 43, 67, 119, 180
  individual 48–9, 152, 167, 180
  for Peirce 168
Crick, Nathan 108–9
crimes 9, 69, 134–5
critical thinking 4, 117, 148, 167, 172–4
cross-cultural relationships 200–1 n.64, 201 n.69
cultural attitude 81, 137, 139, 143, 154
cultural democracy 139, 143, 148, 150–9, 165, 177. *See also* democracy

cultural diversity 3–4, 10, 48, 80, 82
cultural dynamics 4, 60, 71, 89
cultural identity 49, 98, 102, 104, 162, 178–9
cultural memory 113, 116–26, 129, 131, 133, 135–7, 176
cultural pluralism 7, 21, 33, 44, 49, 140–1, 149, 176
cultural relativism 7, 142, 149, 151–2, 154
cultural systems 47, 201 nn.65–6
cultural values 1, 7, 30, 42, 53, 68, 71, 89, 91, 96, 134, 139–40, 145, 156, 162
culture wars 49–50, 165
cybernetics 30, 39–41
  of semantics 198 n.47

Dadaism 61
daimon (moral guide) 9
Dale, Edgar 238 n.78
dance/dancing 4, 11, 14–17, 19, 21
  community (roundel) 24–5
  dancer(s) 16, 20, 24–7, 191 n.64
  elements of (Plato's) 25–6
  spiral successive movements 20
Davis, Zachary 206 n.24
Dean, William, "Radical Empiricism and Religious Art" 214–15 n.48
Delsarte, Francois 19–20, 188 n.39, 188 n.45
Delsarte Method of elocution 17, 19–20
democracy 6–7, 9–10, 27, 71, 73, 77, 81, 88, 91, 95, 106, 133, 175–6. *See also* cultural democracy
democratic building therapies 178
demos 9
De Polignac, Edmond 190–1 n.63
Dewey, John 1–4, 7–8, 29, 58–9, 67–8, 107, 153, 156, 175, 178, 180, 183 n.1, 210 n.11, 211 n.17, 222 n.46
  on Addams's work 216–17 n.5
  and aesthetics 89, 91, 205 n.14
    naturalistic aesthetics 92–7, 176
  on art 217–18 n.12
  Art as Experience 5, 82, 85–6, 90, 92, 97, 103–4, 210 n.10, 213 n.36, 214 n.45, 217 n.6, 222 n.44
  Cahill on 92–3
  A Common Faith 73
  communicative art 92–6
  cosmopolitan/cosmopolitanism

  aesthetics 103–7
    naturalism 96–103
    pedagogy 107–11
    pragmatic 92–6
  "Creative Democracy: The Task Before Us" 175
  on culture 210 n.8
  democratic habits 175–6
  on education 89–91, 97
  The Essential Dewey, Volume 1 183 n.11, 213 n.37
  imagination 67–8, 79, 211–12 n.25
  intercultural values 91–2
  and Kahlo 97, 99
  Nature 82, 95
  Pappas on 91
  poiesis 167
  pragmatic naturalism 106
  The Public and Its Problems 107
  relative process of value-making 155
  religious experience 72–6, 78–80
  and Trotsky 97
discrimination 4–5, 22, 139, 158, 164, 189 n.54, 200 n.59, 230 n.4
diversity 7, 48, 137
  cultural 3–4, 10, 48, 80, 82
  social 4, 90
Dix, Otto 58, 60–1
  Fischer on painting of 69–70
  "Lustmord" 69
  Lustmord (Sex Murder) 208 n.51
  "Randegg in the Snow with Ravens" 64
  and Scheler 61, 70
Dubois, W. E. B. 147, 152, 160
Duran, Jane, *Toward a Feminist Epistemology* 225 n.35
Durer, Albert 101
Dussel, Enrique 90, 220 n.37
  ontology of social justice 103–7
  The Underside of Modernity: Apel, Ricoeur, Rorty, Taylor, and the Philosophy of Liberation 221 n.38
Dylan, Bob 35, 54
  "A Hard Rain's Gonna Fall" 52–3, 202 n.82

Eastern Orthodox religion 81, 83, 87
Ecce Homo self-portraits 100–1
education 5, 7, 53, 134
  art 89, 159

creative 108
  Dewey on 89–91
  mode of 109
  rural 109
Eisele, J. Christopher, "John Dewey and the Immigrants" 221–2 n.43
Eliot, T. S. 30, 34, 36, 40, 193 n.18, 195 n.29
  anti-Semitism 36–7
  and Gray 37
  "Journey of the Magi" 37–8
  and Julius 36–7
elite/elitist/elitism 9, 33, 53, 79–80, 85, 114, 120, 144
Emerson, Ralph Waldo 121
encaustic painting technique 82
epistemology 49, 67, 142
  Addams's 113–14
  feminist 115–16, 123, 126
  Royce's 32, 40
Esposito, Maurizio 153
esthetic understanding 12, 21, 184 n.15
ethics 14, 21–3, 28, 31, 39, 115, 117–18, 143, 145, 158, 220 n.37, 229 n.66, 232 n.22, 240 n.7
  Addams's 129, 132–3, 178
  bioethics 151, 153–4, 156–7
  ethical aesthetics 4, 11, 16–17, 24
  ethical evolution 28
  ethical frameworks 49
  Locke's 155, 161
  Peirce's 167–8, 171
  scientific 30, 39–45
  of self-realization 141
  social 117–18
eugenics 128, 158, 236 n.64
European Union (EU) 85
evolution 13
  evolutionary aesthetics 13
  evolutionary love 13–14, 17, 26–8
  universal symbols of 17–23
  modes of 13

fallibilism 93
feeling-modes (content of values) 145, 232 n.22
feminism/feminist 4–5, 115, 131, 134, 174
  activism 134
  cultural memory 113
  epistemology 115–16, 123, 126
  vs. militarism 120, 122

Ferrante, Elena 136
  Elena (fictional character) 131–4
  Lila (fictional character) 131–4
  My Brilliant Friend 134
  Neapolitan Novels 114
  Neapolitan Quartet 131–4
Film Council of America 160
first-order aesthetic experience 16
Fischer, Ilse 69–70
Fischer, Iris Smith 19–20
Fischer, Marilyn 114, 118, 129
Floyd, George, murder of 180
folk music/songs 30, 49, 51–3
  Dylan's 52–3
  genre 52
Frazier, James George 124
French Revolution 85
Freud, Sigmund 162
Friedman, Randy L 208 n.4
Fuller, Margaret 121

Gapon, Georgi 80–1
gay identity 49, 139, 145, 154, 162–4
gender 4, 7, 9, 30, 89, 120, 139, 143
  injustices 178, 180
  transgender 143, 157–65
German Magic Realism 60
gestures 12, 16, 19–22, 187 n.36
  dancer's 24–5
  of Nagasaki Peace Statue 26
God 37, 72, 81, 84
  Aztec symbol of 101–2
  Huitzilopochtli (god of war) 102
  Ixchel 102
Gottsched, Joann Christophe 54
graphic realism 61
Graves, Mark 42, 45, 47, 49, 200 n.62
  classics 201 n.67
  cross-religion relationship 200–1 n.64
  ethical frameworks 49
  human activity, systems of 46
  on loyalty 48
  Mind, Brain and the Elusive Soul: Human Systems of Cognitive Science and Religion 46, 200 n.61
Gray, Piers 37, 195–196 n.34
  "T.S. Eliot and Josiah Royce" 193 n.18, 195 n.33
Green Peace activism 201 n.74

Grosz, George 61
gymnastic harmony therapy 20

Harris, Leonard 142–3, 155, 164, 231 n.10, 231 n.12, 239 n.89
Harrison, Jane
  Ancient Art and Ritual 125
  on rituals 124–5
Hawkins, Erick 21
  The Body as a Clear Space 16
hermeneutics 3, 14, 24, 31, 33, 60, 72, 79, 82, 89, 160, 195 n.33
Hip Hop culture 179
Hispanic culture 105–6, 110
Hogarth, William 19
Holy Spirit 80–1, 86
homo faber 63, 77
human activity, systems of 46
human cooperation 156–7
human nature 21, 61, 72, 81, 89, 95, 105, 146, 163, 175, 180
  and religious/political value-making 82–8

icons/iconography 12, 80–5, 88, 100–1, 179, 213 n.40
  Byzantine 72
  Eastern Orthodox 80
  The Holy Mother 86
  Madonna of Humility 150
  Our Lady of the Gate of Dawn 87
  Saint Sergius and Saint Bacchus 84, 215 n.51
  Theotokos 86–7
  Vilnius 87
idealism 17, 30, 130, 168, 175, 195 n.32
imagination (artistic process) 5–8, 15, 62, 67–8, 78–9
imaginative value-making process 4
  and art 60–2
immigration 216 n.3
  illegal 110–11
  immigrants 7, 9, 85, 120, 129–31, 134–6, 147, 163
  immigration problems 89–90, 104, 107, 109
  Ryder on 95–6
  US immigration policies 106
indigenous communities 89, 98, 105, 107, 111

Indios/Latin American ontology 104
Inness, George, *Sunset in the Woods* 60
institutional thinking 113, 116, 120, 122
intercultural values 30, 38, 89–92, 96
interpretations 3, 14, 16, 18, 21, 24, 30, 35, 44, 47–9, 55, 58, 87, 128, 192 nn.11–12. *See also* reinterpretation
  and communication 46
  Oppenheim on qualities of 31
  Peirce's 14, 19, 21, 24
  Royce's 4, 7, 30–4, 36, 38–49
  Scheler's 69
  of signs 16, 31–3, 50–1, 186 n.27
  Tatar's 69
interpretive musement 32–3, 37, 43, 47–50, 55
inverse invention method 45
invisible enemy 180
Izquierdo, María 219 n.28

James, Henry, Sr. 60, 205 n.11
James, William 2–3, 7–8, 57, 61–2, 65, 68, 140, 173, 180, 182 n.10, 186 n.25, 196 n.35, 204 nn.9–10, 205 n.11, 206 n.23, 211 n.22
  and aesthetics 57–60
  Alexander on 67
  Essays in Radical Empiricism 186 n.26
  the fringe 61, 63
  ideas cum rebus 62–3, 66
  individualism 62
  meliorism 65, 68, 175
  and Peirce 184 n.17, 186 n.28
  pluralistic phenomenology 173
  The Principles of Psychology 66–7
  problem-solving process 174
  psychology 6
  pure experience 5, 59–60, 66
  religious experience 72–6, 78
  Soul 67
  unity of consciousness 59–60
  Varieties of Religious Experience 203 n.1, 211 nn.15–16
  view on history 3
  What Makes a Life Significant 78
Jastrow, Joseph 18
Jim Crow era 139, 150
Johnson, Sargent, "Mother and Child" 150
Joslin, Katherine 124
  Jane Addams: A Writer's Life 116

Julius, Anthony 36–7
Just, Ernest Everett 6, 142
  bioethics 151, 153, 157
  The Biology of the Cell Surface 234–5 nn.45–6
  cellular biology 142, 151–2
    cellular federalism 156
    epi-genetics 150–7
  embryology 152
  and Locke 143, 150–1, 154–5, 157
Just, Hedwig Anna Schnetzier 153–4

Kahlo, Frida 5, 91, 219 n.25, 219 n.29
  and Christianity 100
  cosmopolitan/cosmopolitanism
    naturalism 96–103, 109
    pedagogy 107–11
  and Dewey 97, 99
  The Diary of Frida Kahlo 220 nn.34–5
  Ecce Homo genre 100–1
  intercultural values 89–91
  My Dress Hangs There 99
  Self Portrait on the Border between Mexico and the United States 99
  self-portraiture of 89, 100–2, 110
  Self-Portrait with a Thorn Necklace and Hummingbird 100–2
Kallen, Horace Meyer 233 n.33
Kant, Emmanuel 77, 153, 209 n.7, 212 n.30
  and Arendt 213 n.33
  imagination 79
  Kantian aesthetics 72, 77
  sensus communis 72, 77
  "Transcendental Ego of Apperception" 74
Khanenko National Museum of Arts, Kiev 84
King, Martin Luther 129
Kosciuszko, Tadeuze, landmark proclamation (the Proclamation of Potaniec) 87
Kvit, Serhiy, on EuroMaidan revolution 71

LaFarge, John 60
Lakhani, Nina 221 n.40
landscape painting 61, 64
Langer, Suzanne 204 n.3
Laufs, Stefanie 160

Fighting a Movie with Lightening: "The Birth of a Nation" and the Black Community 237 nn.75–6
LBGTQ community 164
liberation 73, 81, 104–6, 164, 220 n.37, 221 n.38
liberty 85, 87–8
literature 54, 113–14, 202 n.79
  feminist 5, 131
  and history 123
Locke, Alain 2–7, 9, 29, 160, 178, 180, 233 n.29
  Byrnes on 234 n.44
  "Concept of Value" 140
  cultural democracy for 158–9, 165
  "Cultural Relativism and Ideological Peace" 155
  on culture 141
  and DuBois 152
  "Dynamic of a Genetic Theory of Value" 142
  feeling-modes (content of values) 145, 232 n.22
  feeling qualities 144–6
  "Freud and Scientific Morality" 238 nn.82–3
  "Frontiers of Culture" 232–3 n.27
  " A Functional View of Value Ultimates" 235 n.52
  genetics 142
  Harlem Renaissance 140–1, 143, 147, 155, 164
  "Intro to Superiority Creeds and Race Thinking" 236 n.66, 237 n.70
  "Intro to 'Types of Social Change'" 236 n.67
  and Just (Ernest Everett Just) 6, 143, 150–1, 154–5, 157
  The Negro in Art 150
  The New Negro: An Interpretation 147
  The New Negro, Harlem Mecca of the New Negro 147
  promotion of Black culture 139–40, 143–4, 147, 149, 152, 160, 231–2 n.16, 237 n.76
  psychograph 230 n.3
  on race 151
  and Reiss 147
  self-culture 141

skepticism 140
social values 162
"The Talented Tenth" 144
on transcultural value 161–2
transvaluation 142, 146, 154, 162
value analysis 154, 156, 179
"Value and Culture" 231 n.12, 232 n.21
value reciprocity 139, 142, 149
"Values and Imperatives" 142–3, 232 n.18
value-theory 139–41, 143, 145–6, 155, 161, 164–5
view on history 4
Lossky, Vladimir 81
Lowe, Sarah M., "Introduction" 219–20 n.33

Macaulay, Alastair 27
MacKaye, Steele 19–22, 188 n.39, 188 n.45, 189 n.50
Mahowald, Mary Briody, *An Idealistic Pragmatism: The Development of the Pragmatic Element in the Philosophy of Josiah Royce* 196 n.35
Manning, Kenneth R. 230 n.4
Marks, Jonathan, *Is Science Racist?* 157, 236 n.64
McDermott, John J. 186 n.26
Mead, George Herbert 114, 125–6, 133, 136
  "Fragments on the Process of Reflection" 127
  "The Imagination in Wundt's Treatment of Myth and Religion" 226 n.47
  on memory 126–9
  The Philosophy of the Act 227 n.53, 228 n.59
  Philosophy of the Present 127, 226–7 n.51, 229 n.65
  sociality 127
  "The Social Nature of the Present" 226 n.50
Mead, Helen Castle 126
Mehring, Frank 147–8
meliorism 5, 13, 22, 65, 68, 95, 167, 171, 175
memory/memories 126
  Addams's 113–14

collective 4, 51, 114–16, 123, 127, 129
cultural 113, 116–26
Ferrante's use of 114
of refugees 135–6
and social change 131–7
as social event 126–31
thinking 123
women's 131–4
Mesoamerican culture 89–90, 101–2, 104, 109–11
metaphysics (metaphysical) 19–20, 54–5, 59, 64, 101, 127, 173, 192 n.5, 205 n.11, 227 n.55, 240 n.7
Mexico 96, 99, 102
Mexican cultures 100–1
migrants/migration 90, 109, 111
militarism 114–15, 120–2
Modern Dance 15–16, 23–4. *See also* American Modern Dance
modernism/modern culture/modernity 37, 77, 104
Molesworth, Charles 231 n.10, 231 n.12
Montaguini, Leone 40
  Harmonies of Disorder: Norbert Wiener: A Mathematician-Philosopher of Our Time 196 n.37, 197 n.42
morality 48, 53, 70, 117, 130, 140, 154, 164, 168, 174, 180, 209 n.7, 210 n.10
moral judgments 117, 144, 148, 172, 209 n.7
Morris, Mark 21
  Socrates 14, 23–8
Münsterberg, Hugo 140
Murray, Gilbert, *Euripides* 124
music genres 52, 179
myth(s) 116–17, 121–2, 124–6, 129–30
  of Devil Baby 129–31
  of Ixchel 102
mythology 90, 101, 104, 107, 124

Nagasaki Peace Statue, Japan 26
nationalism 49, 215 n.54
Native Americans 104, 109–10, 140–1
naturalism 2–3, 25, 95–103, 106, 110
naturalistic thinking 123
Nature 82–8, 95, 105–6
Nazi/Nazism 64, 69, 133, 150, 217
Negro 151, 160, 230 n.4, 239 n.90

Neo-Zapatista movement 106
Nietzsche, Friedrich 205 n.16
Northrop, F. S. C 16, 186 n.25

occupational therapy 178
O'Connor, Francis V. 109–10
Odysseus 117
O'Hara, David 169
　"Peirce, Plato and Miracles" 168
ontology 14, 21, 35, 46, 65, 95, 107, 110
　of social justice 103–7
Oppenheim, Frank 31–2
　"Graced Communities: A Problem in Loving" 191 n.4
Oupensky, Leonid 83
　The Theology of Icons 81

paidea 106
pantomime 20–2, 189 n.48
Pappas, Gregory 91
Peace Statue, Nagasaki, Japan 26
Peirce, Charles Sanders 2–3, 5, 7, 20–1, 23, 26, 32, 44, 68, 180, 183 n.1, 186 n.25, 191 n.65, 192 n.13
　belief 170
　community/community-building 168–9, 171–2
　creativity for 168
　"The Doctrine of Chances" 188 n.37
　drawing
　　duck/rabbit drawing 18
　　eidetic 17–23
　　perception/interpretations 14–19
　　serpentine lines 18–19
　　stonewall 18, 20
　"Evolutionary Love" 12–13, 22, 24, 184 n.9, 185 n.20, 187 n.28, 189–90 n.56
　"The Fixation of Belief" 240 n.9
　"How to Make Our Ideas Clear" 182 n.3
　"Immortality in the Light of Synechism" 27
　and James 184 n.17, 186 n.28
　"The Law of Mind" 185 n.18
　on modes of evolution 13
　"The Normative Sciences" 239 n.5
　opinion 170
　on pantomime 21–2, 189 n.48
　"Philosophy and the Conduct of Life" 23, 190 n.58

poiesis 167–8
science/scientific method 6, 13, 19
semiotics 4–5, 7, 11–12, 16, 18–20, 32–3, 172
sign-making, components of 12
"The Three Normative Sciences" 184 n.15
"Trichotomic" 4, 12, 19, 21, 187 n.29, 189 nn.48–9
universal love 11–12, 17
view on history 3
"What Is a Sign" 186 n.27, 187–8 n.36
Peirce, Juliette 19
perceptions 17–20, 32–3, 36, 53–4, 58–9, 68, 74, 88, 103, 167, 169, 196 n.35, 217 n.6, 222 n.44, 226 n.45
personal identity 49, 94, 161–2, 165, 179
personification 125, 226 n.45
phenomenology 4, 11, 15–16, 18, 59, 61, 63, 173, 184 n.17, 187 n.31, 215 n.48
philosophical tenets 180
phrenology 158, 236 n.64
Plato 14, 23–4, 26, 63, 190 n.58, 190 n.63
　Apology 9
　cosmological matter 168
　elements of dance 25–6
　Phaedo 24, 191 n.65
　Phaedrus 24
　Symposium 17, 24
poeisis 167
popular culture 30, 51, 53–4, 61, 114, 120, 140, 159, 179
post-expressionism, German 60
postslavery culture 140
pragmatic aesthetics 2–3, 6, 10–11, 57–9, 170, 172, 175, 181, 183 n.1
pragmatic cosmopolitanism 92–6, 104
pragmatic naturalism 146, 216 n.2
pragmatism 1–2, 11, 58, 61, 169, 174, 186 n.25
　absolute 40
　pragmatists 2, 5, 7, 77
　Scheler and 61–2
prejudice(s) 9, 29, 41, 77, 139, 158–9, 161, 165, 168, 179–80
primitivism 21, 146
pro-Russian separatists 213 n.40

race/racism 6–7, 9, 29–30, 41, 151, 162, 236 n.64
  Locke on 151, 178
  murder of George Floyd 180
  racialist science 150, 157
  racial justice/injustice 147, 171, 178, 180
  racial prejudices 29, 158, 165, 179–80
  segregation 140, 144, 176
radical democracy 106
radical empiricism 16–17, 67, 185 n.17, 186 nn.23–5
Rap music 179
realism/reality 6, 15–16, 37, 55, 60, 103, 148
  fictional 131
  graphic 61
reflective thinking 77, 119
reinterpretation 17, 19, 24, 27, 52–3, 108, 123–4, 172, 228–9 n.61. *See also* interpretations
Reiss, Winhold 233 n.29
  Black culture 147–9
  Brown Madonna 148–9
  The Librarian 147
  The New Negro: An Interpretation 147
  The New Negro, Harlem Mecca of the New Negro 147
  The School Teachers 147
religiousness 72–8, 209 n.6
  Maidan ethos in 2014 80
  religious aesthetics 73
  religious attitudes 72–6, 78
  religious experience 72–6, 78
  and value-making 75–6
    religious/political 82–8
Riena 133
Rioni 131, 136
rituals 117, 124–5, 195 n.33
  of funerals 126
Rivera, Diego 96, 98–9
Rooney, Phyllis 174
Royce, Joshua 2–3, 5–6, 8, 54–5, 140, 172–3, 180, 193 n.14, 194 n.26, 195 nn.33–4, 196 n.40, 197 n.42, 199 n.55
  absolute pragmatism 40, 196 n.34, 197 n.42
  "The Aim of Poetry" 34

The Basic Writings of Josiah Royce, Culture, Philosophy and Religion 194 n.23, 196 n.36
Beloved Community 8, 48, 201 n.72
community (community of interpretation) 55, 173
"A Comparative Study of Various Types of Scientific Method" seminar 40
and Graves 49
interpretation 4, 7, 30–4, 36, 38–49
"loyalty to loyalty" 31, 46–8, 142, 173
music/poetry/time 34–8
The Problem of Christianity; Lectures Delivered at the Lowell Institute in Boston and at Manchester College 30, 34, 38, 47–8, 50, 54, 182 n.9, 191 n.3, 192 n.5, 192 n.13
Race Questions Provincialism and Other American Problems 29
science/scientific method 38–9
  ethical characteristics of 43–4
semiotics 30–2, 34–5, 39, 48, 51
"Shelley and the Revolution" 35–6, 194 n.25
"Shop Talk" 193 n.17
spiritual journey 38
view on history 3
and Wiener 38–49
The World and the Individual (1900–1901) 39, 197 n.43, 199–200 n.59
Ruskin, John 118
Ruyter, Lee Chaifa, "American Delsartism: Precursor of an American Dance Art" 20
Ryder, John 95–6

Santayana, George 140
Satie, Eric 24, 26–7, 190–1 n.63
Saviano, Robert 134, 136
  Gomorrah 134–5
Scheler, Max 4, 57, 65, 206 n.24
  on art (*poiein*) 63–6
  axiology 57, 63
  Cognition and Work: A Study Concerning the Value and Limits of the Pragmatic Motivation in the Cognition of the World 61, 205 n.18
  and Dix 61, 70

Formalism in Ethics and Non-Formal Ethics of Values 65
life-community 68, 70
"Metaphysics and Art" 61, 204 n.5
"On the Rehabilitation of Virtue" 203 n.1
personalism 63
phantasy 62, 64–7, 69
and pragmatic aesthetics 57–62
on thinking 206 n.31
vital soul 62, 64–7, 70
science/scientific method 1, 4–6, 11, 13, 19, 30, 36, 38–9, 64, 120, 164, 200 n.59
cellular biology (*see* Just, Ernest Everett)
and culture 39
cybernetics 39–41
entropy 41
ethical 30, 39–45
evolutionary 117
racialist 150, 157
as valuing process 150–7
second-order aesthetic experience 16
Seigfried, Charlene Haddock 114, 121
"Cultural Contradictions Jane Addams's Struggles with the Life of Art and the Art of Life" 223 n.4
self-expression 141, 143–4, 159, 200 n.59
self-identity/self-identification 100, 102–3, 107, 111, 126, 139, 141, 156, 159, 161, 164
semiotic process 3, 21–2, 31
MacKaye's 21, 189 n.50
Peirce's 4–5, 7, 11–12, 16, 18–20, 32–3
Royce's 30–2, 34–5, 39, 48, 51
Shelley, Percy Bysshe 4, 35–6
Shusterman, Richard 2–6, 146, 232 n.26
on James's perception of aesthetics 58–9
"The Pragmatist Aesthetics of William James" 204 n.4
sign-making process 27
aesthetics and art as 14–17
components of 12
Simmel, George 141
Simmons, Seymour 188 n.37
social change 3, 29, 36, 47, 77–8, 99, 104–6, 126–7, 131–7, 144, 177

social justice 6, 29, 44, 50, 72, 115, 118, 131, 148, 150, 177–8, 202 n.74
ontology of 103–7
social occupational therapy 178
Socrates 9, 23, 190 n.63
soma-aesthetics 15, 17, 20
Soria, Chris, *IX Chel* 110
spirituality/spiritualism 3, 17, 27, 34, 38, 45–7, 49–52, 60, 81, 101, 215 n.48
Stalin, Joseph 96–7
Stebbins, Genevieve 20–2, 188 n.45
Stein, Gertrude 34
Stern, Bernhard Joseph, "Intro to Superiority Creeds and Race Thinking" 236 n.66, 237 n.70
Stewart, Jeffrey C., *The New Negro: The Life of Alain Locke* 231–2 n.16
Stikkers, Kenneth W. 63
Problems of a Sociology of Knowledge 206 n.19
storytelling 5, 118–21, 123, 125–6, 129
surrealism 60–1, 218 n.18
surrealist art movement 103
Swedenborg, Emanuel 60
Swedenborgism 60
symbolism 21–2, 72, 85
synechism theory 11, 14–17, 22, 27, 184 n.13, 185 n.18, 185 n.20, 189 n.50

Tarvin, David 108–9
Tatar, Maria 69
Thomas, Dylan 168
Tibol, Raquel, *Frida Kahlo an Open Life* 218–19 n.22, 222 n.49
Tonalism 60
totalitarianism 79, 96
tradition(s) 37, 73, 75–6, 201 n.67, 209 n.6
religious beliefs and 76, 78–9
Western 49, 101
transvaluation 133, 142, 144–6, 148–9, 154–5
transgender struggles as 157–65
Trotsky, Leon (Trotsky Commission) 97, 103
Tsar, Nicholas 80–1
tychasm (chance), evolution 13
Tynbee, Arnold 158

Ukraine 71, 85
  cultural artifacts of 2014 Maidan 71, 80
  democracy 71, 81
  Kiev 72
  Maidan revolution 71, 78, 86
  Orthodox churches in 83
The Ukrainian Institute of America 214 n.40
The United Nations 136
The United States 5, 9, 41, 99, 110, 137, 140, 170, 197–8 n.45
  immigration problems with 89–90
  white supremacy movement 176
universal symbols of evolutionary love 17–23
universal/world peace 4, 14, 23–6, 28, 43

value-making process 1, 6, 15, 31, 46, 72, 120, 132, 139, 143, 146, 154–6
  and art 5, 92
    as relativistic value-making 144–50
  creative 170
  cultural 75
  democratic process 132–3
  ethical 33
  human nature and religious/political 82–8
  imaginative 4, 60–2
  music genres 179
  pragmatic 153
  and religion 75–6
  science as 150–7
  theory of Royce 31–4, 36
  through film (filmmaking) 157–65
    The Birth of a Nation 159–60
    Moonlight 162–4, 239 n.87
    The Quiet One 160–2, 238 n.80

value pluralism 142
value reciprocity, cultural 139, 142, 149–57
Viola, Tullio 18, 188 n.46
  "Bistable Images and the Serpentine Line: A Chapter in the Prehistory of the Duck-Rabbit" 187 n.31
violence 72, 99, 107, 109, 111, 116, 134–5, 137, 176
  cultural 104, 140
  domestic 102, 133
  institutional 115
  symbolic 130–1
  against women and children 113–14

Weimar Republic 61, 69
white supremacy movement 176
Wiener, Norbert 30, 197 n.42, 199 n.49
  cybernetics 30, 39–41
  Ex prodigy: My Childhood and Youth 196 n.40
  The Human Use of Human Beings: Cybernetics and Society 40, 42, 197 n.41
  and Royce's seminar 40, 42
  science/scientific works 38–49
Wild, John Daniel, *The Radical Empiricism of William James* 204 n.9
Wilkoszewska, Krystyna 205 n.14

Zaatari refugee camp 135–6
Zalizniak, Maksym 87
Žižek, Slavoj 85
  "What Europe Should Learn from Ukraine" 215–16 n.54
zoonpolitikan 77